New Work Patterns

Putting Policy into Practice

New Work Patterns
Putting Policy into Practice

Patricia E Leighton
Michel Syrett

PITMAN PUBLISHING
128 Long Acre, London WC2E 9AN

A Division of Longman Group UK Ltd

© Patricia E Leighton and Michel Syrett 1989

First published in Great Britain 1989

British Library Cataloguing in Publication Data
Leighton, Patricia
  New work patterns: putting policy into practice.
  1. Work patterns
  I. Title II. Syrett, Michel, 1957–
331.25'7

ISBN 0 273 02864 2

All rights reserved; no part of this publication may be reproduced, stored in a retrieval system, or transmitted in any form or by any means, electronic, mechanical, photocopying, recording, or otherwise without either the prior written permission of the Publishers or a licence permitting restricted copying in the United Kingdom issued by the Copyright Licensing Agency Ltd, 33–34 Alfred Place, London WC1E 7DP. This book may not be lent, resold, hired out or otherwise disposed of by way of trade in any form of binding or cover other than that in which it is published without the prior consent of the Publishers.

Typeset by J&L Composition Ltd, Filey, North Yorkshire

Printed in Great Britain at The Bath Press, Avon

To Owen and Alun, to whom
'flexibility', 'peripherality'
and the various work patterns discussed
in this book have become
far more familiar than 'striker,
sweeper and 4:2:4'.

Contents

	Introduction	1
1	**New work patterns: concept and reality**	3
	The old agenda: economic push	4
	The new agenda: social pull	5
	Government policy and legislation	11
	Management communication and control	13
	Categories of work patterns	14
2	**Assessing employment needs**	18
	Organisational goals	18
	Issues to consider	21
	Issues relating to specific work patterns	29
	'Social-pull' patterns	42
	Summary points	53
3	**Preparing for different work patterns**	55
	Changes to management systems and procedures	55
	Gaining the support of the organisation	59
	Issues raised by specific work patterns	62
	Summary points	81
4	**Redeployment and recruitment: the management of change**	83
	Introducing change	83
	Restraints on change	87
	Consultation, negotiation and notification of change	94
	Recruitment	100
	Summary points	114
5	**Employment law and worker contracts**	117
	Employee or self-employed?	117
	The contract document	118
	Incorporating work characteristics	121
	Contracts for Category A workers	121
	Contracts for Category B workers	134
	Contracts for Category C workers	137
	Summary points	140
6	**Management and development**	141
	Central administration versus local discretion	141

	Communication and control	143
	Changes to internal relationships	147
	Changes to external relationships	150
	Appraisals, promotion and training	151
	The manager's role: changes, training and preparation	158
	Summary points	164
7	**Pay and benefits**	165
	Topics for consideration	166
	The approach and demands of law	166
	Special provisions	167
	Areas where the workforce can be treated similarly	176
	Pay, benefits and Category B workers	187
	Summary points	188
8	**The work environment**	191
	The general legal framework	193
	Responsibilities to the workforce: some specific topics	196
	Responsibility for the conduct of workers	204
	Summary points	204
9	**Industrial relations**	206
	Specific responses to new work patterns	208
	Conclusion	214
	Summary points	222
10	**Disputes and termination of contracts**	219
	Ending contracts with Category A and B workers	219
	Breaches and termination of contracts: the courts	223
	Breaches and termination of contracts: the tribunals	226
	Ending contracts with Category B and C workers	238
Index		241

Introduction

The climate in which the consideration, use and effective management of new work patterns is discussed has changed radically during the past five years and will continue to do so in the 1990s.

Traditionally, the use of new work patterns has been motivated by economic factors and in particular the dominant need for employers to reduce their labour costs. This motivation remains. Temporary workers, part-timers, many categories of homeworker and sub-contracted services have all been used by employers throughout the 1980s as ready sources of labour which have not involved a high level of commitment, in terms of pay and job security, to the individual. Little or no attempt has been made to integrate or support these categories of worker in the organisation.

These attitudes are beginning to change. The prospect of widespread skill shortages in the 1990s, both in terms of crude numbers and mismatch between the demand and supply of skills knowledge and experience, have forced employers to re-evaluate the role and status of 'atypical' workers. The needs and aspirations of workers have become critical, not just in terms of reward and job satisfaction, but also through increasing concern for the quality of the work environment and a more professional and coherent approach to the management of the work contract itself.

The aim of this book is to re-assess the role of new work patterns in a labour market where the demand for skilled labour greatly exceeds the supply. The opening chapters identify the trends and pressures facing employers, especially those coming from workers. Subsequent sections set out the options for organisations wishing to achieve flexibility in the context of a greater awareness of employee needs. The latter half of the book provides detailed practical guidance on the management systems required to underpin greater use of new working arrangements, covering such critical areas as redeployment and recruitment, employment law, management and development, pay and benefits, the working environment, industrial relations and the termination of contracts. Wherever possible, the text draws on recent and current research, experience and good (or bad) practice.

We cannot, in the space allowed us, cover every issue affecting every work pattern. Readers will note the absence of detailed consideration of overtime flexi-time and shiftworking, which have all been discussed satisfactorily in previous publications. Rather, we have attempted to identify those patterns which have been most affected by current labour market developments and which, as a result, require employers to re-assess the terms of employment, day-to-day management and overall quality of relationship they offer individual workers.

No book is accomplished single-handedly by the authors. We would like to thank Jean Simmons, of the Anglia Higher Education College, for her keyboard skills in drawing up the manuscript, and our publisher Simon Lake for the help, support (and patience) he provided throughout the time we worked on the text.

Patricia Leighton
Michel Syrett
May 1989

Chapter 1

New work patterns: concept and reality

'The published material on future patterns of work is beginning to make up in quantity for what it lacks in quality', wrote an exasperated Director of Personnel at London's International Stock Exchange in 1986, 'Over recent times, the employment profession has acquired a following of journalists and commentators who are set to wring copy out of every modest, exploratory venture on the part of employers to find (exciting) new solutions to (dreary) old problems'.

The Director, Rhiannon Chapman,[1] was commenting on the plethora of books, papers, seminars, conferences and presentations on flexible patterns of work which flooded the market for personnel information in the five years following the 1980–81 UK recession.

In a profession already dependent on information and advice provided by books, trade journals and conferences, a new sub-culture of commentators, business writers and analysts grew up profiting from the latest vogue topic. Since Chapman's remarks, two major books and at least three reports have returned to the subject.

So why another publication on new work patterns when so much has already been written? There are a number of reasons:

- Much of the discussion has centred around a model of strategic planning used by, at most, a very small minority of organisations
- The legal and contractual implications of 'flexibility' are founded on employment law which, in itself, is outdated and increasingly irrelevant to the needs of a changing workforce
- Good practice is often based on a small number of over-cited and sometimes unrepresentative case studies
- Little detailed work has been undertaken on the practical implications of using new work patterns and, in particular, the effects on employment contracts, management systems, career planning, communications and control
- Little attempt has been made to integrate atypical workers into the mainstream of the organisation or create a culture in which they will be accepted – career management and personnel data systems also fail in many instances to make advances for periods away from full-time permanent work

- The needs and practical experience of public sector organisations have featured less strongly – yet the public sector has often taken the lead in pioneering new work practices
- Most debate has centred around initiatives designed to meet specific economic ends – reducing labour costs, meeting or creating extended demand for products or services, etc. Little attention is paid to working practices designed to meet the personal needs of individual workers – yet meeting these needs is an important factor in retaining staff at a time when the number of new entrants to the labour market is falling significantly and organisations are planning their human resource strategy with more care.

THE OLD AGENDA – ECONOMIC PUSH

There is a long tradition of explanations and analyses of the links between labour market trends and the use of various work patterns. Much of the work has centred on the relationship between the so-called primary and secondary labour market, the latter comprising most of the major groups of atypical or vulnerable workers, focusing particularly on the economic factors which affect employers' choice of working arrangement.

Most recently, attention has focused on the concept of the 'core' and 'peripheral' workforce.[2] The essence is that organisations need to be flexible in their use of labour to be competitive at a time of rapid growth and continual change. This is achieved by employing a core of 'firm-specific' employees with secure employment rights and benefits but who are prepared to be flexible about, say, where and when they work and in what function. To cope with uncertain product growth or demand for services, core workers are supported by peripheral staff of varying kinds who provide both numerical and functional flexibility and who (by implication) have access to few of the benefits and little of the job security enjoyed by their core colleagues.

The result, according to this analysis, is a workforce that responds quickly, easily and cheaply to unforseen change; can be contracted as easily as expanded; allows work time to match precisely job requirements; and allows unit labour costs to be held down to manageable proportions.

Developed at a time of uncertain economic recovery immediately following the UK recession of 1980/81, this perception of employment practice presupposes a ready supply of labour which is both malleable and not too demanding in terms of pay and work conditions. Not surprisingly, it has attracted criticism[3] and there are some commentators who doubt that the core/periphery approach to manpower planning provides a real explanation of employers' recent policies.[4]

Indeed, evidence of a strategic and coherent approach to manpower issues generally remains slight. In so far as there has been a conscious development of core and peripheral workforces, it has tended to be in the public sector. The National Health Service, local government and the education service in particular provide good examples, not least through their reliance on professional locums, agency staff, sub-contracted services and supply teachers. Legislative change affecting the public sector will probably increase the use of this kind of peripheral worker in the 1990s.

A growing issue arising from the core/peripheral concept is the impact of workforce change on specific skills and occupational qualifications. This is largely beyond the scope of this book. However, it has to be borne in mind that change is multi-dimensional. The need for flexibility implies a requirement that individuals move out of traditional skill areas, grading structures and professional responsibilities. Again, these are issues affecting the public sector at least as much as the private.

THE NEW AGENDA - SOCIAL PULL

Social and labour market changes have created a new agenda for the consideration, use and effective management of new work patterns. The most important developments are:

- An increased demand for flexibility from individual employees, reflecting a radical change in the aspirations and physical make-up of many UK (and other European) workforces.
- Declining numbers of new entrants to the labour market which make it all the more important for organisations to anticipate and meet these demands.

Demand from individual workers

Labour market analysis in the mid-1980s failed to place enough emphasis on the increasing demand for new work practices among the workforce itself. The main demand has been from women. The significance of increased female participation in the workforce, particularly among working mothers, has still to be appreciated, as has the steady decline in the numbers of economically active men (see Figure 1.1).

By 1990, women will make up half the total workforce. Moreover, they will be concentrated in growing sectors of the economy. A recent survey of future employment trends in the City, for example, found a growing percentage of female staff in banking, securities dealing, insurance, software services, accountancy and management consultancy.[5] An earlier report on future growth in the services sector predicted that two-thirds of all new jobs will be filled by women.[6]

The same report also found that a third of all new workers are also likely to be part-time staff. This is hardly surprising. The growth of part-time working has gone hand-in-hand with increased female participation in the economy. Britain has the largest part-time workforce in Western Europe. Nearly six million people work part-time. Nine out of ten are women. Four-fifths are low paid and many have no basic employment or social

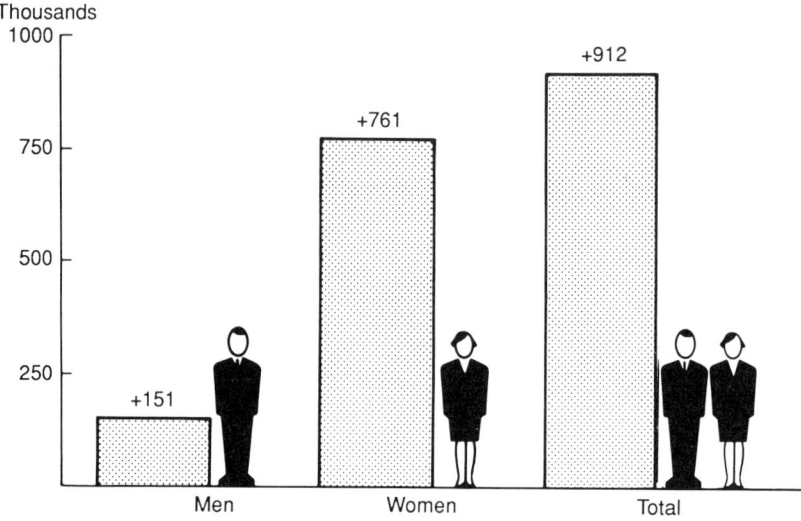

Fig. 1.1 Main changes in Great Britain's labour force: 1987–95 (*Source:* Centre for Research in Employment and Technology in Europe)

security rights. In these circumstances, it is easy to portray women as 'victims'. Yet it is also clear that women's attitudes to and perspectives of work are significantly different from those of men.

This is clearly illustrated by the steady influx of women into professional and managerial positions – where the terms of employment are much closer to those of men. Large employers now automatically recruit and train significant numbers of women in most managerial and professional career groups – some banking and retailing organisations have annual female graduate intakes of over 40 per cent.

Despite offering favourable career opportunities and commensurate levels of pay, most of these employers still lose the majority of their female professionals when they choose to start a family. Like their counterparts in less skilled occupations, qualified female staff find themselves choosing between statutory maternity leave followed by an immediate return to work, or no work at all. Most give up work altogether and hope to resume their careers later on.

This represents a vast waste of money and loss of skills and experience. The training costs alone can be staggering – one major management consultancy, for example, invests £35 000 in training on each of its key consultants over the first five years of their employment. Furthermore, women in managerial and professional jobs are less likely to return to full-time work than their counterparts in lower grade jobs, who tend to take shorter maternity leave.

Faced with this dilemma and operation in a labour market where the demand for skilled staff greatly exceeds the supply, forward-looking employers have begun to adapt their terms of employment and career management systems to meet the needs of their female staff.

The result is a series of new initiatives incorporating job-sharing, homeworking, professional part-time work and formal career break schemes. The initiatives have come particularly from the public sector, most notably the NHS, the Civil Service and local authorities (all suffer from severe skill shortages and fail to retain key staff). But a growing number of private sector organisations, particularly in the finance and retail sectors, have followed their lead.

However, 'supply-led' work initiatives are not just a woman's issue. In a recent lecture on future industrial relations,[8] Sir Adrian Cadbury commented:

'Further evidence for the rise in individualism lies in the increasing demand for flexible hours and for patterns of work which enable people to combine their work with other activities, in ways which are not possible under standard shift patterns. The idea that employment means full-time paid work from leaving school until state retirement age is rapidly breaking down. There is more interest in continuing education, in working for voluntary organisations and in having more than one job. What is difficult to disentangle is how far the increasingly fragmented pattern of working is a consequence of the structural changes in companies ... and more freedom about when and where they work and how they are rewarded. The driving force is likely to be the need for companies to cut their costs and to maintain their flexibility, but the ready response to a greater variety of arrangements over pay and hours shows that they meet individual needs as well – certainly the pressure for flexitime came from employees.'

The most commonly publicised symptom of this 'individualism' has been a doubling of self-employed workers since 1979. But this is only one aspect of a broader desire among employees of both sexes to exercise greater control over their working lives.

In a study published in 1988,[7] the British Institute of Management asked its members what kind of company appeals to them most. Only 24 per cent cited a large organisation. Asked which kind of company they intend to work for in five to ten years' time, 65 per cent indicated they wished to be in small companies, medium sized ones or running their own.

Those who intend to set up on their own or move down in the scale of size tended to be the younger and better educated – under thirty-five years old with an MBA or at least a degree. One in three of the respondents were also unhappy with the effects of the job on personal and family life.

A similar trend was identified by the recruitment consultancy Reed Employment in a survey published one month later. It showed that an increasing number of office workers choose temping as the next best thing to self-employment.

In the seventeen to twenty-three age group, the survey found a diminished commitment to the traditional idea of a job. 'Quite honestly I would give anything not to work', said one interviewee. 'All I need is the cash to go off and do what I want.'

For this group of respondents, work is merely what finances the prime objective of leisure, and temping provides the best opportunity to do so in such a way that it can be enjoyed as soon as enough money has been built up, rather than when an employer says a holiday can be taken.

Committed temps surveyed in age groups from twenty-three upwards fell into three categories. Some might spend several months temping and regard that as a way of trying out a variety of jobs, types of employers, office environments and working neighbourhoods until they find one that suits them. Others see it as a more wide-ranging form of training and career development than they would get from most organisations as an employee – an experience that will enhance their value in the marketplace and widen their options when they look for a permanent job. The third group is more traditional – slightly older women with young families who for that reason are unable to take on regular full-time work.

Changing demographic trends: retention over recruitment

Staff employed in atypical arrangements are still a minority of the workforce. But their importance, and the potential demand for more flexible work patterns which exist among existing (and future) full-time staff has been made more critical by labour market trends which place an equal emphasis on the needs to *retain* key staff as well as recruit them.

After ten years of steady increases, nearly one million people were of school leaving age in 1983. By 1993 that figure will have fallen by 35 per cent. Between 1982 and 1987 the decline was only slight and had the welcome effect of reducing local areas of high unemployment. The real reduction – a massive 27 per cent fall – is concentrated at the turn of the decade (see Figure 1.2). Moreover, this is not a development confined to the UK. With the notable exception of Ireland, most European countries will experience a similar fall.

In the early 1990s the consequences for some employers will be profound. Already the nursing profession is unable to attract sufficient school leavers, while many YTS schemes in the South East have empty places. Banks, some of which recruit up to 5000 school leavers a year, are facing similar problems. In the long term, the main sources of professional and managerial talent, higher education establishments, may be unable to meet employers' expanding needs – UK graduate output is set to fall by about 10 000 by 1997.[9] The necessity to keep and make better use of existing human resources is already high on the agenda of many organisations.

A study *Employer Responses to the Decline in School Leavers into the 1990s*[10] surveyed twenty organisations with a total of over a million employees. Some expected to be able to maintain school leaver recruitment with current entry standards; others hoped to do so with lower qualification requirements.

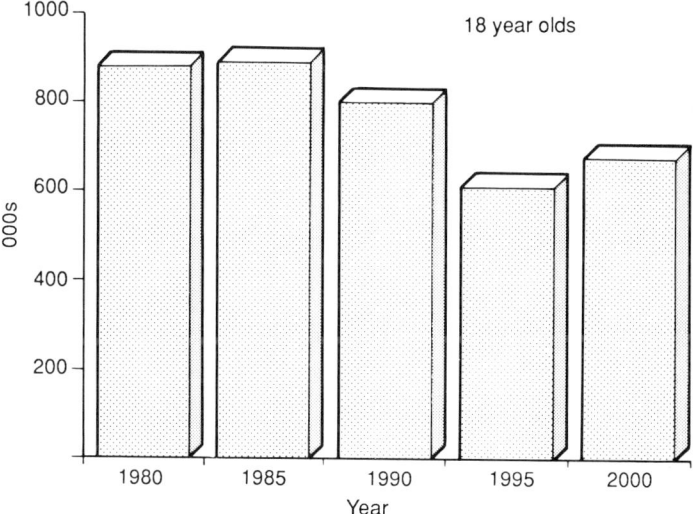

Fig. 1.2 Youth labour supply 1980–2000 (Source: Institute of Manpower Studies)

Two important responses from service-sector employers are directly relevant to this book:

- Many will turn to other sources of labour to replace school leavers. The most favoured group were *women working part-time*. Employers in the survey recognised that they would have to increase the attractiveness of work to these groups. This type of response included improvement in the quality of part-time work and greater opportunities for combining employment with raising children
- Employers also wanted to reduce the need for school leavers by improving the retention of all employees. The plans included improving training and career prospects through better opportunities for part-time work and an improvement of its perception.

A further incentive for employers to consider new working arrangements has been the fragmentation of the UK into local and regional labour markets. Employers experience increasing difficulties in moving key staff from one location to another due to variations in cost of living and house prices – particularly between the South East and the remainder of the country. This has aggravated still further local skill shortages. The problem has been particularly acute for multi-site organisations with a national framework for pay and benefits.

Although a general progression towards regional pay policies and more imaginative (and responsive) relocation support has been one effective response to this problem, a greater emphasis on career management and flexible working is also being widely considered.

In the public sector, local authorities and the Civil Service have introduced new work patterns as one response to the skill shortages caused by the North/South divide. A survey by the Local Authorities Conditions of Service Advisory Board in 1987[11] found that 91 per cent of local authorities in the South East have undertaken an examination of new work practices. Of these, 53 per cent already use job-sharing, 53 per cent contract work out, 47 per cent employ part-timers and 53 per cent use other new working arrangements.

A key factor in employers ability to 'prepare for the future' will therefore be their willingness to adapt working arrangements to meet the changing personal and domestic needs of their staff; and the improvements of working conditions and terms of employment for their atypical workers.

This will involve abandoning over-rigid career management structures and allowing staff to move between a variety of different work patterns while retaining their commitment and economic contribution to the firm. The risk of losing staff is still there, but it is also present with permanently employed full-timers. Too often, employers use the inherent organisational difficulties of new work patterns as a scapegoat for their own bad communication, high turnover, lack of commitment and poor performance. The real fault lies more with the corporate culture and quality of human resource management.

High turnover, lack of commitment and poor communications are certainly common to many employees working on a part-time or temporary basis. But this is often because atypical workers receive terms of employment and rates of pay well below those of permanently employed full-timers. Atypical workers are excluded from the social culture and fabric of the organisation. Frequently, they do not receive routine perks and bonuses, do not benefit from staff social or leisure facilities and are excluded from staff outings or social events. Their achievements are not highlighted in employee communications literature; their progress is not linked to any formal system of career or performance appraisal; and they are deliberately excluded from company training provision and opportunities for promotion.

One of the unintended effects of the concept of core-periphery working was to reinforce this short-sighted attitude and make it respectable. The application of the term 'peripheral' to categories of staff such as job-sharers, homeworkers and contract staff, who are often firm-specific and perform 'core' functions, only served to encourage the image of 'flexible' workers as unreliable and uncommitted. This attitude not only prevails among personnel and line management. It also extends to supervisors, trade union officials and full-time workers who work directly with atypical staff.

Is it any wonder that these workers feel uncommitted and have higher levels of turnover than their full-time contemporaries? How can they feel loyalty when the firm, in its culture and management, shows scant commitment to them?

In summary, organisations will only succeed in retaining atypical workers and their commitment if:

- they make it easier to transfer from one working pattern to another without sacrificing career continuity
- they ensure parity in working terms and conditions between all categories of staff and the extent to which they are integrated into the fabric, structure and culture of the organisation.

To achieve this, management systems and career structures require 'bottom up' direction. More sophisticated two-way employee communications and appraisal systems should establish working arrangements best suited to the needs of individual workers. Out-dated working arrangements designed solely for the needs of permanent full-timers and imposed from the top, should be abandoned or adapted.

This will not just benefit atypical workers. It reinforces the bond between the organisation and all its workforce. To work, it requires a radical change in attitude from both senior management and the human resource function. As one commentary recently put it[12]

'Radical self-development may produce people who do not fit into the organisation's career structure so easily. Ambition is a very subjective concept. Very able people may decide that they do not wish conventional 'upward' development. ... People may also wish to be recruited later on in life or work in an unusual way – for example, at home or on a part-time basis. They may wish to take an unpaid sabbatical to further their education. These 'exceptions' will become far more commonplace and will need far more debate in organisations where employees are given greater discretion over how they manage their working lives. An inevitable result would be more varied contract of employment. ...'

Nor is this process confined to employers. Employers' policies are in part a reflection of the attitudes of the trade unions who, until recently, actively opposed the introduction of many new work patterns and also of the insurance and pension companies who excluded many flexible workers from their policies. Employers' policies also reflect a system of employment law which is becoming totally irrelevant to up to half the working population; and the attitudes of the various providers of information and advice to the personnel function – professional institutions, research establishments, trade publications and consultancies.

These institutions need to reflect the changing social needs of a workforce which has transformed over the past twenty years. Many employers are already making changes but at a pace too slow to remove the barriers of inequality which still underpin employer–employee relationships.

GOVERNMENT POLICY AND LEGISLATION

There is a popular conception that a highly interventionist system of legal protections for workers will curb recruitment and inhibit management discretion. This view largely explains the systematic deregulation of the labour market since 1980. Reforms have weakened wages councils, lengthened qualifying periods for basic statutory rights, such as unfair dismissal, and have led to increased vulnerability for certain groups of workers, especially temporary and part-time staff. At the very stage when atypical workers were comprising a considerably enlarged proportion of the labour market, statutory protections were being withdrawn, and concentrated on the core. In reality, there is little or no evidence that law has such an inhibiting effect. Most research shows that recruitment and personnel policies are only rarely influenced by lack of legal protection for workers.

The post-1980 situation is only a refining of an established tradition in employment law. The die had been cast in 1965 with the Redundancy Payments Act which prescribed a two year qualifying period for employees and which provided the highest levels of compensation for long serving and older employees. The 1971 Industrial Relations Act, which introduced unfair dismissal rights used a similar format. Atypical workers were not outside the law by accident; they were deliberately excluded. Legal protections were reserved for the full-time, loyal and long-serving employees.

The current position is that although it is unlikely that there will be further deregulation, there is little chance of greater legal protection other than those required by the European Community. Critics of the present legal system have not yet developed a coherent strategy for change. Some suggest a return to protections via collective action, others a labour law code. The issues are complex, but at present the law leaves managements largely free and responsible for their own employment policies.

Two areas stand out as having impact. They are European law and anti-discrimination measures. In recent years the Treaty of Rome has had an increasing impact on our legal system and employment. European legal traditions are markedly different from our own. They are more interventionist, more broadly based and directly enforced, and often provide greater protection for various groups of atypical workers. For example, French and German attitudes on regulation of temporary work are not only more protective but increasingly colour the European Community law more generally. Further change will come from the Community, especially from 1992.

Anti-discrimination legislation has had major impact on the labour market. Legislation regarding pay, conditions, occupational benefits, recruitment and promotion has improved the situation of many non-core staff, largely because women are heavily represented. The simple equation that women = part-time work has enabled challenges to be made to decisions to make part-timers redundant first, to refuse job-share proposals, to limit membership of occupational pension schemes to full-timers and/or long-serving employees. If policies, in effect, treat women less favourably than men, claims can be brought. Many managerial policies and long established practices have been declared unlawful. Perhaps the major blow was the 'equal value' aspect of the equal pay legislation. This has tackled some of the disadvantages of job segregation into women's (lower paid) work. As will be discussed in Chapter 7, the impact of case law in this area has been considerable on pay grading and scales.

These areas apart, law not only provides few rules but government policies have intensified deregulation in the public sector. Recent legislation has required more sub-contracting and greater flexibility generally, but it has also prevented some employers prescribing terms of work in the contract for the supply of labour (Local Government Act, 1988).

Despite this situation, law does have an important role to play in the management of new work patterns. This is because although statutory protections have relatively little relevance, the law of contract and more traditional legal remedies remain important. Indeed, there has been a revival of claims for damages, use of injunctions and other procedures, not least as a response to the 'gap' left by statutes.

Managers will have to be conscious of the role of County Courts and the High Court as well as industrial tribunals. This is especially so during the process of introducing changes at the workplace. Some areas of law, such as that relating to health and safety, must also be taken seriously when considering new work patterns. Law will therefore permeate the whole book but will tend not to appear in separate units. Law is simply one of the factors and influences to take on board.

MANAGEMENT COMMUNICATION AND CONTROL

Just as employment law, and thus contracts of employment, have been designed around the model of a continuously employed full-time worker, so corporate management and communications systems have followed suit.

Experiments with new work patterns have often broken down, or failed to achieve their full potential, because key management procedures designed for full-time staff do not adapt well.

Many new working arrangements require well-designed reporting systems to set objectives and monitor progress; recruitment criteria which place a greater emphasis on *how* a job is undertaken; and line managers who have project management and teamworking skills and an ability to compare labour costs more accurately.

Employee communications literature, formal appraisal procedures and remuneration policy should reflect and incorporate the contribution of atypical workers. They will need to be represented on staff associations or trade unions, safety councils and other employer–employee liaison bodies. They will also need greater access to training and promotion.

Changes to management and communication procedures will need to be discussed and agreed with line managers, trade union officials, supervisors and full-time employees who will be working with atypical workers. As with any management of change, the commitment and support of senior management is essential.

This book will examine the issues highlighted in this chapter in greater detail. It will explore the major reasons why organisations use new work patterns and the principal arrangements in regular use.

It will examine the adaptations and innovations that need to be made to existing management and communications systems; and the contractual implications of each working arrangement in the light of the changes currently being made to employment law.

The purpose is to open up a range of options which organisations can then tailor to provide solutions to specific problems. This is likely to be increasingly necessary:

- at a time when relationships between employing organisations and their staff are becoming more individualised and complex;
- in a labour market where the demand for skilled labour greatly exceeds the supply and where the organisations have to hold on to and make better use of their existing human resources:
- and where individuals are increasingly demanding working arrangements which fit in more easily to the changing personal demands of their life-styles.

As Rhiannon Chapman concluded in 1986:

'Companies do not readily adopt imported practices. They need to develop and mould their own in tune with the particular organisational culture each has endorsed. ... But personnel people build their careers from a reactive base of experience, and it is helpful to be given some encouragement to think ahead, exploring and anticipating options which our organisations may need to have available to them. When a requirement arises, it is often at short notice, when it is already too late to put in hand the necessary modifications to procedures, behaviours or management style!'

CATEGORIES OF WORK PATTERNS

Flexible working is a general term. However, not all so-called flexible patterns are new. The use of casual, freelance and sub-contracted labour has a long tradition, especially in certain occupations. Some patterns and opportunities are less familiar, such as job-sharing, high-technology home-working and career break schemes. It is the re-appraisal and/or extended use of some of the traditional work patterns which justifies categorising them as 'new'. At the same time 'flexible work' comprises a wide range of work patterns often with a confusing variety of titles. For example, those who work from or at home can be called 'distance workers', 'homeworkers', or 'networkers'. Self-employed professionals can be 'freelancers', 'agents', 'consultants' or 'contract workers'. Temporary staff can be 'casual', 'fixed term' or 'short term'. The word 'temp' is widely used to connote staff supplied by an employment business which is itself often (erroneously) called an employment agency. There is debate about the correct phraseology for sub-contract labour – some see 'contract' as correct and see no need to use 'sub'-contract. In some occupations, the system is called 'labour only' sub-contracting, or the 'lump'. Many workers with the same label can be either employees or self-employed, for example 'casual' and 'distance workers'. For the purposes of this book, some order had to be brought to the confusion.

It is accepted that there are two direct and practical factors influencing categorisation:

- The contractual relationship
  Employment policies will be influenced to a greater or lesser extent by the legal and tax implications of:
  – whether the worker is employed or self-employed
  – how long and for how many hours per week they work.
- Managerial relationship
  Employment policies will be influenced by factors such as:
  – whether work is on or off site
  – whether workers are subject to the direction of third parties
  – the length of engagement
  – the purpose of engagement
  – the number or variety of workers involved.

However, underpinning these factors are some common denominators which shape attitudes more generally. They are:

(a) Control – the extent to which day-to-day supervision is possible and desirable
(b) Integration and dependence – the extent to which workers are 'bonded' into the financial and organisational culture.

For the purposes of this book we have divided work patterns into three categories which indicate a gradation of control, and integration/dependence. Employment status is ultimately the key factor. The three categories are as follows:

Category A: Directly-employed workers
– part-time work (supplementary and substitutional)
– job-sharers
– flexitime
– sabbaticals, career break schemes
– homeworking
– annual hours contracts
– fixed term contracts
– fixed job contracts

– own-pool temporaries.
Category B: Self-employed workers
– casual workers
– freelance workers
– consultants
– Schedule D homeworkers.
Category C: External workers
– agency workers
– sub-contracted labour
– seconded workers
– Government subsidy workers.

Category A workers are dependent on the organisation and controlled by it, even though workers may only be there for a short period or on a limited basis. The relationship with Category B staff is one of inter-dependence, typified by the employment of consultant or freelance staff who provide specialist skills or advice. Category C workers are the legal responsibility of another employer, though not necessarily as employees. They are technically independent of your organisation and yet workers will have to be integrated to some extent and there are a wide range of legal and managerial issues resulting from this.

We recognise that categorisation in this way may not be entirely satisfactory but would argue that each group presents sufficient discrete managerial issues to make the categorisation viable. Some categories figure more prominently in some chapters but have little coverage in others. For example, consideration of Category C issues is prominent in Chapters 2 and 3, where strategic and preparatory issues are considered. They are relatively neglected in Chapters 5 and 7, where contractual and pay issues have most relevance for Category A workers. Put succinctly, 'up-front' planning is vital for Category C and some of B. Day-to-day and development issues dominate discussion for Category A.

Traditional legal and managerial analyses have tended to focus on the 'vertical' employment relationship. They have examined personnel policies and their impact on individuals or groups of employees. This book argues that the new workforce requires greater consideration be given to 'lateral' as well as 'up-down' matters. The impact of work patterns on colleagues, on other work patterns and on third parties (such as clients and customers) will be examined. The diversification of the workforce requires flexible attitudes and planning, as well as rigorous evaluation.

References
1 Chapman, R., Review of *New Patterns of Work* (Gower, 1985) in *Manpower Policy and Practice*, Vol. 1, No. 3, Spring 1986.
2 Atkinson, J. 'Flexibility, Uncertainty and Manpower Management', IMS Report No. 89, Institute of Manpower Services, 1984.
3 Callaghan, B., 'Unions: the economic outlook', *Manpower Policy and Practice*, Vol. 1, No. 4, Summer 1986.

4 Henley Management College, 'Employment agencies and the future of work', a study conducted for the Blue Arrow Group, 1987.
 5 Rajan, A. and Fryatt, J., *Create or Abdicate: the City's Human Resource Choice for the 1990s*, Witherby & Co., 1988.
 6 Rajan, A., *Services – The Second Industrial Revolution?* Butterworth, 1987.
 7 Peppercorn, G. and Skoulding, G., *Profile of British Industry, The Manager's View*, British Institute of Management, 1988.
 8 Cadbury, Sir Adrian, *Industry and Employment*, Foundation for Business Responsibilities, 1987.
 9 Pearson, R. and Pike, G., *The Graduate Labour Market in the 1990s*, Institute of Manpower Studies, 1989.
10 Meager, N. and Metcalfe, H., *Employer Responses to the Decline in School Leavers into the 1990s*, Institute of Manpower Studies, 1988.
11 Roberts, G. and Mellor, D., *Local Authorities' Responses to Shortages*, Local Authorities Conditions of Service Advisory Board, 1987.
12 Hirsh, W., 'Self-development: opening Pandora's box', *Manpower Policy and Practice*, Vol. 3, No. 2, Winter 1987.

Source material

ACAS, *Labour Flexibility in Britain*, 1988.
Casey, B., *The Extent and Nature of Temporary Work in Great Britain*, Policy Studies Institute, 1987.
Cair, H., *Changing Patterns of Work*, Workers' Educational Association, 1984.
Department of Employment, *Building Businesses ... Not Barriers*, Cmnd 9794, 1986.
Department of Employment, *Employment for the 1990s*, Cm 540, HMSO, 1988.
Department of Employment, 'Employers' labour use strategies: First Report of the 1987 Survey', *Research Paper No. 63*, 1989.
'Growth and utilization of part time labour in Great Britain', *Employment Gazette*, September 1984, p. 391.
Hakim, C., 'Trends in the flexible workforce', *Employment Gazette*, November 1987, p. 549.
Labour Force Surveys, Department of Employment, 1982.
Leighton, P., 'Marginal Workers', in Lewis, R. (ed.) *Labour Law in Britain*, Blackwell, 1986.
Leighton, P., 'New workers: old laws', *Manpower Policy and Practice*, Vol. 1, No. 4, 1986, p. 16.
MacInnes, J., 'The question of flexibility', *Research Paper No. 5*, Department of Social and Economic Research, University of Glasgow.
Martin, M., 'Renewing the options for flexibility', *Personnel Management*, June 1987, p. 42.
Men and Women, Equal Opportunities Commission, 1984.
'Women part-time workers: evidence from the 1980 Women and Employment Survey, *Employment Gazette*, September 1984, p. 409.
Yeats, J., *Retaining Specialists*, IMS Report No. 145, Institute of Manpower Studies, 1988.

Chapter 2

Assessing employment needs

ORGANISATIONAL GOALS

In common with human resource policies generally, the introduction of new work patterns should be directly linked to organisational goals. Those responsible require a comprehensive understanding of:

- The main objectives, activities and constraints of the organisation
- The way in which individual working arrangements impact on and are affected by them.

Key areas are set out below:

Level and nature of demand
What demands are made of the organisation?
What are the human resource implications in terms of skills required and working hours?
What fluctuations in demand is the organisation subject to?
Does it vary according to the time of day, month or year?
Is fluctuation consistent or unpredictable?
Which categories of staff are most affected?

Labour costs
Compared to other organisations, are overall labour costs high or low?
In each category of staff, what components of labour costs are made up from:
– basic salary
– statutory payments (NI contributions, etc.)
– holidays, sickness, injury and maternity
– voluntary social welfare benefits (inc. pensions)
– subsidised services, benefits in kind, training
– personnel administration
– office accommodation and facilities?

Production or service capacity
Is the organisation making maximum use of capital equipment, production capacity, office facilities and/or business premises to meet organisation goals?

Centrality of function
For each category of staff:
- how central is their work to the principal objectives and functions of the organisation?
- how much discretion do they have in performing their responsibilities?
- what impact does the function have on the organisation?
- is the function relatively autonomous or closely integrated with the work of other employees?
- is the function performed primarily on-site or off-site? Has it the capacity to be performed off-site using office technology?
- what reporting and communication systems are involved?

Labour market requirements
Does the local labour market supply most of the organisation's skill needs? Which skills are particularly difficult to recruit and retain?
Are the organisation's skill needs drawn from sectors of the labour market with a growing proportion of women or other minority groups likely to be attracted to new working arrangements?

Equal opportunities requirements
Is it the official policy of the organisation to promote equal opportunities? Are existing employment policies implicitly discriminatory under existing legislation (see Chapter 5)?

Social needs and career aspirations of workforce
What are the career and domestic issues most likely to affect the existing and future workforce's choice of working hours or arrangements:
- the need to combine career or job continuity with the domestic responsibilities of looking after children or a sick relative
- the desire or need to take time off in order to retrain or engage in some kind of continuing education?
- the need for less demanding working hours because of physical or mental disability
- the desire or need to work from home, work on a self-employed basis, or maintain a greater degree of control over their working life?

Industrial relations constraints
Do existing agreements with trade unions constrain certain working practices or patterns? How do the responses of individual unions vary from one work pattern to another?
What is the policy of *each* national union to the introduction of new work patterns?
What is the attitude of local officials? Is there any divergence between the two?

External policy constraints
What are the external policy constraints affecting human resource options within your organisation? Do they, for example, relate to:
- government policy or guidelines (for example, those influencing the use of contract services in local government and equal opportunities in the Civil Service)?

20 NEW WORK PATTERNS

Work pattern	Organisational Goals							
	Economic					Social		
	To meet extended demand	To reduce office overheads	To make better use of capital equipment	To reduce labour costs	To increase sources of labour	To aid retention	To promote equal opportunities	To reward long service
CATEGORY A								
Flexitime								
Shift working								
Part-time								
– Supplementary								
– Substitutional								
Job sharing								
Career Break Schemes								
Sabbaticals								
Temporary workers								
Public subsidy trainees								
Homeworking								
CATEGORY B								
Self-employed								
Consultants								
CATEGORY C								
Agency workers								
Secondments								
Sub-contractors								

Fig. 2.1 (A)   New work patterns and organisational goals

ASSESSING EMPLOYMENT NEEDS 21

Work pattern	Economic				Organisational Goals		Social	
	To meet extended demand	To reduce office overheads	To make better use of capital equipment	To reduce labour costs	To increase sources of labour	To aid retention	To promote equal opportunities	To reward long service
CATEGORY A								
Flexitime								
Shift working								
Part-time								
– Supplementary	✓				✓			
– Substitutional	✓				✓	✓		
Job sharing						✓		
Career Break Schemes						✓		
Sabbaticals								
Temporary workers								
Public subsidy trainees								
Homeworking								
CATEGORY B								
Self-employed			✓					
Consultants								
CATEGORY C								
Agency workers				✓				
Secondments								
Sub-contractors								

Fig. 2.1 (B) New work patterns and organisational goals. An example (medium-sized book retailer)

- multinational corporate policy (for example, affecting the human resource policies of a UK subsidiary)?
- EC Directives (for example, those relating to deployment of and the terms of employment offered to part-time, contract and temporary staff)?
- legal constraints, both national and international?

In the first chapter, we found that two underlying causes for the move to flexibility were the 'economic push' of organisations to introduce cost-effective human resource policies; and the 'social pull' of a labour force which, collectively and individually, wants a greater degree of control over the way in which they work and employment patterns which reconcile their occupational and personal goals or responsibilities.

Common organisational goals can therefore be summarised under two main categories:

Economic
- to meet or encourage extended demand
- to cope with fluctuating demand
- to increase production capacity
- to aid recruitment and retention
- to reduce labour costs and office overheads.

Social
- to promote or comply with equal opportunities
- to meet social and domestic needs (child-care, career breaks, continuing education, early retirement, etc.)
- to increase motivation and commitment.

Categories of staff: how they meet organisational goals

In the first chapter, we also summarised the common patterns of employment which have emerged. We divided them into three categories:

Category A – directly employed workers
Category B – self-employed workers
Category C – external workers (employed by a third party)

These categories of worker can be used to meet key organisational objectives using the model illustrated in Figure 2.1.

In general, overtime, shiftworking, supplementary part-time work, temporary, contract and agency working are largely used to meet economic objectives. Shiftworking and part-time work are used to meet extended demand, make better use of capital equipment, extend production capacity and cope with predictable fluctuations in demand. Overtime, temporary work and agency work are more often used to deal with unpredictable fluctuations in demand and seasonal peaks. Contract work is used to reduce labour costs.

By contrast, career break schemes, sabbaticals, job sharing and substitutional part-time work are most used to meet the social pressure of the workforce for greater equal opportunities and more control over their working hours and/or career development. But in meeting these socially driven demands, organisations are also solving economic difficulties. In a labour market where the demand for skilled labour often exceeds the supply, these working arrangements enable organisations to increase their sources of labour, retain key staff and enlarge the skills at their disposal.

In a similar way, the use of self-employed workers and directly employed homeworkers also meets both economic and socially driven objectives. They provide organisations with a means of reducing labour costs through the better use of workplace facilities and premises. At the same time, they meet individual employees' aspirations for greater control over the work, and a means of reconciling occupational and personal needs or responsibilities.

Using the model – an example

The mix of economic and socially driven objectives can be illustrated by looking at how the model applies to a specific organisation – a medium sized book retailer with a small chain of branches throughout South East England (see Figure 2.1(B)).

A significant reason for the company's growth during the 1970s was the ability of its West End outlets to extend their opening hours to the early evening, on Saturdays and during Bank Holidays. Supplementary part-time staff, working between 12 noon and 3pm, provide additional support to the full-time staff in some of the smaller branches during the increase in demand generated by lunch-time shoppers. Substitutional part-time staff help to extend the opening hours of the mainstreet stores, working evening, afternoon and evening and Saturday shifts. These shifts are used, therefore, to meet extended demand and increase sources of labour by offering working hours attractive to students, working mothers and retired or semi-retired people of both sexes.

The various branches of the company also use contract workers to perform specific tasks, and thereby reduce labour costs. These include a contract cleaning company and a firm specialising in window dressing.

At Head Office, the company has responded to demographic skill shortages by offering key female managers a formal career break scheme and limited opportunities for job sharing. A small number of clerical staff are also employed on a permanent part-time basis as a means of retaining valued employees who would otherwise have left the company when deciding to start a family. Temporary agency staff are used to cover for expected and unexpected absences of permanent full-time staff.

ISSUES TO CONSIDER

A number of issues need to be considered if new work patterns are used to meet corporate objectives:

Labour costs v. demand

If flexible working patterns are introduced for cost reasons, there needs to be an accurate understanding of how the organisation's labour costs interrelate with the predictability of the demand for its products or services.

The aim of many organisations is to introduce measures that will shift the balance away from fixed towards variable costs to allow greater flexibility in financial planning and to better meet the demand for its goods and services. Getting the right mix of staff in terms of skills and money is therefore extremely important. An analysis of comparative labour costs undertaken by Henley Management College in 1985 found that the significance of labour costs within different organisations varies in relation to such factors as capital intensity, predictability of demand and the location of premises, not all of which are under management control.

The study found that non-wage costs are extremely variable and need careful analysis. Taking government estimates of labour costs in the production and construction industries over the past twenty-five years as an example (see Table 2.1), there has been a very slight decline in recent years but these costs still represent about 16 per cent of the total. Taken as a percentage of pay, they total 31 per cent in the case of manual workers and 36 per cent in the case of non-manual staff – well over a third.

Table 2.1 Labour costs in the production and construction industries

	Wages and salaries	Statutory National Insurance	Voluntary social welfare	Other costs	All
1964	91.9	3.6	3.1	1.5	100
1975	87.5	6.4	4.2	1.9	100
1981	81.6	8.9	5.6	3.9	100
1983	82.3	7.5	6.1	4.1	100
1984*	83.9	7.3	5.8	3.0	100

* Manufacturing only

Source: Employment Gazette, 1984

The study also found that these figures could be analysed in a variety of different ways. Statutory payments represent the most unchangeable element and one that may be increasing as the proportion of higher paid employees grows within organisations. The occupational pension cost of these for long-service employees is another large and unavoidable expense. A final unavoidable expense is the cost of holidays and absence which in some organisations may amount to more than 12 per cent of costs on top of wages and salaries (see Table 2.2).

Government statistics do not reflect the whole picture. Organisations have adopted many other forms of rewarding staff which do not increase pension and other pay-related benefits. This includes the provision of subsidised services such as meal tickets, canteens and staff restaurants, season-ticket loans, housing loans and medical care facilities; and the

Table 2.2 Components of labour costs as percentage of pay

	Manual %		Non-manual %	
Holidays, sickness, injury, maternity	12.3		12.6	
Statutory payments (including NI; employers' liability; redundancy)	11.4		10.5	
Voluntary social welfare benefits (including pensions)	5.5		11.1	
Subsidised services, benefits in kind, training	2.20	31	2.24	36
		15		15
Total on-costs		46%		51%

Source: Rothwell, S., *Comparative Labour Costs of Employing Permanent Staff and Using Temporary Workers Through Agencies*, Federation of Recruitment and Employment Services, 1985.

provision of company cars which currently cost most organisations between £2000 and £3000 per year per unit.

Finally, there is the question of personnel administration costs. These include all the costs associated with recruitment and termination of employment (including statutory and voluntary redundancy payments), as well as wage payment, grievance handling and welfare administration. Estimates of such on-costs vary from 0.5 per cent to 35 per cent but government statistics indicated an average of 15 per cent in 1985.

Taking all these on-costs together, this means that up to 50 per cent needs to be added to hourly wages to estimate the true cost of employment.

Example – Rank Xerox

The best example is the labour cost equation which prompted Rank Xerox to introduce networking into their organisation. The organisation found that direct wage payments accounted for less than a third of total labour costs in their Central London office with a further third being taken up by the outlay for office facilities. This meant that an employee receiving £10 000 a year (pre-tax) was actually costing the organisation £27 000 a year. Furthermore, the organisation argued that whereas salary payments are controllable, add value to the organisation and motivate staff, office facilities are inflationary, uncontrollable, add no value and do not motivate.

The labour cost equation will be directly affected by fluctuations in the demand for the organisation's product or services. This was illustrated by a risk analysis model developed by Sheila Rothwell at Henley Management Centre which compares different levels of labour costs and demand fluctuations and the varying mixes of core and peripheral staff which will best meet their needs.

Ms Rothwell's model indicates careful evaluation of a range of factors and can be applied to our own classifications of new working patterns.

26 NEW WORK PATTERNS

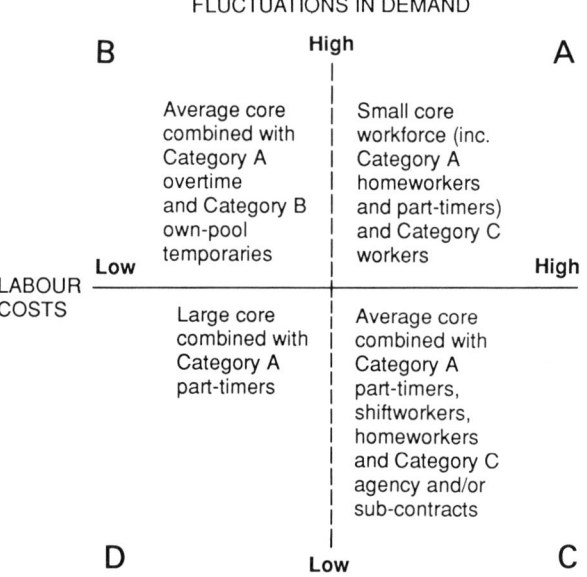

Fig. 2.2 *Labour costs versus demand: a risk analysis*
(*Source:* adapted from Rothwell, S. 'Comparative labour costs: getting the right mix', *Manpower Policy and Practice*, Vol 1, No. 3, Spring 1986)

Although it would be ill-advised to use it slavishly, it provides an interesting insight into effective use of work patterns (see Figure 2.2).

The model divides organisations according to their labour levels and the fluctuations in demand they experience. There are four main categories:

Organisations with high labour costs and high fluctuations in demand (A)
Category A workers are expensive to maintain and will frequently be underused. The need here is for work patterns that will reduce on-costs and enable the workforce to be increased and decreased quickly and cost-effectively in line with demand.

A very small core is therefore most suitable, including off-site Category A workers to reduce overheads and the imaginative use of part-time contracts to avoid overmanning and under-utilisation.

Fluctuations in demand should ideally be met by Category C external workers (such as agency workers and sub-contracted staff) to ensure a quick response to deployment needs. These are preferable to Category B workers since the recruitment and personnel charges are transferred to external agencies thereby reducing still further unnecessary labour costs.

Organisations with low labour costs but high fluctuations in demand (B)
Here the need for a flexible response to fluctuations in demand remains but lower labour costs mean that this can be provided using workers directly

under the organisation's control. Accordingly, an average core workforce can be used with fluctuations being met either using the incentive of overtime or Category B workers such as temporary workers.

Organisations with high labour costs but a low fluctuation in demand (C)
Here the needs are reversed. A more structured and planned approach to manpower planning design is less prone to fluctuations in demand because they are entirely predictable. Accordingly, an average sized core can be used using a combination of Category A part-time and shift working arrangements to cope with extended demand to daily working hours, and homeworking or networking arrangements to reduce office overheads and facilities costs. To respond to seasonal predicted peaks, Category B temporary working arrangements may be useful to avoid unnecessary personnel administration charges. Where high costs are continued and there are retention/recruitment problems, job sharing may be helpful.

Organisations with low labour costs and low fluctuations in demand (D)
Here the organisation's economic circumstances will allow it to employ a fairly large core workforce with fluctuations and extended demand being met by a combination of Category A overtime and flexitime arrangements and the imaginative use of part-timers.

This analysis merely suggests changes in emphasis to manpower policies. Certain uses of new working patterns may be used in all four types of organisations. For example, specialist consultants may always be used for particular projects and temporary agency workers to cover for holidays, sickness, and unexpected absenteeism.

Maintaining career continuity

Decisions about new forms of employment cannot be taken in isolation from the organisation's total employment policy and its philosophy about how it treats its workforce. Indeed, too great an emphasis on policies designed to reduce labour costs leads to a perception of employees as *costs* to be minimised rather than *assets* to be developed.

As we have frequently noted, many working arrangements are introduced in response to the social 'pull' of existing staff or potential applicants who wish to work on a flexible basis for personal reasons.

The incentive for introducing new working patterns of this nature has been given a distinctly commercial perspective by growing recruitment costs; the increased level of initial and continuous training required to maintain the right skills needed in the organisation; and a reduction in the numbers of young people entering the labour market, making it necessary for organisations to make the maximum use of their existing workforce.

In designing effective career management systems, it is worth remembering that people's requirements for flexible working arrangements vary at different periods in their lives.

28　NEW WORK PATTERNS

A professional worker's needs might possibly follow the pattern below:

20–25 years	Studying for technical or professional qualifications – happy to work full-time but requires study leave.
25–30 years	Building post-qualification work experience. Happy to work full-time
30–35 years	Starting a family – need for mid-career break for domestic, child-care or education purposes (possibly through sabbaticals and career break schemes). This may need to be followed by a part-time commitment under a professional part-time or job-share arrangement.
35–45 years	Immediate domestic pressures lessen. Desire to consolidate career development and reach positions of seniority. Happy to work full-time.
45–55 years	Children leaving home. Open to the idea of consultancy, counselling or networking business either because career development has peaked or from a desire to broaden career horizons.
55–65 years	If still with organisation, open to a steady staggering of work in immediate run-up to retirement.
65 plus	Looking for some part-time working arrangement either to supplement pension or to keep occupied.

Another profile might look as follows:

16–20	Working full-time as a junior in hotel and catering as a trainee chef.
20–25	Trained and working full-time for leading UK organisation.
25–30	Child-care responsibilities. Working part-time and employed as a 'casual' for special functions and seasonal demands.
30–40	Continuing to work on a casual basis but launching small catering business from home on self-employed basis. Business thrives.
40–45	Manages a leisure unit, on a sub-contract basis, part of the hotel chain originally employed in.
45–55	Recruited on a consultancy basis to develop links of organisation with small business and advise on management needs and policies!
55–	Works full-time towards retirement as regional manager for the organisation.

The difficulty is that many career development policies conflict directly with employees' personal needs. Many workers want more flexibility in their working patterns for personal reasons between thirty to thirty-five. This is precisely the time when most organisations demand a full-time commitment because, for example, management development programmes expect staff in that age range to make a quantum leap to senior positions or from a specialist to a generalist position.

The career dilemmas of working mothers is only the most visible example of the dilemma. At various times in their careers, workers of both sexes may want to change their working patterns to take up consultancy work, to cope with physical or mental disability or to take up some form of continuing education.

New work patterns can therefore be used to maintain the career continuity of workers. It might also offer better and varied opportunities to staff. The result will be a greatly reduced turnover and a more effective and long-term return on the resources invested in training and development.

ISSUES RELATING TO SPECIFIC WORK PATTERNS

Employers need to have a proper understanding of the benefits and disadvantages of introducing individual working arrangements and a clear picture of the choices at their disposal. For the remainder of this chapter, we will look at the issues and study a number of work patterns which impose significant changes to management and communication systems. We shall begin with those work patterns which have been largely used for economic reasons.

Temporary work

Anecdotes about the relative advantages and disadvantages of temporary workers abound. A few general points are worth making:

- Strictly speaking, there is no concept of a 'permanent' contract in English law. The true distinction is between a contract of indefinite and one of definite length
- Temporary work ranges from the highly skilled, for example, in medicine ('locums' are included), computing, and engineering, to cleaners, salesmen, waiters, fruit pickers, and ice-cream sellers during Wimbledon fortnight. Consequently, temporary workers are a mixed group and present varying issues for management
- The motivation for choosing temporary work varies. A high proportion of temporary workers, especially women, are temporary out of choice and not seeking permanent work. They enjoy the variety, freedom and lack of commitment to a particular enterprise. A minority, especially men, accept temporary work because of the unavailability of permanent work. They look for work as an opening to a more secure post and may therefore be a useful source of proven and easily recruitable labour
- In some circumstances the situation requires that the contract *has* to be temporary (for example to provide cover for maternity leave). Yet, many circumstances allow the employer to choose whether a vacancy is filled on a limited or permanent basis
- Expectations of temporary workers will vary considerably depending on whether they are primarily used for functional or for numerical flexibility.

The short-term research worker, computer or design engineer will bring valuable skills and experience and the day-to-day demands on them will be considerable. Casual cleaning, catering and agricultural workers will probably attract lower and less complex expectations. All will have to adapt quickly to an organisation's management style and culture, and to the varying attitudes of fellow workers.

Advantages

- Lower wage costs and other wage-related expenses in terms of occupational benefits
- Lack of legal regulation will mean that workers can be employed more informally
- Contracts can be terminated more easily. Periods of notice required by law are short and temporary workers are rarely protected under job security law – those whose contracts are for a specific task (fixed-job contracts) are especially vulnerable
- Collective agreements rarely provide detailed terms for temporary staff, leaving individual management considerable discretion
- Lower recruitment costs
- Fixed-term contracts can be tied in more effectively to specific corporate objectives.

Many of these features are particularly attractive to new enterprises or those with an uncertain future. A study of computing firms in 1982[1] showed that new and family-owned firms often employed workers on a freelance/casual and self-employed basis until they had a secure market position. The change to permanent contractual arrangements was a mark of their firm 'having arrived'. Many still relied on local or professional registers or agencies to recruit workers to specific projects or particular needs.

Disadvantages

- Higher levels of absenteeism than with permanent staff
- Lower levels of commitment and loyalty
- Increased management problems
- Risks of disruption and impact on the quality of work or service.

Dilemmas

- How to recruit and manage temporary staff economically and yet achieve effective quality and screening
- How to keep overheads and wage costs relatively low yet motivate workers
- How to maximise efficiency of workers who are working for short periods

- How to achieve variety and flexibility and yet establish efficient management systems sensitive to the needs of individuals
- How to retain the impermanent concept of the relationship yet build up sufficient loyalty.

Overall, temporary work is most effective where professional and occupational loyalty is marked and therefore a powerful motivator overcoming ambiguous feelings of loyalty to the firm. Occupational commitment is a feature of work at the highest skill levels, and also the lowest. Skilled engineers or doctors will have professional standards which guide their work regardless of the contractual arrangement. Experienced bar and banqueting staff will have less marketable skills but often considerable experience and an unwritten code of loyalty. Both of these category of staff have strong traditions of working under contract. More problematic are categories of workers where there is a strong tradition of permanent work. Professions in the public sector increasingly subject to temporary engagements are the areas where insecurities and resentment are likely to breed most easily.

Self-employed workers

Self-employed workers includes groups classified as casual, freelance, under contract, and agents. In some occupations, for example, journalism, music, the building trades, selling, mini-cabbing etc., there are long traditions of employing workers in this manner. Experience in other occupations, such as insurance and catering, is more variable and individual employers have made differing choices. Although it is likely that employers have clear views as to whether to employ on Category A or B basis, it is important to keep the process under review and assess its effectiveness.

Advantages

- Savings on National Insurance, injury insurance and the administration of PAYE, SSP, and related matters
- Savings on personnel management costs in terms of contract documentation and other material, and often recruitment costs
- Increased productivity and incentives due to the opportunity for higher earnings and perceived advantages of Schedule D taxation
- Less demand for close supervision
- Lower or lack of training and developmental costs
- Avoidance of most employment law provisions, e.g. maternity pay, guaranteed pay and rights to time off
- Lower level of responsibility for health and safety regulations
- Savings on occupational benefits
- Ease of termination of arrangement
- Greater likelihood of provision of equipment, uniform and the like by the worker

These advantages can be most significant in areas where the work is skilled and requires updating; and where motivation and output are central. Selling, and creative occupations are typical. However, many employers find that incentives can be provided for directly employed workers not simply in cash terms but through profit sharing, time off arrangements and a high level of participation in the enterprise. Greater flexibility by employers regarding pay and occupational benefits can challenge some of the traditionally associated advantages of self-employment.

Disadvantages

- Increased liability to pay higher level of basic pay
- Less control and supervision of work and product
- Likely higher level of turnover and lack of continuity
- Increased managerial costs of harmonising work with the enterprise and its other workers
- Lack of availability of many employment law rights of the employer regarding restraint of trade, confidential material, disciplinary matters and indemnities
- Possible increase of risk of accidents, injury and damage, demanding higher insurance premiums
- Lower level of loyalty and less integration in the culture of the enterprise
- Possible risks to the reputation of an enterprise through its association with 'cowboy' operators and the hidden/informal economy
- Possible problems of recruitment at times and/or in places where workers seek secure employment.

The disadvantages of self-employed labour are often less obvious. Some concern quality rather than cost. Others turn on less direct management costs. It is tempting to ally self-employment with independence and enterprise, especially on short-term projects or in occupations demanding drive and energy. However, turnover and drop-out rates are high. Although the training and other investment costs have probably been low, there are other costs to be borne in terms of disruption, communication, familiarisation and standardisation. It is surprising how many employers shrug their shoulders at the unreliability and even harm inflicted by self-employed workers and disregard the consequent cost in terms of replacement and possible loss of goodwill.

Dilemmas

- How to retain loyalty while offering little security and occupational benefits
- How to allow for enterprise and independence while maintaining control
- How to assimilate the self-employed worker sufficiently without unduly increasing managerial costs

- How to provide effective overall management which is equal but different from that for employees
- How to maximise the efficiency and output of the worker when they are notionally independent and an equal contracting party and wishing to extract the 'best deal' for you
- How to provide tailored support and facilities without compromising the interests of the organisation.

There are no obvious answers, especially at a time when pressure from workers to be self-employed is growing. Before changes are introduced, the employer must ensure that quality as well as output will be maintained and that apparent cost savings are real.

The experience of two life insurance companies will illustrate these points.

Examples

1 Company A, a multi-national based in North America, employs workers as agents on a self-employed basis. They have an expensive recruitment programme, followed by intensive residential training. Agents are given a 'franchise' to market life insurance and a few 'warm' contracts. Most have to find their own market but are paid a generous 'fee' on all sales. They have a 90 per cent staff turnover per year. This is tolerated on the basis of 'survival of the fittest', the good agents producing adequate income to support the recruitment programme. Career development is through higher earnings and access to the few managerial posts: other overheads are minimal as the agents work from home using their own 'phone, and other equipment. The 'core' office staff and premises are small, though the organisation works from a prestigious location.

2 Company B, also a multi-national, employs virtually all staff on employment contracts. Line managers have two contracts. One is at basic salary and concerned with managing agents and dealing with office administration. The other is a contract to sell policies. The company has a complex training and staff development programme and discipline is strict. Most of the agents follow up leads provided by the company, though they can make independent sales. Pay is based on a salary with incremental points. But there are considerable opportunities for commission on sales and other incentives in terms of free holidays, cars and attendance at prestigious functions with awards to successful employees. Staff turnover is below 50 per cent. The company sees its policies as effective in attracting, retaining and achieving good output by employees. A balance exists between providing some support and security, and encouraging enterprise and hard work. It is conscious that the insurance industry can easily attract a bad name through 'fly by night' reps.

From the customer's viewpoint, it would be hard to detect the impact of the contrasting management policies. Both companies were firmly committed to their choice.

Consultants

Consultants, along with sub-contractors, represent the most obvious form of third party intervention at the workplace. Both groups usually provide a specialist function; both usually have high levels of autonomy. Some may work for only a few hours; others may have long-standing contracts. In all cases, the relationship and those contracts require careful anticipation and planning. Given that consultants and sub-contractors both supply a functional need, it is necessary for present purposes to distinguish their role.

Consultants are used for two basic reasons:

- For diagnostic purposes, where they undertake an evaluation of the needs, shortfalls, potential and development of an enterprise. Consultants may simply diagnose and leave or participate in policy implementation following their evaluation
- To provide specialist advice or services on a continuing basis.

Sub-contracting will imply the delegation of a discrete function to another enterprise. That function may be the supply of goods and/or services and will generally be undertaken on a regular or continuing basis.

Traditional areas of consultancy are finance, legal, computing, marketing, design and highly specialised professional skills, such as medicine. Using consultants is often a long-standing and only rarely reviewed activity. The processes applied to the choice and evaluation of legal advice will rarely be the same as those applied to management consultants. It will be necessary, therefore, to review the use and effectiveness of currently used consultants as well as to consider extension of consultants into new areas of work.

Consultancy is increasing, especially in the public sector. As it continues to grow, those able and willing to offer advice and skills on a consultancy basis will be drawn from a wider area. For example, more and more academic institutions offer services to employers following pressure to become self-supporting. There will be an increasing choice of consultants, and new areas will open up. Well-trodden areas, frequently not at the heart of an enterprise, may be overshadowed by use of consultants in core or central activities. Already, personnel managers are frequently supported (or supplanted) by consultants in key areas of their work.

Despite the increasing use of consultants, research and analysis of their use and impact is fairly limited. Advantages and disadvantages are often presented in an anecdotal way, or on the basis of relatively limited investigation. Many are self-evident. Much will obviously depend on the size of an enterprise, its overall policy, nature of business and its management needs.

Benefits

- To provide expertise which is lacked in-house
- To provide a quick response
- To save costs
- To widen the expertise of in-house staff
- To highlight inadequacies in personnel and practices

- To transform managerial attitudes particularly when inflexible and unresponsive to the needs of the market or employees.

Points to consider

- A clumsy or insensitive introduction of consultants can do untold damage. Some consultants have gained the whole profession a bad name. Stories of 'fly-by-night' so-called experts abound, as do allegations that consultants merely confirmed the obvious or were simply being used by senior management to divide or remove staff
- The use of consultants in some areas of work is less likely to cause tension than others, especially where strong traditions of an in-house role have not developed. Computing and advertising are often such areas. If consultants are used in training, production and promotional areas, or for purely diagnostic purposes, tensions can easily arise
- Consultants need to be warned about pre-existing rivalries or tensions, and of vested interests. They will need to be alert to assertions that they simply picked employees' brains and packaged the ideas to their client, the employer. At the same time, pretentious or empire-building proposals will be unwelcome and often a waste of money.

Generally, the evaluation of the enterprise should focus on the following questions:

- Are you aware of, and can you clearly define, an un-met functional need or operational shortfall?
- Do you lack adequate or appropriate in-house skills, including in-house third-party roles?
- Are you clear about your motives for, and attitudes towards, using consultants?
- Are the conditions at the workplace likely to allow mutual trust to develop between you and the consultants?
- Is the consultancy role to be primarily diagnostic or a separated and complementary activity?
- Do you have the relevant skills to choose and negotiate with consultants?
- Does the enterprise have or can it develop appropriate mechanisms and structures to monitor and/or respond to consultants' work?
- Does the enterprise have or can it develop awareness and skills on the part of in-house staff to effectively relate to consultants?
- Is use of consultants going to be worth the effort, and/or will it distort the balance of the workforce generally?

Where consultants are currently used by the enterprise it may be helpful to consider the following issues:

- Have you ever reviewed or re-negotiated the consultancy contract?
- If so, did the re-negotiation cover matters other than fees?
- Have you established clear criteria for efficient performance?

- Are the criteria met or broadly met?
- Are you aware of any problems or tensions caused by the use of consultant(s)?
- Does/Do the staff member(s) responsible for liaising with the consultants make reports on their efficiency?
- Are they and you satisfied with overall attitude and performance?
- Have relevant skills developed in-house since the contract was negotiated?

Sub-contracting

Sub-contracting is likely to be the most controversial and problematic of work patterns. In the private sector, many areas of work, such as cleaning, maintenance, decorating, and catering, and specialist areas like lift installation and maintenance, have traditionally been sub-contracted. But the enormous growth of the practice in the public sector has led to publicity and debate.

There are no obvious answers to the questions about sub-contracting: the central issue is whether it is compatible with the culture of your organisation and will lead to greater efficiency. There is no value in sub-contracting maintenance or computing management, if the costs, in terms of industrial relations strife, discipline and quality of service, outweigh the notional contract costs. The debate on use of sub-contractors therefore centres on the relative importance of cost versus quality. Only if the latter can be maintained will the apparent economic advantages be realised.

There are a whole range of options on offer regarding the use of sub-contractors, which leave various gradations of control to the employer. An employer can buy a whole service – equipment, management, and staff – combined. In this case, you have to be very sure of the quality of the sub-contractor, as you have no 'lever' over them, other than through the contract, once they have taken over the function. You can retain the plant and equipment, but buy-in the management and/or workers. You can buy-in the management but employ the workers as your own employees.

You can retain the employees, but buy-in the use of equipment, such as for printing, computing, transportation and storage. You can run the main activity on an in-house basis but sub-contract for support services, for example, jobs in the secretarial and financial areas. The list is almost endless, and will require careful consideration by management of its own needs. It also requires an appraisal of what 'management' implies in the context of all or some of the service being contracted. The managements' skills will have to adapt, and move from 'people management' to 'project management'. These skills will be very different and will require specific preparation and training (see Chapter 6).

One of the major problems about sub-contracting, especially for public sector managers, is that the enterprise is both buyer of the service and producer of it. This dual role is not always easy to reconcile and perform. It may lead some employers to conclude that sub-contracting undermines essential areas of control and is not worth the effort. Sub-contracting is clearly a complex aspect of the flexible enterprise, and raises a number of central issues regarding the role of management. Many enthusiasts point to a number of clear advantages. Few of the claimed advantages are as clear cut as first imagined.

Advantage 1: Cost savings

Most of recent data is almost inevitably drawn from the public sector, especially the NHS and central Government. The research indicates that savings of between 30 per cent and 60 per cent can be anticipated through the sub-contracting process. Areas such as cleaning, refuse collection, catering (including school meals), laundry work, ground and building maintenance, have been analysed on a 'before and after' basis. Cost savings can be achieved through labour and administrative costs, with contracts being performed by fewer workers, often with less generous employment arrangements than those available for in-house staff. With the weakening of the power of wages councils, the absence of minimum wages levels and a broadly non-interventionist approach by law, the sub-contractors have wide discretions on fixing a cost for the contract, and there can be pressure and obvious advantages to clients to go for the cheapest contractor.

Within the private sector, costs efficiency often arises through the fact that the service, for example, security or window cleaning, is highly specialised and does not warrant the retention of regular staff, or the cost of the associated overheads. On a purely cost basis, there are services, for example, those in the technical and medical areas, which ought to be considered candidates for sub-contracting. This is especially so where there are wide choices available of appropriate and experienced sub-contractors. Cleaning and security are obvious cases in point where there is a plethora of organisations operating in the sub-contracting market. Indeed, many organisations *only* operate on this basis.

The re-evaluation of services through the tendering process is likely to save on costs, as opposed to sub-contracting itself. Studies of the NHS show that where contracts are won by in-house units as well as sub-contractors, savings arise across the board. In-house units are just as likely to be cost effective as outsiders. Analysis of the savings showed that the major cause was redefining the job specification, with greater labour productivity as the second most important factor. In some cases, redefining the work to be done leads to a reduction in the extent or quality of a service or function. This factor must be carefully balanced, especially where the consumer/customers are quality conscious; or where mistakes, for example in computing, could be disastrous. In some cases, redefining a specification would lead to shortfalls which had to be made up by other workers in the enterprise – a factor which will add to costs.

Sub-contractors often allege that comparisons between performance of in-house units and sub-contractors fail to take account of the full cost of in-house staff and equipment. For example, administrative and personnel costs are not properly accounted for, giving in-house units advantages in the tendering process.

When assessing the relative cost of using your own staff, rather than sub-contracting, it is vital to take into account the following costs over and above labour and capital:

- Recruitment costs
- Training costs
- Costs of protective clothing and uniforms, etc.
- Administrative and medical costs, and expenses connected with occupational benefits
- Management's cost of devising the specification and managing the sub-contractors
- Maintenance and renewal of equipment and plant.

Research indicates that the specification and day-to-day management are key areas, and ones that can be both skill and time consuming. It may be necessary to introduce new procedures to accurately define these and other costs. Cost savings may well occur through the scrutinising of the function itself. This ought to take place, even without sub-contracting. Evaluating cost savings in comparison with an efficient in-house unit or capacity is essential.

Advantage 2: Improved output and efficiency

The basis of this is that contracts are for a specified period and are subject to renewal, often in a competitive situation. With or without an in-house bid, this will sharpen edges. At an extreme level, some employers will hire and fire contractors, especially where there are many firms in the market. Cleaning and catering are examples, particularly in city areas. Realistically, many sub-contractors are non-unionised, or have relatively weak unions. Collective bargaining is not an issue. Despite labour turnover being at levels of over 50 per cent, per annum, in some occupations, many contractors are able to remain highly competitive, especially in relatively unskilled areas of work.

Sub-contracting can lead to greater efficiency but the quality of work provided by sub-contractors should be scrutinised carefully. In-house disciplinary codes, promotion possibilities and occupational benefits, will not be present when applied to sub-contracted staff. Various organisations, especially trade unions, have monitored and categorised the alleged failures of sub-contractors. The sanction of ending the contract is there but this will probably cause disruption and there may not be a substitute available to take over the 'failed' contract. In-house staff are more aware of the specific needs of the enterprise, more familiar with its culture, more committed to its success and more likely to work efficiently. There are many examples cited of ancillary workers in the NHS who, as in-house workers, viewed themselves as part of the total health care 'team' but who were distanced and more aware of occupational boundaries when working for a sub-contractor.

The extent to which the service or function is integrated in the enterprise more broadly is therefore crucial. If the function can be hived off, is highly specialised or can be performed off-site this will not be a key factor. The style and quality of work may not have to complement that of other in-house activities, and will be less likely to give rise to tension and complaints.

Many sub-contractors are long established and are familiar with the particular demands of this type of activity. Many belong to professional or trade associations, and conform to codes of practice. The Contract Cleaning and Maintenance Association and the Computing Services Association are examples. They cover approximately 60 per cent and 80 per cent of the sub-contracting market, respectively. They are very image conscious and members should be more reliable than non-members.

Public subsidy trainees (YTS)

Most analyses of the flexible work include trainees as part of the peripheral workforce. This might seem surprising. The current two year YTS scheme appears somewhat rigid, highly structured and vigorously monitored by the Training Agency (TA); and provides training programmes which, although they aim to produce transferable skills, are closely determined by onerous contract terms.

An enterprise has to decide whether to participate in the scheme.

Advantages

- Provides a source of cash (though may not be adequate)
- The cash can be used to offset training costs
- Can be useful in labour and skill shortage areas
- Considerably aids recruitment and recruitment costs
- Improves in-house training and procedures
- Can improve the image of an enterprise
- Can provide a source of cheap labour
- Can release permanent workers from routine jobs, and improve customer/client service
- Provides links with educational institutions and other employees.

Experience shows that the majority of advantages to employers are in terms of recruitment (67 per cent of trainees are taken on by the employer at the end of the scheme) and in assisting to redress skill/labour shortages. Many employers appreciate the advantages of using the scheme to plan manpower more effectively and to recruit 'proven' employees. The possible effect on training itself is particularly motivating. The external demands on an enterprise will likely lead to an evaluation of current training programmes, particularly in a context of accommodating the off-the-job training and vocational awards which now have to play a part.

Improvements may well come about through a sharpening of existing programmes and the necessary addition of new elements, such as health and safety training. The experience of YTS may lead to an evaluation of all the training needs of an enterprise and result in more training and re-training of core and other workers which will ultimately lead to increased skills and flexibility. Thus, the 'knock-on' effect of YTS may well be the most valuable.

Disadvantages

- High levels of bureaucracy involved in setting up and administering the programme
- Interference by the TA at the workplace
- Control by TA over training
- Rigidity of some training schemes
- Trade union and other pressure to 'top-up' pay to trainees
- Pressure to provide employee status for trainees.

The training demands and control by the TA are considerable, and they will be discussed further in Chapter 4. In order to be admitted to the scheme an employer has to meet considerable demands in terms of levels of staffing, accommodation, the nature and supervision of the training itself and health and safety. The paperwork and time taken to deal with visits by representatives of the TA can be substantial. Since the introduction of the two-year scheme a number of previous providers of training, especially some local authorities, have withdrawn, finding these demands too onerous and intrusive.

With the two-year scheme there has been increased pressure to 'top-up' pay, especially for the second year of training. During the second year the TA allowance to trainees is £35, compared to the average wage of a seventeen year old of approximately £75 per week.

Relatively few employers provide 'top-ups' though some provide other benefits, such as staff purchasing discounts. Employers, especially some in the retail trade – e.g. Empire Stores, Littlewoods Mail Order – pay the rate for the job in year two, as do some ICI plants and Fords. Similarly, local authorities, such as Peterborough District Council, Salford Council, Sheffield, Knowsley, and Harlow Councils, pay the rate for the job, and often trainees are moved automatically into permanent posts when vacancies occur.

Employers clearly have choice as to whether to top-up pay and whether to give 'employee' or 'apprenticeship' status. Some employers provide contracts of employment because of trade union or political pressure not to 'exploit' young workers. Other employers, especially in skill shortage areas will see the advantage of integrating trainees quickly and effectively into their organisation. This might encourage them to put more energy into the scheme and the trainees to be more committed in their work.

Dilemmas

To be a sponsor or an Approved Training Organisation (ATO)? Employers only now can enter the scheme as an Approved Training Organisation. Currently there are over 3000 operating as ATOs. The ATOs arrange the programmes of training and receive an annual management fee and basic grant for each trainee. ATOs can be individual employers – though most are large organisations, group training associations, voluntary organisations, local authorities, training boards or private agencies. They liaise with educational institutions, and the YTS Certification Board (YCB), which validates the vocational awards to be obtained through the scheme. There is some confusion and controversy over this issue. Although there is an ongoing review of vocational qualifications, the views of employers as well as trade unions have been given a low priority, and they have no representation on the YCB. Critics have said that the YCB will merely perpetuate the ethos of the traditional awards bodies, such as City and Guilds, BTEC, and the Royal Society of Arts. This could lead to inflexibility and a lack of innovation in training programmes, with the changing needs and policies of employers going unrecognised.

Although trainees can be recruited directly onto an employers' programme many come via the local careers office. In all cases the terms of work are strictly laid down by the TA. Some trainee places, for example, for disabled workers or for employing difficult trainees, qualify for additional grants to employers over and above the basic training grant for trainees.

Is it worth entering the scheme? Much will depend on individual factors at the enterprise. Obvious ones are pre-existing training schemes, ease of recruitment, the highly individualised culture of an organisation, and size and nature of the workplace. Whether the scheme provides sufficient flexibility is open to debate, both in relation to the operation of the scheme and the skills and attitudes it develops. It will not be an easy source of income, especially when offset against the vast bureaucracy and levels of control. As one writer put it, when posing the question whether employers should join: 'If the answer is "no", check that it is not an easy way out, that problems, difficult as many are, are not just an excuse. If the answer is "yes", then there is a crusade to undertake but more on strategic than factual issues'.

In the context of the flexible workforce, there must remain other questions about whether to use the YTS scheme. With its emphasis on traditional full-time work and a rigid training programme, with no leeway for suspension of the scheme, and with change to other training programmes difficult to effect, the issue arises whether it is compatible with the atmosphere and objectives of flexibility. This may not lead to the conclusion that one should not join, but may make harmonisation of YTS training, and other training and promotion procedures at your workforce more difficult. Insofar as flexibility is a matter of attitudes, the YTS scheme, as currently operated, may present a considerable hurdle to many employers, other than those with specific training needs or other factors.

'SOCIAL PULL' PATTERNS

As we saw earlier in the chapter, organisations are introducing a number of new work patterns specifically to meet changing social needs and obligations of employees. These include:

- Formal career break schemes and sabbaticals
- Job sharing and professional part-time working
- Homeworking
- Secondments.

In some cases, the initial reason for the introduction of these schemes has been to support already established equal opportunities policies, often at the prompting of staff associations or white-collar unions with a strong female membership.

The majority of organisations have followed suit for different reasons. To avoid additional labour costs and to combat skill shortages caused by shrinking numbers of new entrants to the employment market, UK employers are trying to improve their performance without greatly adding to their number of employees. Retention is becoming as key an issue as recruitment. There is a growing awareness that the loss of a skilled trained member of staff represents a dual cost, in terms of the lost investment in expenditure on training and development for the person leaving and the recruitment and development costs of taking on a successor.

The result is a greater emphasis on career management and the effective use of internal labour markets. Employment policies incorporating some or all of the schemes above are seen as a means of maintaining employment or career continuity during periods when employees are unable or unwilling to work full-time for the employing organisation. In some instances (for example, in the case of job sharing and secondment) these work patterns are also used to stagger older workers' hours in preparation for retirement; and give younger employees formal time out to further their education or work in a different environment (often as part of a planned programme of career development).

Career break schemes

Option One: with guaranteed re-entry
The number of normal career break schemes *guaranteeing re-entry* at the

same level or in the same job after a fixed period of absence is still very limited. In most cases, the scheme is confined to a small number of candidates with a very high career potential. These schemes have a number of common characteristics:

- A clear definition of eligible groups
- Minimum service requirement, for example, five years and, often, a requirement that candidates should have, say, twenty years of working experience ahead of them when they return from the break
- One break only allowed with a fixed maximum length (e.g. five years)
- Provision for candidates to keep in touch with the organisation during the break through regular meetings, counselling sessions and/or a requirement work on a part-time basis at staged intervals.

Advantages

- Providing the rules and eligibility have been clearly spelt out, the process becomes easy to administer and gain acceptance, even in the most bureaucratic culture
- There is no need to re-design jobs and therefore limited disruption
- Organisations where managers are still hostile to women combining careers with child-care will inevitably use discretionary policies (see below) to a very limited extent; a formal scheme operated efficiently from the centre of the organisation (rather than at the discretion of local managers) can guarantee that at least some women can take a longer career break and return to employment
- By being so visible, such schemes may in time also change attitudes more easily.

Disadvantages

- Schemes guaranteeing re-entry are only suitable for a very small number of valued employees – there is a critical trade-off between the size of the eligible group and the degree of certainty over re-entry which can realistically be guaranteed.
- Numbers may also be restricted because of the administrative costs – participants will need to be kept in touch with the organisation's development during their absence and will almost certainly require re-training on their return.
- A total break in employment followed by a compulsory return to full-time employment may not be what many women actually want; unless the return is staged using homeworking, job sharing, part-time work or other flexible arrangements, the drop-out rate may be high. In certain circumstances, the obligation to return to full-time work may be considered by tribunals as discriminatory under the Sex Discrimination Act (see Chapter 5).

Option Two: schemes offering discretionary return
The alternative is a more discretionary policy which offers 'serious consideration' to ex-employees who wish to return to work but no guarantee of re-entry.

Advantages

- The scheme can be offered to a much wider range of employees – there is less danger of the policy being seen as discriminatory or elitist
- It is easiest to apply to jobs which are less skilled and firm-specific – re-entry in this case is less of a problem provided the organisation has a growing workforce.

Disadvantages

- The relationship between the ex-employee and the organisation is unclear
- The success of the scheme is dependent on the co-operation of local managers – if they are hostile to the idea of women returners or are unable to offer comparable employment then the scheme may well be perceived as little more than meaningless paper policy
- A discretionary policy is much less likely to work for those on career ladders where jobs are usually filled by internal promotion and where the problems of re-integration after up to five years' absence is much harder to manage.

In summary, career break schemes have had a mixed success since their introduction in the late 1970s. Few organisations are happy to risk large numbers of re-entrants knocking on their doors in five years' time when they are uncertain about their future growth. Many women also prefer a gradual part-time return and may not necessarily want to concentrate their child bearing and rearing into one five year period.

In addition, career break schemes are almost always introduced and eligibility designed with career mothers in mind. Male employees may have their own reasons for wishing to have time out or stepping off the career ladder: e.g. supporting and sharing in child rearing, further education, travel, etc. Organisations are equally liable to lose them if they cannot provide sufficient flexibility in their career management.

Options for organisations designing or improving career break schemes therefore include:

- Combining a 'guaranteed re-entry' scheme for fast-track managers and/or long-service employees with a more discretionary policy available to a much wider section of the workforce
- Ensuring that the scheme(s) are either administered centrally (e.g. in the case of guaranteed re-entry) or monitored centrally to gauge their success

- Ensuring that local managers are made aware of the policy and, where their discretionary role is a critical part of the policy's success, that their commitment has been secured
- Ensuring that participant's re-entry is made simpler and that the process is better managed by:
  - staging the return to full-time work through job sharing, homeworking and part-time employment
  - adequate and early agreement over return to work, covering timing, specific job description, and work location
  - careful job replacement or liaison with local managers to ensure that a suitable vacancy exists at the right time
  - offering the possibility of either (a) a longer single period of leave (e.g. seven years) or (b) more than one shorter period (e.g. three years) to allow the individual more flexibility in matching career breaks to personal needs.

Example: Kent County Council

A good example of the greater flexibility that can be built into career break schemes is included in the policy introduced by Kent County Council in 1988.

The Council's career break scheme was introduced as part of a package of measures to aid the poor promotion prospects of key professional female staff – and, in particular, women teachers working for the authority.

The returner scheme enables teachers taking a career break for domestic reasons to return to employment at the same status at which they left. Posts are protected for seven years providing the returner undertakes ten days' supply teaching each year and attends in-service training designed by the Authority specifically for their needs.

The scheme has a number of characteristics which make it particularly noteworthy. Firstly, it is retrospective. Teachers who left the Council within five years of the scheme's introduction were encouraged to return and all teachers then on maternity leave were sent information.

Secondly, the length of break – seven years – is markedly longer than periods offered under other schemes; this was specifically because the working party responsible for setting up the programme felt that women would need this length of time if they were to have more than one child.

Thirdly, it is possible for teachers to take up the scheme more than once, provided there is a two year gap between the breaks. The scheme is also open to male staff, although the provisions only enable the break to be taken for domestic reasons (e.g. child rearing, looking after a dependant relative) rather than to enhance career prospects (for example, by taking up further education).

Part-time work and job sharing

Many organisations have extensive experience of part-time workers and, whereas in some occupations, such as retailing, cleaning and market research, part-timers dominate the workforce, others have a strong tradition of full-time work only. Frequently, but not necessarily, occupations resistant to part-time work will also be reluctant to introduce job sharing.

However, it is vital to appreciate that although job sharing is a form of part-time work its essence is the division of a full-time post and its pay, benefits and prospects.

It is generally thought that the advantages of part-time work are:

- Saving on wage costs
- Higher output by workers
- Coverage of specialist, on-going tasks
- Lower level of training and recruitment costs
- Less intrusion by employment law.

Disadvantages

These are usually expressed as follows:

- Less commitment to the organisation
- Higher levels of turnover and absenteeism
- Relatively higher administrative and management costs.

Some of these views are not proved conclusively, especially the assertions about commitment. However, they are widely held and tend to colour attitudes towards the introduction of job sharing. Increasing use of part-timers is already a feature of the labour market, and will continue, especially in service industries and for specialist skills.

Job sharing has developed over the past few years and has become established in parts of the public sector and is making inroads in the private sector. For some time it has been thought that job sharing was appropriate for middle to lower level white-collar work where job tasks and working could be easily divided. Secretarial, administrative, medical and para-medical work were dominant. However, recent research shows that job sharing is being effectively carried out by managers in a range of high level, policy-oriented and creative posts. It has broken through into senior posts in central government, the media and the caring and other professions such as planning, law and engineering. The practical arrangements vary considerably and are less and less based on traditional patterns of Monday to Wednesday for sharer one and Wednesday to Friday for sharer two.

However, research is beginning to identify the advantages as well as likely problems associated with job sharing. Clearly, the culture of an organisation, especially its labour market position and its attitude to equal opportunities matters has great influence.

Advantages

It seems likely that major advantages of employing job-sharers are:

- Increased work output by the sharers – the sum of the two part(ners) in the job often add up to more than the whole post. Job sharers are conscious that full-timers suspect they are onto a 'cushy number' and they

work harder to refute this. A typical comment was, 'I have less time for socialising. If I chat at work its purely about work – I never go out to lunch'
- An aid to recruitment and retention of employees. Many employers face severe problems in this area, and many of their actual or potential staff cannot or do not want to work full-time. Managers might say, 'We kept two able people we'd have lost otherwise'. The retention of staff who might not return after maternity leave or take early retirement from a full-time post is the most important aspect
- 'Two heads are better than one.' Many jobs are enhanced by the presence of two employees, especially where they are complementary or contrasting. Policy and creative areas especially benefit and jobs which are routine or unexciting for a full-timer can be acceptable on a part-time basis
- Increased flexibility. Flexibility can arise through the individual skills of the sharers providing a wider range overall. Sometimes it arises through the willingness of sharers to cover the whole post for short periods, or to deputise for the other on occasions
- Less time off work. Most job-sharers make medical and similar appointments on their days off. Labour cost savings can be considerable.

Although using job-sharers can be highly beneficial, and even in senior and supervisory posts it is likely that where work is project based and peaks over relatively short periods of time, for example, a week, job-sharers are hard to absorb. There are also a few types of work where third parties have to relate to one individual and who would find two people in a post highly confusing.

Disadvantages

- There can be a loss of continuity in a post – the 'two Monday's syndrome'
- Some job-sharers can be unresponsive to crises or peak demands, when compared to full-timers
- Increased personnel and administrative costs. These largely derive from the need to effectively plan and implement a job share, and for additional communication facilities.
- Increased investment of time by managers, research indicates that managers will happily contribute to job sharing, especially where it solves other managerial problems.

Homeworking

As we have already seen, homeworking is a generic term covering a wide range of individual arrangements. The main ones include:

Employees working 'from' home: staff in this category include travelling sales representatives, researchers, homebased journalists

Employees working 'at' home: these are often 'teleworkers' linked to their organisation through computer terminals

48 NEW WORK PATTERNS

Self-employed or contract staff: also included in this category are networkers who are 'retained' by the organisation on a part-time basis and are free to take up consultancy or freelance work during the remaining time.

Advantages

- Office costs, including those linked to working space and regular travel, are reduced, often dramatically; although it may be necessary for homeworkers to spend part of their time working on site (see below)
- Homeworking often enables employees to dovetail their work and domestic responsibilities; it also provides a middle option between on-site and self-management, enabling them to achieve a greater degree of control over their working hours or techniques without sacrificing their financial security.

Dilemmas

- Many homeworkers feel cut off from the social mainstream of the organisation; they may need regular access to office facilities and data; and their work will have to be based on regular briefings and appraisal. For all these reasons, it may be necessary for them to visit and work occasionally (or even regularly) on the organisation's premises
- Additional training may be needed:
  – for homeworkers, to enable them to regulate their own work and use new equipment
  – for line managers, who may require greater teamworking and project management skills
- Management and communication systems, performance appraisal, reporting systems and selection criteria will need to be redesigned or improved to allow for a more sophisticated form of off-site supervision and control.

Secondment

Organisations have experimented with secondment for a number of reasons. The main ones include:

Corporate social responsibility: secondment plays a key role in many organisations' CSR policies. It is seen as being 'good value' for money since a secondee worth up to £25 000 pa is more valuable to the host body than a similar cash grant

External public relations: secondment is seen by many organisations as cost effective public relations although the majority who perceive this benefit do not exploit it in a heavy-handed manner

Internal public relations: secondment is seen as good internal public relations, 'it shows employees we care', etc. However, this does not always have the desired effect, with many employees regarding the practice with suspicion and managers resenting the loss of skills

Career development for key managers: a growing number of companies regard secondment as a means of giving valued or key staff the opportunity to acquire new skills and experience. One of the training managers recruited to the Stock Exchange's job-share scheme, Jean Lammiman, for example, was subsequently seconded to the City University as deputy director of their consortium MBA programme – principally for career development reasons

Other staffing reasons: organisations use secondments to solve particular staffing, some of the more common include:
 – *pre-retirement* as a means of preparing older workers or easing them out
 – *surplus employees:* as a means of easing out staff for whom there is no work (for example, in the case of a merger, internal re-organisation, or plant closure)
 – *avoiding conflict:* to ease personality clashes
 – *assessing individuals:* this reason often being linked to systematic career development (see above)
 – *career break:* to re-motivate employees who have peaked in their careers or been in one job too long.

Although British organisations' use of secondment does not match that of US or Australasian counterparts, it has been growing steadily over the past fifteen years.

A recent survey of 122 companies by the Centre for Employment Initiatives (CEI) found that nearly half (sixty-five) were found to be seconding staff to non profit-making organisations. Major banks were found to be the most enthusiastic practitioners.

Five hundred and thirty staff were involved. The ratio of management to other staff was 7:1. There were almost twice as many pre-retirement secondees as other categories. Male secondees predominated and nearly all secondees were on a full-time basis usually for periods exceeding one year. Twenty-four companies purposely used secondment for career development purposes.

Traditionally, secondments have been for periods of two years or more, but an increasing number of 'host' organisations can offer shorter, flexible assignments tailored to meet the training needs of the organisation and secondee.

Action Resource Centre (ARC), the principal agent for seconding arrangements, recently launched COMPASS (Community Project Assignments) in Leicester. The scheme, backed by the Home Office and Leicester Task Force, offers clearly designated assignments of between one and 200 hours for young managers.

The assignments, based in local community organisations, can be undertaken on a part-time or full-time basis and involve anything from a half day per week for a number of months, or block release. Assignments can be undertaken by a group of employees or on an individual basis. They are supported by a structured monitoring and appraisal system based on the main aims of all three parties. The scheme is now being taken up by other ARC branches around the country.

Two main options are available to organisations wishing to second their staff to 'host' bodies:

Option One: 'single ticket' schemes
Here staff are seconded to organisations as a staged means of terminating the contractual relationship with the employee, this can be undertaken on a full-time or part-time basis usually for a period of up to two years.

Advantages

- Like job sharing, this kind of secondment has been used very successfully to ease older workers into retirement – if care is taken to match the employee's talents and pre-retirement aspirations to the host organisation's needs
- Re-entry is not a problem – although care should be taken to monitor regularly the secondee's progress if the relationship between the three parties is to be properly managed.

Dilemmas

- The over-use of this kind of secondment to solve 'difficult' staff problems will give the arrangement a bad reputation among younger employees and line management. Secondment will become associated solely with 'failures' and this will restrict the number of volunteers if the arrangement is also being used as a management or staff development tool (see below).

Option Two: 'return ticket' schemes
Here employees are seconded to the host organisation for a fixed period (on a part-time or full-time basis) and are re-deployed in the seconding firm on their return, either in their previous job or in an alternative position.

Advantages

- This kind of secondment can be used to give key employees 'time out' in their formal careers and to re-motivate members of staff who have peaked in their careers or been in their job too long
- Used properly, it can prove a valuable part of a formal training and development programme – exposing key employees to different environments and providing important skills which they can use on their return.

Dilemmas

- Like career break schemes, secondments can fail badly in their objectives

if re-entry is not managed effectively – regular assessment and liaison is required with both the secondee and their prospective local managers to ensure that the secondee is confident that he or she will return to an appropriate job
- Re-entry aside, the management will only work well if:
  - the objectives and aims have been clearly thought out and understood by all parties
  - the work experience and projects during the secondment have been directly linked to the secondee's career in the seconding organisation

This may require a considerable input of time and financial resources, possibly including the cost of additional training.

Examples

Two case studies taken from the CEI study illustrate the benefits of secondment and the pitfalls if the process is not planned and administered with care.

Case Study 1: Success

☐ *Irene, a twenty-five-year-old secretary, had worked in a high street bank for eight years and was getting to feel 'stale'. She voiced her desire for a change at her annual appraisal meeting and her personnel officer suggested the secondment opportunity to her branch manager.*

Irene's initial feeling was one of suspicion mixed with excitement but, when she reacted with interest to the possibility, an interview was arranged with the bank's community affairs department. There then followed a visit to and formal interview with the host, a national organisation concerned with youth training and employment. The whole process took two to three months.

The bank had been seconding staff since the early 1970s but this has become more structured in recent years and now forms part of a planned 1 per cent 'social responsibility' budget. Details of secondment opportunities are circulated by the community affairs department to personnel departments, and this secondment arose from the host's desire to replace an existing secondee.

The host describes secondment as 'part of [our] fabric'. It promotes secondment opportunities to companies on the basis of its experience and professionalism; as a proper exchange with both parties having something to offer.

Irene worked for two weeks alongside her predecessor. At first she found the environment very different and was frightened by the workload and need to use her initiative. However, she felt well supported by host staff, and her job description was, she believes, comprehensive. There was an induction day at head office three months after Irene started but she felt it was not very relevant. Appraisals with the bank's personnel staff were maintained during the secondment and regular appraisals were conducted by the host, also involving bank personnel. At one appraisal, Irene was invited to go on a course for trainers run by the bank. Her role then developed to include organising and delivering teaching courses in secretarial skills and she also learned and then taught word processing. At her final host appraisal, Irene's return to the bank was discussed and the bank's personnel officer felt that a role in training might be appropriate. Irene put in a formal application for a new post and returned to a job which, as she put it, 'I would never have considered otherwise'. However, the months before her return were a worry – primarily caused by a concern that she might have to return to her old job as a secretary.

Irene says her secondment has been the happiest working time of her life. She feels she has gained enormously in confidence, particularly in her relationships with other people. Added to this she has obtained specific new skills which have led directly to a new and rewarding job back with the company. The host organisation also judged the secondment as a success and believed it played a valuable role in challenging Irene and raising her confidence.

Case Study 2: Failure

☐ *'Jim', aged fifty-eight, retired from his post as general manager in a division of a large company where he had worked for twenty years. His secondment was for two years to an environmental organisation but ended after seven months.*

Before leaving the company and whilst looking for alternative paid work, Jim was asked by the personnel director if he would consider secondment. The idea appealed to him; he needed financial security to maintain domestic commitments and finding other work would take time. The company's Community Affairs Department, operating a long-standing secondment policy, had already agreed to make a secondment to the host organisation, in preference to making a grant to help them develop in new localities. At a brief informal meeting, Jim was introduced to the host. He agreed to be a secondee and accepted in principle a pension plus top-up salary arrangement with the company.

A job description 'of sorts' was given to Jim before he started work, but the haste with which the secondment arrangements were made – six weeks from interest to joining – meant that he was not asked or expected to make any contribution to it. The company insisted that the host operated a three-month probation period, something which Jim found unpalatable after so long as a senior manager. The Community Affairs Department handled all the process and decisions about the secondment, including setting its length and Jim felt he was presented with a fait accompli. The host organisation believed that the company had specifically chosen and 'matched' Jim to fit its needs. Immediately before taking up his post, Jim was told by the company that the top-up part of his salary was to be reduced, effectively cutting his promised income in secondment by 35 per cent. At this point, Jim would have refused to go, except that he had no time or funds to make other work arrangements.

Jim was given a two-hour induction by the manager of the host organisation and thereafter was expected to find his own feet. During his initial two months Jim met new and existing business contacts to develop the host's activity in a new territory. But whilst doing so, Jim discovered that he was not expected to make any direct input into the specification of his tasks.

Jim felt increasingly frustrated by the way he was cut out from making a personal input into the objectives and operation of the host organisation, and with the under-utilisation of his talents and experience. He also felt unhappy with the style of the host managers, 'I felt I was operating in a vacuum'. Despite these reservations, Jim persisted in his tasks. The company laid down no special or 'clear' contact mechanisms for Jim and he felt it was 'left very much up to me'.

At the end of the three-month probation period, Jim talked with the host managers. The meeting went well: no serious problems were raised and Jim discussed some ideas for internal improvements. Subsequently, however, one of the managers explained to Jim that he was unhappy about how he was performing. Jim was surprised, 'This was the first indication to me of their tenseness'. He sought to improve his working relationship with the manager. Unknown to Jim, the host management had approached the company to complain about his performance. Jim first knew of *this a month later when a letter from the company arrived saying that his probation period had been extended to one year. Jim tackled the host managers and tried to talk matters through, but ended up by resigning.*

SUMMARY POINTS

- Evaluation of the current use and future introduction of new work patterns should take place in the context of:
  - the demands made on the individual work unit and/or organisation as a whole
  - current and future labour costs (which should include non-wage and managerial costs such as those of managing effectively Category C entrants and workers)
  - the current and future labour supply
  - the opportunities and constraints posed by new technology and other related workplace innovations
  - the culture and reputation of the work unit and/or organisation
  - existing collective and/or individual agreements with the current workforce
  - the personal needs of the workforce (particularly in the context of effective career management)
- The process of evaluation or consideration should involve as wide a range of people as possible. Traditional attitudes to new working arrangements and existing practices should be re-examined and, if necessary, amended through a systematic process of education and consultation.
- Particular interest groups which should be involved in any discussions include:
  - senior management (if the practice is to be introduced on an organisation-wide basis)
  - line management
  - trade unions
  - employees likely to have regular contact with the 'new' workers and/or are likely to be directly affected by the new work practices

Reference
1 Leighton, P., 'Contractual arrangements in selected industries', Research Paper 39, Department of Employment, 1983.

Source material
Deakin, B. and Pratten, C., 'Economic effects of YTS', *Employment Gazette*, 1987, p. 491.
Hartley, K. and Ruby, M., 'Contracting out in Health and Local Authorities', *Public Money*, September 1985, p. 23.
IDS, *Reorganising Working Time*, Study 417, Income Data Services, 1988.
Industrial Relations Review and Report, *Part-timers – pressures for change*, IR–RR 422, 16 August 1988.

Competitive Tendering, Institute of Personnel Management, 1986.
Kakabadse, A., *How to Use Consultants*, MCB Publications, 1986.
Kolderie, E., 'Contracting out as an approach to management', *Local Government Studies*, Jan/Feb 1987, p. 1.
Leighton, P. and Winfield, M., *Does Job Sharing Work?*, Industrial Society and Essex Institute of Higher Education, 1988.
Leighton, P. and Rayner, C., *Job Sharing in South-East Essex*, Essex Institute of Higher Education, 1986.
Leighton, P., *Sub-contracting for Services*. A report for the ILO, Essex Institute of Higher Education, 1985.
Mackay, L., 'The future – with consultants', *Personnel Review*, Vol. 16, No. 4, 1987, p. 3.
Meager, N., *Temporary Work in Britain: its Growth and Changing Rationales*, IMS Co-operative Work Programme, Institute of Manpower Studies, 1985.
Milne, R., 'Competitive tendering in the NHS: an economic analysis of the early implementation of HC(83)', *Public Administration*, Vol. 65, 1987, p. 145.
Preedy, J., 'What you should expect of consultants', *Personnel Management*, Vol. 16, No. 4, 1987, p. 3.
Contracting Out in the Public Sector, Royal Institute of Public Administration, 1984.
Shaw, G., 'Whither two-year YTS?', *Personnel Management*, June 1987, p. 33.
Syrett, M., *Temporary Work Today*, FRES, 1985.
Syrett, M., *Employing Job Sharers, Part-time and Temporary Work*, IPM, 1983.
Torrington, D. and Mackay, L., 'Will consultants take over the personnel function', *Personnel Management*, February 1986, p. 34.

Chapter 3
Preparing for different work patterns

At a recent conference on flexible working,[1] one delegate commented, 'Flexible work patterns are a good litmus test for the organisation's efficiency. In establishments where employee communications are good, job descriptions are accurate and management systems well thought-out, new working patterns will bring considerable benefits. If any of these are lacking, atypical working will highlight the gap far more clearly than conventional full-time arrangements'.

This is largely true. Hard experience shows that organisations cannot get away with lax personnel practices simply because the arrangements are new or atypical. Once establishments have identified the working structures that best suit their organisational needs, they need to introduce specific management systems and training to ensure that these new working arrangements are introduced without disruption and are properly administered.

Two important processes are involved:

- Assessing the changes required to existing management systems and what new procedures need to be introduced
- Gaining the agreement, commitment and acceptance of key interest groups within the organisation who are likely to be most affected by the change.

CHANGES TO MANAGEMENT SYSTEMS AND PROCEDURES

If new patterns of work are likely to be introduced on any large scale, existing procedures will need to be adapted or replaced. Key areas include communication and control, pay and performance, appraisal and assessment, training, career development and re-entry and recruitment.

Communication and control

If much of the work is based on output, or conducted off-site, and staff are given greater responsibility for managing their own workload, control and communication systems need to be tight and well-defined. Key points include:

- Formal reporting systems are required to set objectives and monitor progress. These may include fixed meetings on a regular basis which off-site workers are expected to attend, regular days off which they are expected to work on-site, daily telephone reporting and the more imaginative use of electronic messages. The same requirement may well apply to flexible workers on-site; job-sharers, for example, need 'overlap time' built into their working hours to enable them to brief each other on aspects of the work for which they are jointly responsible. Wherever possible, these requirements need to be fixed or arranged well in advance
- Induction and routine employee communication systems should ensure that all flexible workers receive the same start-up information, staff facilities and sources of assistance as their full-time counterparts. This is particularly important for external field sales staff and all those Category B staff who work on-site, including contractors and their workers, secondees and temporary agency staff (bad induction and poor back-up is a common complaint among office temporaries).
- Greater emphasis should be placed on team working and project management procedures which link staff working on a variety of different projects and from different locations – procedures which facilitate conflict handling and problem solving.

Pay and conditions

Pay and performance will need to be far more closely linked. Key issues include:

- Job targets and requirements will need clearer identification and clarification, as in the case of field sales staff
- Whilst many contractors, teleworkers, fixed term and part-time staff will continue to be paid on the basis of time – so many days or hours per week, month or year – managers will need to ensure the right level of quality or output for the salary or fee paid
- Job evaluation systems and salary structures may need to be completely overhauled. When negotiating remuneration packages, traditional perks (such as travel assistance, canteen facilities, etc.) may need replacing by those more suited to workers' needs – for example, low interest loans, advice services, access to training facilities)
- Many traditional perks will remain desirable and these should be included in the remuneration packages of non-standard as well as core staff. These include sick pay, health insurance, pensions, cars and holidays. Effective means of calculating and dividing these terms of employment on a pro rata basis will need to be devised (shared car pools, for example, may need to replace individual car allocation). Often, this will mean extensive negotiation with insurance companies and other

financial institutions providing standard policies which currently exclude those working under a certain number of weekly hours or not working on-site
- Remuneration policies should take into account tax and social security issues. As will be discussed in Chapters 4 and 7, the tax status of many flexible workers, particularly those that work off-site or variable hours, may be ambiguous. Organisations may need to establish regular liaison with local DHSS or Inland Revenue offices to establish whether different categories of staff are subject to Schedule E or D status
- Non-financial rewards may also prove very attractive to certain categories of flexible worker. Publicity references or recommendations will be highly valued by consultants, contractors and freelancers if they are seeking work with other companies. Recommendations will also benefit secondees who wish to improve their standard in their parent organisation.

Appraisal and assessment

If new work patterns are to be properly integrated into the organisation, traditional appraisal and assessment procedures should be extended to all work patterns at the organisation over any length of time. Key issues include:

- Systems for determining merit pay, agreeing future goals, providing career (or other) counselling and determining productivity are all relevant to most categories of workers
- These systems should be redesigned to reflect the particular output, aspiration and circumstances of different kinds of worker. They should also be able to define more clearly whether a failure to reach targets or professional standards is due to the worker or shortcomings in the design of their working arrangements (where failures occur in job-share schemes, for example, it is not always easy to establish which sharer, if either, is at fault). A more rigorous attitude to fixed term, casual and homebased staff should be evolved. The fact that often such workers are not highly paid does not affect central issues.

Development and training

Although development and training policies may not be applicable or cost-effective in the case of flexible workers on short-term assignments, they should certainly encompass more permanent contract, distance or part-time staff. Key issues include:

- Failure to extend training to flexible staff which may place a greater barrier between them and other staff and lead to industrial relations difficulties
- Training policies should incorporate new delivery mechanisms to meet

the needs of staff working off-site or unusual hours. Distance or open-learning systems are particularly effective
- As a matter of principle, organisations should be designed to enable all workers to achieve promotion and work their way to senior levels in the organisation
- Wherever appropriate, there should be appraisal schemes to allow all workers to apply for promotion to senior full-time positions and not experience discrimination purely on the basis of their part-time or other status
- If possible, opportunities for promotion should be further extended to enable workers to continue in their present pattern of work. Examples exist of job-sharers who have been promoted jointly into the next grade.

Accommodation and premises

The implications to the use of the organisation's premises will need to be carefully considered. Key issues include:

- A variety of part-timers, contract and temporary staff working on the premises for atypical hours means that office accommodation and facilities will need to be shared more widely and carefully planned and monitored rostering used for the allocation of the facilities
- The cost of office space and equipment will need to be accurately assessed and related directly to the needs of the growing number of staff who may spend a large proportion of their working time off-site. Recent research shows that even with job-sharers the accommodation and equipment issues need to be thought through. They may or may not want to share the same desk or equipment; colleagues who cover for the absent sharer may need to be in the same office or unit; organisational information may need to be circulated in different ways or by, say, greater use of noticeboards; there may need to be investment in telephone answering machines or tape recorders. These issues require discussion with all those involved with job-sharers at the workplace.

Example
Preconceptions about labour costs can cloud judgements. A study of sub-contracting for cleaning in one London health district showed that there had been insufficient consideration of the 'transactional' role of a hospital manager. He found that virtually all his time was spent dealing with complaints about the contractors, to the detriment of his other responsibilities. Some of his more routine work had to be covered by temporary staff.

Research also shows that the presumption about higher costs when employing job-sharers may also be misconceived. The increased personnel and administrative costs are more than offset by the fact that all the job-sharers made medical and similar appointments on their days off.

Financial control

As we saw in Chapter 2, cost analysis is vital to the effective use of flexible staff. Key issues include:

- Managers will need to work much harder at understanding their total labour costs, not only when deciding what pay packages to offer but also in deciding which work patterns to develop. Alternatives should be properly costed and the likely benefits carefully examined
- Budgets for the discretionary use of casual, agency, and contract staff should be strictly controlled and their use directly related to agreed corporate objectives.

Recruitment and selection

Recruitment and selection policies will need to be adapted to incorporate a much more diverse range of potential staff. Key issues include:

- The sources of potential applicants: these will be, in many cases, different from those used by full-time staff. Recruitment techniques and procedures should reflect this
- Selection criteria should place a greater emphasis on *how* a job is undertaken as well as *what* is being undertaken. In the case of job-sharers, teleworkers, contractors and consultants, this will mean that applicants' skill to self-start and manage their own workload will be a crucial factor
- For both these reasons, job specifications should be clearly defined. Managers responsible for drawing these up will require good analytical skills and training in appropriate job analysis and work specification skills.

Management preparation

Changes and adaptations to management systems will have considerable effect on the role of line management. A key issue is the ability of managers to define, delegate and specify tasks, this will need to be greatly improved. They will become 'co-ordinators' and 'orchestrators' rather than 'doers' and their interpersonal skills will be at a premium in their handling of a greater variety of staff.

GAINING THE SUPPORT OF THE ORGANISATION

Like any major management of change exercise, the introduction of new patterns of work should be preceded by a comprehensive education and training programme to gain the support of key interest groups within the organisation. These include: *senior management; trade unions; managers and supervisors; full-time staff working alongside the new workers.*

For most new work patterns to succeed, the support of *all* these groups is required, not just that of the majority.

Senior management

As we have already seen, the scale of change required to properly implement new working is considerable. It will need adequate resources to introduce and these will have to be fought for and justified. In addition, clear indications from the top that the move towards new work patterns is supported by decision makers within the organisation will help to overcome residual opposition among managers in lower levels.

The objectives linked to greater manpower flexibility have already been explored in Chapter 2. These objectives need to be explored in any corporate decision making process, preferably at the time changes to organisational direction are being discussed. Too often, human resource considerations are only raised after organisational objectives are fixed. This is a dangerous approach to adopt. The move to different work patterns is often a strategic rather than a tactical issue. There is much value to be gained from developing and publicising opportunities policies within the organisation which are seen to be supported 'from the top'.

Trade unions

To examine the implications of changes on industrial relations inside your own organisation, it is necessary to set this against the changing attitude of trade unions to this issue generally during the past five years.

The emergence of new work patterns has posed a number of problems for trade unions. There are some obvious difficulties:

- Recruiting and organising new workers is much more difficult to achieve. Some of the reasons include the tenuous relationship that often exists between the worker and the employer; the frequent isolation of these workers, the unorthodox patterns of attendance, the self-employed status of many of them, and the distance between employer and place of work implicit in the use of sub-contracted workers
- Legal protection for new workers is very modest (see Chapter 1) compared with the rest of Europe. This leaves the unions reliant on collective bargaining to push for better conditions for these workers. Not all unions have shown a keenness to do it
- Bargaining strength among staff is likely, nevertheless, to be undercut by the relative over supply of workers on the external market – with the obvious exception of skilled and professional workers who are being bought in because of the lack of equivalent full-time staff
- Attitudes towards new and atypical workers among full-time staff have sometimes been hostile, both because they are seen as a threat to existing full-time jobs and also because they are perceived to enjoy better

conditions of work. Worker competition between full-time and other staff could develop as a result. Collective solidarity could further be reduced.

Despite reluctance and ambivalence on the part of many unions and their officials it is clear that the support of the union for new work patterns remains crucial, especially from the perspective of the employee. Opposition will make the 'social pull' work patterns hard to implement.

Full-time staff

Finally, there are the attitudes of existing full-time staff to consider. Full-time staff's attitudes towards non-core staff have often mirrored the prejudices of line management. They are seen as 'outsiders', 'unreliable', 'uncommitted', 'on a cushy number', and are often perceived to enjoy better conditions of work.

Example: Job sharing in Holland

In 1982, the Dutch Government's enthusiasm for job sharing was tempered by the failure of a major experiment by Bedrijfswagenfabriek DAF BV. In an interview with International Management, *one of the management board directors explained, 'It didn't work. The full-time workers didn't like it. The part-timers were only getting paid for part-time work, so there was no reason for the full-timers to be jealous on that score. But they were jealous because the part-timers had more freedom'.*

The problem may well have been regional (the director also pointed out that social attitudes dictate that men have full-time jobs in the South Netherlands). But the attitudes of full-time staff are very important, not least because the introduction of new working arrangements could have a direct impact on the day-to-day running of their work unit (see Chapter 6).

Formal programmes

To obtain the support of all the relevant sectors of your organisation, it is well worth investing in a formal education and training campaign designed to overcome prejudice and practical management difficulties. This programme could incorporate:

- films or slide shows
- talks by managers and employees from other organisations who have been involved with the successful introduction of the particular work pattern
- easy access to written literature and research on the subject
- visits organised for senior and line management to establishments which operate successful schemes
- articles in house journals or on staff noticeboards and in annual reports (incorporating supportive messages from the organisation's chief executive).

All the above should be followed by full and frank group and individual discussion to clear misconceptions and misunderstandings.

An education campaign can also be used to alert existing full-time staff to the availability of flexible working, particularly when new patterns of work are being introduced as a recruitment or retention aid.

The support of all relevant interest groups with the organisation is essential. Traditional hostility to change is still very widespread on both sides of industry and overcoming this will probably prove the most difficult stage of the whole exercise.

An illustrative case study: the social workers

A recent study of job sharing included an evaluation of the efficiency of sharing a social work post in a multi-disciplinary paediatric and maternity team. Sharers worked closely with a well-known teaching hospital. The job was stressful and often crisis driven. The job-share post was in a team of seven professionals. The proposal to job-share had the support of the unit manager, but support from senior management was lukewarm until two consultant paediatricians 'were very much in favour ... and wrote to the manager in social services'. One job-sharer commented, 'That was the end of the opposition'.[2]

The union was also supportive. However, despite careful negotiation with team members some reluctance remained on the part of colleagues. They voted not to split any further posts. It is likely that although the manager saw job sharing as an opportunity to 'examine systems of dynamics', colleagues had not been ready for the implications of job sharing and the burdens on them. It is essential to thoroughly work through the likely practical issues which any new work pattern presents to colleagues, be it homeworking, self-employment, or job sharing.

ISSUES RAISED BY SPECIFIC WORK PATTERNS

The preparation of organisations for particular working arrangements raises specific issues. These are covered by the various sections below. The list is confined to work patterns generating substantial organisational change. Those that fit easily into existing management systems, such as flexitime and shiftworking, are not included.

Preparation for career break schemes

Policy and Communication

Clear guidelines about the scheme should be drawn up covering:
– categories of employee who are eligible (occupation, length of service, grade, etc.)
– whether selection is automatic or discretionary (if discretionary, at whose discretion?)

- how long a break is allowed
- whether each individual is eligible for more than one break (if 'yes', how many and between what intervals?)
- whether re-entry is guaranteed (if so, at what grade?)
- what methods (if any) are to be used to keep the employee or ex-employee in touch with the organisation
- whether the individual will have the option or the obligation to work part-time during the break
- what effect this is likely to have on the individual's pension rights and/or other long-term occupational benefits

These guidelines should be agreed and, if possible, drawn up in agreement with: senior management, local managers, trade union representatives and/or employee associations. Particularly if the policy is discretionary, local managers' agreement and acceptance of the policy is essential if the scheme is not to end up a worthless piece of paper.

Once the policy has been agreed, it should be communicated to all staff who may become eligible in the short or long term. Eligibility, application procedures and sources of further information should be clearly identified.

Career appraisal

- career appraisal programmes should be used to identify those women (and men, if they are eligible) who are likely to want to take a career break in the short or long term
- appraisal sessions should emphasise that a decision to take a career break is not likely to affect the individual's right to promotion and development.

Personnel data
- records should be kept of individuals who have expressed an interest or specific intention to take a career break
- individuals on formal schemes with a guaranteed re-entry should be recorded as a special category of employee
- separate periods of service by individuals who take extended breaks or more than one break should be recorded on one career record
- periods of part-time and full-time work should be recorded on one career record
- the legal implications of the break should be spelt out.

Liaison during the break
Regular meetings (at least once a year) should be arranged between the individual, the personnel department and the local manager to discuss:
- whether the individual is still happy to return
- an adequate and early agreement over the return, covering time, specific job and work location

Any change in circumstances (either in the individual's willingness to return or in the ability of the organisation to provide suitable employment) should be identified well in advance.

Preparation for job sharing

Two issues are worth close examination:

- The introduction of a formal policy
- The re-design of the job specification.

Formal job-share policies

In the promotion of job sharing, much emphasis has been given to the need or desirability of a formal job-share policy. Recent research indicates that this is by no means a prerequisite. Many organisations which have introduced formal policies have little or no actual job sharing. By contrast, many of the most prolific users of the work pattern do so without a policy.

Hackney Job Share Project recently summarised the relative advantages and disadvantages of introducing a policy:[3]

Advantages

- A policy provides guidance and procedures for resolving management issues – this saves managerial time and reduces unnecessary conflict
- Fewer *ad hoc* decisions means less scope for favouritism: reducing disparities means fewer disputes over terms and conditions
- A public commitment by the organisation makes it easier to overcome any internal resistance.

Disadvantages

- A policy requires initial input of management time at the time of its formation and during its negotiation
- Negotiating details with workplace representatives may be a lengthy process
- Policy negotiations may get linked to other negotiations on the bargaining agenda
- Can be inflexible and cause disputes if too widely drafted.

Much will depend on the numbers of job-sharers the organisation expect to recruit and the cultural considerations determining the execution of management policy.

In small organisations, or larger firms using job sharing occasionally, the time spent on designing and negotiating the policy may not be justified by the number of sharers. Equally, a formal policy fits best into organisations used to formal decision making processes. It is no coincidence that job-share policies have been most widely used in the public sector, where management systems and employment have been governed by systematic regulation: over half of all local authorities have formal policies. The concept may fit less well into private sector organisations, where a formal policy on any form of management practice is the exception rather than the rule.

Any policy should cover the following points:

- Statement of intent, setting out the aims of the policy
- Guidelines on which positions are open to job sharing
- Procedures for establishing job-shares involving existing employees
- Recruitment and selection procedures
- Procedure if one sharer leaves or is dismissed, or if only one sharer is appointed
- Personnel procedures and contractual aspects.

The policy should be developed in consultation with and with the agreement of key interest groups in the organisation including senior management, line management, trade union representatives and staff associations. Careful consideration of and agreement on the principles governing job sharing at the outset will save considerable complications once the scheme is in operation. The most important aspect is to ensure that the policy is real, not cosmetic, and is widely known and implemented.

Assessing/redesigning the job specification
Either in response to an unprompted application or as a deliberate course of policy, any initial move to convert a full-time position into a job-share requires a complete redesign of the job specification. In relatively unskilled jobs involving little discretion, this may merely entail the imaginative restructuring of working hours. Some of the most common divisions of working time include:

- Split week on a 2½/2½ day basis (with a possible overlap of working hours on Wednesdays to facilitate joint liaison between the sharers)
- Split week on a 3/2 day basis (e.g., Monday to Wednesday, Thursday and Friday)
- One week on/one week off with the shift change taking place either at the beginning or the middle of the week
- Mornings/afternoons

In more skilled work, a division of the job by task as well as time might also prove necessary. General points to consider include:

- At what hours does the job need to be covered? Is 9–5 Monday to Friday absolutely necessary? Would a more flexible arrangement excessively inconvenience customers, service users or colleagues? Do the potential benefits of this kind of flexibility outweigh that inconvenience?
- Would it be useful for both sharers to be at work at the same time, either to provide a short overlap time or to provide extra cover at peak periods? Overlap time is useful if both sharers need familiarity with each other's work to obtain continuity of approach, for example, on jointly undertaken projects, supervisory responsibilities, or agreeing management policies. It also allows supervisors to share together when necessary
- The division of the workload should take account of the nature of the work and the sharer's particular skills. Work can be allocated by project, task, client or any other relevant basis.

Example

A very senior, policy-orientated, post was job shared in a central Government department. It had been a developing job-share in the sense that over a two year period four employees had been part of it. Initially it was split on a 50/50 basis but eventually the post was expanded to 1/2, each job-sharer working a three day week. This allowed them to spend one day a week together, which was the day of the key departmental meetings. Managers and colleagues reported very high levels of productivity and the arrangement maintained continuity.[3]

Preparing to use consultants

Employing consultants often involves their offering advice which you are free to ignore, or getting them to perform a distinctive and self-contained professional task for the organisation. There are likely to be fewer problems regarding image or reputation of an organisation than with sub-contractors.

The overriding need of the organisation and the consultant is to clearly define the expectations of the parties. Organisations must be both discerning and coherent about the use of consultants, especially as the decision is generally taken at a senior level, but the day-to-day contact is often with middle management or supervisors.

The various stages in preparing for the consultation and preparing the organisation may vary according to the nature of the work and the length of the contract. Clearly, the rules of discipline applicable to employment relationships are not available for consultants. There are few possibilities of correction if the contract was misconceived, inadequate or imprecise. The basic requirement is to anticipate the working through of the relationship, and its impact on individuals and the organisation.

As well as defining the precise nature of the project it is important to provide in writing or otherwise a clear impression of the nature of the organisation. This is especially true if the consultant has to relate to member(s) of the workplace who are themselves atypical or flexible. For example, if consultancy work is referrable to job-sharers the implications have to be clarified. If a consultant is used for managerial, financial or technical matters, it is important that manpower policies are adequately explained, including the working of equal opportunities initiatives.

The various preparatory stages may look as follows:

- Agree and state the objectives of the consultancy. This may require a thorough investigation and involve surveys by actual or potential consultants
- Agree the costing and length of project or on-going contract
- Determine the manager responsible for the consultancy work
- Decide how much information and resources is to be made available to consultants.
- Establish effective lines of communication
- Establish monitoring arrangements and performance targets

- Determine the preference/options when the consultants' performance is inadequate
- Prepare and, if necessary, provide training for those dealing with or affected by the consultants
- Make sure that physical accommodation is available and appropriate and decide whether there is to be access to social or occupational facilities, such as car parking and restaurant, as well as secretarial support
- Establish procedures for dealing with complaints or tensions between consultants and in-house staff.

Preparing for secondment

Hard experience shows that employing organisations and hosts need to develop their policy and practice towards secondment with greater care. In particular, the objectives, expectations and implications for both seconding and host organisation must coalesce. Points of good practice to consider include:

Seconding organisations
– Seconding organisations should spell out in detail the corporate/organisation reasons for secondment (e.g. public relations, staff skills and experience development, manpower flexibility, promotion, long-service reward) and the social and community rationale.
– Seconding organisations should clarify the extent and value of contributions that employees can make by participating.
– Seconding organisations should identify precisely how secondments tie in with 'mainstream' internal processes such as training, staff appraisal and promotion.
– Communication must be improved in both quality and quantity within the seconding organisation and between all parties, particularly concerning objectives and evaluation.
– Objective setting in matching and selection is crucial: seconding organisations should ensure hosts apply recognisable and valid selection practices, even if this means the rejection of certain secondees.
– Contact and support needs to be properly supervised: agreements should be made before secondment concerning how, where, how often and from whom, it is available.
– Normal appraisal systems should be linked to the evaluation of secondments covering objectives set and competencies acquired.
– Arrangements for termination need to be agreed *before* the scheme is initiated: this should involve agreed timetables and set procedures about who is responsible for deciding how and when the secondment will end.
– Arrangements for re-entry must be properly designed to facilitate the secondees re-induction into the firm, de-briefing and follow-up.

Host organisations
– Host organisations need to familiarise themselves with the seconding

firms' policies and practices to identify how and why they make secondments.
- Host organisations should develop new and more imaginative project and task activities directly linked to the secondee's career path and future responsibilities.
- Host organisations need to adopt the same (or better) professionalism in objective setting, job descriptions and monitoring for secondees as they do with their own staff (possibly with the support of the seconding organisation's training department).

Example: Project Fullemploy

Project Fullemploy, a charity that aims to improve the employment prospects of minority ethnic communities in England and Wales, provides training for young adults, supports community and economic development among black communities and offers equal opportunities consultancy and training.

It carries out its programme in partnership with voluntary and community-based organisations, with central and local government and with the private sector. Secondments have always featured strongly in this process. The charity currently (1988) uses twenty secondees to support the activities of its 200 staff.

Fullemploy's secondment manager stresses that potential secondees are assessed as much on their character and mentality as the skills they have to offer. 'We need people who can adapt well to a different culture', she comments. 'Many people from the private sector approach secondments as a charitable exercise and this can often lead to a patronising manner that can severely prejudice their relationship with staff and course members. We have, by our very nature, a central commitment to equal opportunities and our secondees will need a strong awareness of racism and sexism. Sometimes, our interview process results in a recommendation that an individual would make a good secondee, but not with our organisation'.

Originally, secondees were used predominantly in training activities but a growing number now aid Fullemploy's central office administration. The relationship between the secondee, seconding organisation and Project Fullemploy is managed under an established process divided into seven stages:

Consultation
With an individual company/organisation:
- *to explore secondment as a useful resource to the company/organisation*
- *to explore secondment for an identified member of staff, establishing objectives and time scales. The usual duration of a secondment is one year, but Fullemploy is able to offer shorter or longer placements.*

Information visits
By the prospective secondee(s), to:
- *the central office, for an overview of Project Fullemploy's objectives and achievements*
- *the training project/department where a secondment role has been identified.*

The prospective secondee will also be encouraged to spend a full day at the work location as a member of the staff team rather than as a visitor. This will provide a more in-depth view of working in Project Fullemploy.

Formal Interview
- *With a panel of three, comprising the prospective line manager, Fullemploy's*

secondment manager and a member of Fullemploy staff currently fulfilling a role similar to that being considered by the secondment candidate
– This interview will explore in greater depth the issues surrounding Fullemploy's work.

Induction

An individual induction programme is planned for each secondee's first three weeks, including, as appropriate:
– visit to training projects, regional offices, or other central office units, to meet other secondees and explore different training methods and materials, where appropriate
– training in training techniques, preparation of materials and curriculum planning, where appropriate
– racism awareness introductory session.

Appraisals

The seconding company/organisation is encouraged to maintain close contact with their secondee(s) and is specifically invited to participate in all secondee appraisals:
– to contribute, where appropriate, to the objective-setting
– to evaluate for themselves at close-hand the development and achievements of their member of staff.

Written reports of the appraisal interviews are forwarded to the seconding company/organisation.

During secondments of nine months or more, two appraisals are conducted, the first after three months:
– to establish that the secondee has settled in well
– to set objectives for the remainder of the secondment.

The second within the three months before re-entry:
– to evaluate the secondee's performance against the objectives set and the secondment experience as a whole
– to identify clearly any new skill areas that may be of use to the company/organisation upon the secondee's re-entry, where this is appropriate.

During secondments of less than nine months, an informal objective-setting session is held early in the secondment (to which the company/organisation is invited to contribute) and a formal appraisal is held within the final two months.

De-briefing

Within the final three months of a secondment an informal de-briefing session is held to assist the secondee in beginning an evaluation of his/her secondment. This is linked to the impending final appraisal, but the secondee is also encouraged to recognise that the full results of the secondment experience may be evident in different ways some time into the future.

Secondment report

The secondee is requested to write a full report on the secondment, within three months of leaving. Where secondees have returned to their company/organisation, we ask them to comment on their re-entry experience. This focuses on the perceived gains to the individual and both Fullemploy and the employer.

Preparing for agency workers

The management systems used by organisations to regulate the use by organisations of temporary agency workers are often loose and poorly thought out.

70 NEW WORK PATTERNS

The design of these systems is complicated by the very ambiguous triangle of contractual and management relationships that exist between the organisation, the agency and the worker.

The complexity is best illustrated by comparing agency work arrangements to the rather similar triangle of interests that exist in the use of sub-contracted labour (explored in detail later in the chapter).

In the case of sub-contracted arrangements (see Figure 3.1) there is a direct contractual relationship between the contractor and the organisation. Under this, the contractor directly employs any sub-contracted labour and, despite the fact that the workers may discharge their obligations on the client organisation's premises, the contractor is responsible for their recruitment, training, salary administration and supervision.

To all intents and purposes, the contractor controls the worker's output. There is no direct relationship between the client organisation and the worker other than a residual obligation under health and safety legislation.

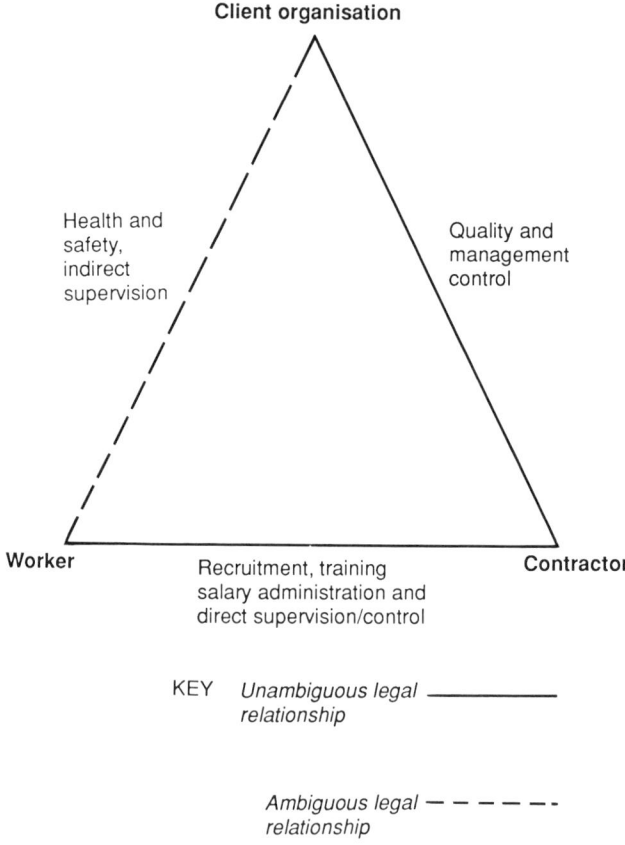

Fig. 3.1 *Triangle of contractual and management relationships (direct supervision/control)*

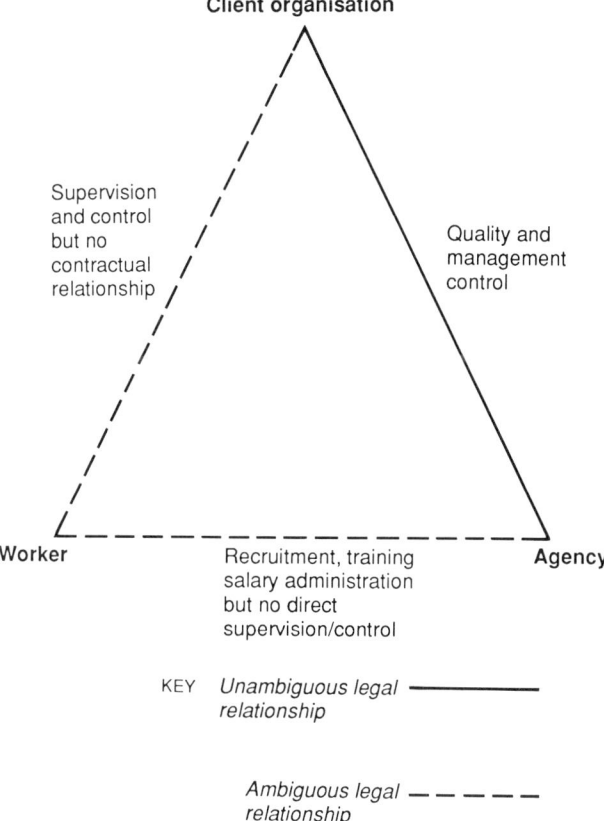

Fig. 3.2 Triangle of contractual and management relationships (no direct supervision/control)

Any management control systems designed by the organisation (for example, governing selection, monitoring progress and checking quality) should therefore be directed towards the contractor.

Under an agency worker arrangement (see Figure 3.2), the triangular relationship is more complex. The direct contractual relationship between the organisation and the agency remains very similar to that with a contractor. But whereas the agency is responsible for the recruitment, training and salary administration of the worker, the client organisation is directly responsible for induction and supervision. This raises problems regarding liability for negligent and other acts, which will be discussed in Chapter 8. However, the employment agency is the employing organisation, despite the day-to-day supervision by the client.

Two sets of management systems therefore need to be considered:

- Systems which govern the selection, briefing and monitoring of the *agency*

- Systems which govern the induction, supervision and monitoring of the *worker*.

Management systems and the agency

The systems used need to cover a number of key areas.

Overall responsibility

A decision should be made over which category of management takes responsibility for the selection, briefing and monitoring of the agency. In smaller organisations, it may well be appropriate for the process to be handled by the personnel department. In this case, they should establish an effective system of liaison with line management to establish temporary help requirements. In larger organisations, the responsibility may well be left to line managers but, conversely, they will need to operate their discretionary use of agency help under agreed criteria as to when it is necessary or appropriate.

Criteria for use

Managers of either category should operate under agreed guidelines. They should be given budgets specifically for the use of hiring temporary agency help to which they are strictly accountable. These should reflect the individual departments and overall establishment's needs for agency labour and be calculated to take into account the organisation's expected peaks in demand. Managers drawing on this budget should have a clear understanding of the relative costs of using agency workers and directly employed staff so that their decisions reflect the most cost-effective option.

Effective liaison

Having selected the right combination of agencies, man$gers will need to set up clear channels of communication with agency representatives. These should ideally be invited to the organisation's premises for briefing sessions and given lists of authorised personnel to deal with, with strict instructions not to accept requests for temporary help from unauthorised managers. Clear written contractual agreements need to be entered into covering such areas as quality control, scaled charges (including discounts for regular or large scale use) and supplementary fees, should the organisation wish to hire effective temporary staff on a permanent basis. This process needs to be updated and reviewed, particularly when there is a change of personnel on either side.

Accurate briefing

If the agency is to be used on a regular basis, managers should ideally provide the agency with an 'induction package', enabling temporary controllers to brief agency staff working for the organisation as to its main activities, house rules governing dress and behaviour and the staff facilities available to agency staff (this can save valuable time during on-site induction). Similar induction packages would also be appropriate for individual departments or for individual managers, if either are likely to be using staff from that agency on a regular basis. For every individual assignment, managers should also provide temporary controllers with information covering:

- The nature of the assignment and its duration
- The qualifications, skills, knowledge and experience required
- The function of the department or individual manager who the agency staff member(s) will be responsible to
- House rules governing dress and behaviour (if they have not already been provided)
- The hours of work and the person agency staff should report to.

Management systems and the worker

Cost and time factors often limit the resources organisations devote to inducting agency staff. Nevertheless, effective induction is important, particularly if the agency temporary is likely to be working for the organisation over any length of time. Managers should therefore ensure that the agency worker is provided with:

- A friendly welcome at reception and clear instructions of who to report to
- Details of the organisation's main activities and house rules (if this has not already been provided by the agency)
- A breakdown of the role of the department they will be working for and/or the manager to whom they will be responsible (particularly if the temporary's task is to provide him/her with personal support)
- Clear and explicit instructions on their tasks, duties and responsibilities and the targets or standards they will be expected to reach – these should be supported where appropriate by job instruction sheets, typical letter styles, etc.
- Details of member(s) of staff they can consult to answer queries and clarify work instructions
- Routine information about lunch and coffee breaks, staff facilities, and health and safety regulations.

If agency staff are hired for any length of time, attempts should be made to integrate them into the organisation's performance appraisal systems which should be adapted to monitor their work. These should link in with their agency's assessment techniques. Proper targets should be set and reviewed.

Staff facilities and membership of staff associations should be extended to long-serving agency workers. More importantly, access to union membership and related leave should be provided if the contract with the agency has been subject to a union agreement, either between the organisation and the union or the union and the agency.

Procedures and systems used to monitor and supervise agency workers should be agreed with all departments regularly needing temporary help and should, if possible, be summarised clearly in a detailed policy statement which both personnel and line managers can refer to. The areas under the policy should cover many of the issues encompassed by counterpart agreements relating to contract work and job sharing.

Summary

The ambiguous relationship between client organisation, the agency and the worker, often makes it difficult to establish which party is at fault when problems occur. For example, if an agency worker fails to meet accepted standards of performance, it could be for any, some or all of the following reasons:

- The agency's selection and screening techniques are sub-standard
- The client organisation has failed to brief the *agency* properly
- The client organisation has failed to brief and supervise the *worker* properly
- The worker's performance is simply sub-standard.

Performance appraisal and management control systems need to be sufficiently sophisticated to enable managers to pinpoint the source(s) of any difficulties. This process is discussed more fully in Chapter 6.

Preparing to sub-contract

This is a complex area. There are differences of approach and detail between the private and public sector, and the nature of the work to be sub-contracted.

The process of sub-contracting necessarily involves transfer of control to a third party, which may lead to tensions with in-house staff and management. It is vital that the preparation, negotiation or re-negotiation is carefully undertaken. If an area of work previously performed in-house is to be sub-contracted there are two main areas of preparation:

- The preparation of the organisation itself, and the mechanics of putting work out to contract
- Dealing with in-house staff likely to be displaced or dismissed as a result of sub-contracting.

Preparation of the organisation and the contract

Major parts of the public sector are required to devise and administer a tendering process, which is generally formal, costly and lengthy. It is often much bound up with a policy of improving the efficiency of an in-house (DLO) unit. The situation in the private sector has been traditionally more variable, with decisions taken often by line rather than senior managers. Partly this can be the consequence of the size of the organisation and its structures, but also because sub-contracting will likely be less controversial in private organisations. There are no simple answers to the question of who should be responsible for sub-contracting and sub-contractors, or how the process should be carried out.

Whether or not there is a formal tendering process the following areas must be considered.

Who has responsibility for sub-contractors?

Much will depend on the scale of sub-contracting, the type of work, the overall managerial policies of the employer and the sector of employment. For example, the fact that sub-contracting in the public sector is sensitive, large-scale and growing, has tended to mean that a generalist committee of, for example, a local authority such as the Policy and Resources Committee has had overall responsibility. Within the NHS, although general managers in hospitals have had a considerable influence, the district health authority have assumed ultimate responsibility, supported by management from the Regional Health Authority.

For preparation to be appropriate it is essential that the committee, unit or individual manager receives input or representation from key areas in the enterprise. Generally, these will be:

- Personnel and industrial relations
- Finance
- Legal
- General administration
- Relevant specialist departments or persons.

It is vital to estimate and integrate the impact on the organisation as a whole. The advice of the safety officer, medical staff, marketing and key customers or clients may well need consideration. Spread the net widely at this early stage, as some clients or customers may be resistant to the use of sub-contractors because of worries about quality. They may want certain factors or guarantees built into the contract. There are no hard and fast rules. However, there are areas of work, for example, highly specialised or luxury areas or the provision of a specific service, that clients expect will be performed by directly employed staff. Some clients view this as a guarantee of quality control. Some organisations advertise that they do not use sub-contractors, or if they do, they are only drawn from a guaranteed source and are carefully monitored. It is important not to ignore perceptions or even prejudices in this area.

Example

A manufacturer and installer of garden and swimming equipment places prominently on their brochure: 'We only ever employ direct labour. It provides you the consumer with guarantees of effective control and quality'.

As well as identifying those who have relevant contributions to make when preparing for sub-contracting, it is important to consider whether the person or group which defines the needs and implications of sub-contracting will also be responsible for its day-to-day management. Within the public sector strong views suggest that the contract preparation role should be separate from the contract monitoring role. This sometimes arises because sub-contract work is often performed in reality by an in-house unit. It must be accountable to the standards specified by another unit, distinctive from the management responsible for performance. The particular need may not be so acute in the case of 'ordinary' sub-contractors, and contractors in the private sector.

Management will want to consider where and at what level the contract will be prepared, negotiated and monitored.

Determining the nature and level of service
This is a more generalised function than that of devising the contract specification. It involves an evaluation of needs, in terms of time, cost and quality. If the function is being sub-contracted for the first time it may be possible to revise standards or to expand the brief expected of sub-contractors. Some sub-contractors, for example, in computing, maintenance, and safety, may be able to offer a wider service than currently performed by an in-house unit or department. Establishing the standards and scope of the contract is a vital exercise, and may lead to greater efficiency in the organisation generally.

For example, when considering a service such as catering or cleaning it may be possible to reconsider when the service is performed (in or out of working hours), whether it is performed on a different basis (using machines, self-service or automated methods) and generally estimating the needs of the organisation and its workforce. It may be possible to transfer costs, for example, by offering luncheon vouchers.

Defining the specification for the sub-contractor
This is a technical and vital exercise. It has three elements:

- Contract control – responsibilities and liabilities of the parties
- Operational specification – how and by whom performed and at what price
- Technical specification – what precisely has to be achieved by the sub-contractor.

With regard to the first aspect a number of options appear, especially regarding the pricing of the contract. All have advantages and disadvantages. The contract can be expressed as:

- A fixed price for a service for a set period – this makes budgeting easy, but may make the contract rather inflexible and encourage cost cutting
- An hourly rate contract – may help when demand is uncertain, but may lead to the contractor extending time. It may be difficult to budget for

- Management fee contract – this will give the contractor flexibility in labour and material usage, but may lead to high costs and difficult budgeting
- Unit pricing – i.e. cash for a specific task which makes budgeting easy but may encourage contractors to cut costs and act to the detriment of quality
- Time and materials – this will probably lead to a higher standard of service but may be expensive and hard to budget for.

These are only examples of types of contract pricing which can be negotiated. Their appropriateness will depend on the needs of the organisation and the type of work being sub-contracted. Sensitive areas of work such as design, promotion, expert computing systems, and finance, may lend themselves to a time and materials contract with strict controls. A relatively less skilled or central area of work, for example, ground maintenance, may suggest a fixed fee contract, where failure to meet standards will lead to its termination and replacement of the contractor.

It is essential that the client identifies its priorities in terms of cost, administration, and quality. The type of contract arrangement may well suggest itself.

The specification

Regardless of whether there is going to be a competitive tendering exercise it will be essential to devise a specification of the work to be done by the sub-contractor. This is especially important when the contract involves a mixture of client input in terms of capital, premises and workers, and contractor input. Responsibility for maintenance, damage to and replacement of equipment, such as laundry and catering equipment must be resolved at the specification stage. Responsibility for transportation, loss and liability insurance, and provision of support services must be clarified and built into the costing as necessary. It is just as vital to budget for situations which go wrong as for a smooth execution of the contract. Failure to anticipate problems will be the most obvious source of dispute when the contract is implemented.

Example

One manager in a large construction company based in London commented that, although he was happy with the way contract cleaners cleaned the company offices, his one major headache occurred one morning when some valuable office equipment was discovered damaged. The suspicion was that the cleaners were responsible, but the real problem was that the specification had not dealt with damage and insurance costs.

Drawing up the specification can be a lengthy process – two years is not unheard of, especially if the enterprise has no previous experience. The exercise may well be the prompt for a thorough evaluation of a whole range of work, not just the area designated for sub-contracting. For example, computerised payroll issues may well be sub-contracted to a computer bureau or a software house preparing payroll programmes. The reason may be to increase security or to avoid the danger of the in-house computer breaking down at a crucial moment, or sudden staff shortages. Devising the specification for the contract also requires a careful review of the personnel role in the organisation, so that time scales, costs and issues of accountability, can be properly considered.

The specification will usually contain two interrelated elements, both requiring careful attention. They are:

- Operational matters, such as nature and length of the proposed work, lines of communication, and accountability, managerial responsibilities, basis of payment, penalty clauses (if any)
- Technical specification – the precise work to be done and the standard expected.

Technical specifications can be very lengthy – one story reports a health authority's cleaning specification being three feet thick when piled on the table! It must be borne in mind that lengthy specifications may well deter contractors, especially given that the average cost of submitting a public sector tender is over £3000.

Defining standards to be met may not be an easy task. It may be necessary to introduce a system of inspection and monitoring rather than resort to vague phrases in the specification. It is also essential to seek advice from those in the organisation best able to define work and standards, and those affected by the area of work. This is particularly important where maintenance and other ancillary services are concerned, which affect a wide range of other workers.

A major problem is that realistic costing can only be based on realistic evaluations of the work to be done, including the standard of performance. Specifications can be used to themselves engender greater flexibility by offering a range of performance options. This in turn, may allow the client to introduce complementary changes. Indeed, the whole tendering process can provide opportunities for fresh ideas and greater efficiency. There may be new ways of combining skills of in-house staff with those of the contractor, or using plant, equipment or working hours in new ways. A flexibly devised specification which makes clear the nature of the overall task to be performed but which allows scope for its performance may be a useful tool. Although this approach may provide longer term bonuses it will require more careful negotiation than the tightly-worded 'closed' formulae often used by public sector employers.

Employers wishing to use sub-contractors to provide greater flexibility in providing specialist functions, or greater efficiency, must ensure that the specification not only conveys the nature of the task but relates to the structure, ethos and culture of the whole enterprise. A rigid or 'insulated' specification and contract may well cause more problems than it cures.

Preparing the workforce
This is often the most taxing matter for personnel managers, especially in organisations where the process of competitive tendering and sub-contracting is novel. Where the decision is to sub-contract previous in-house work, but not allow for an in-house tender, the personnel issues arise through the need to re-deploy or dismiss staff. The legal matters relevant to re-deployment and dismissal are discussed in more detail in Chapters 4 and 10.

Where the contracting allows for an in-house bid, the period of preparation and uncertainty can last up to three years. A typical strategy might encompass the following matters:

- Review of personnel policy and practices where there is to be an in-house bid, to encourage competitiveness and flexibility
- Consultation with both unions (if relevant) *and* the individual workers regarding the likely changes
- Management of the workforce during the pre-contract period, including a possible freeze on vacancies, promotions and other changes
- Consideration of measures to maintain morale and motivation.

This will probably be a difficult period, during which industrial relations can be strained and unrest can occur. However, as experience of the techniques of competitive tendering grows, and as in-house units are often successful, some of the more extreme forms of action have receded. The signs of major changes in the industrial relations climate have affected attitudes to sub-contractors with some public sector trade unions beginning to negotiate with sub-contractors and some traditional private sector unions moving into the public sector. Despite an improved climate, insensitivity can still lead to claims that workers have been out-manoeuvred and perhaps constructively dismissed. The pressure on Direct Labour Organisations (DLOs) to be more adaptable cannot be too severe, or claims for unfair dismissal and other legal redress can result.

Overall, the need for preparation and change at the workplace depends on whether an in-house bid remains a possibility or whether the strategic decision had been taken to have the service provided by third parties.

Preparation of others
A change to using sub-contractors also requires consideration of its likely impact on people both within and outside the enterprise. There should be:

- Consideration of the impact of third party workers on the premises and their access to facilities
- Attention to provision of information regarding safe systems and disciplinary procedures. It is vital to ensure that information is available to individual workers
- Development of procedures to deal with complaints and friction between in-house and sub-contract staff

- Agreement as to the level and nature of intervention in work of sub-contractors' staff by line and other managers
- Preparation of in-house staff regarding sub-contract workers, aimed to identify problems and deal with possible resentment
- To keep key clients, customers, patients and the like, informed of changes and their likely impact. It may be necessary to reassure them of continuing quality of work/service and that the enterprise retains ultimate control. It ought to include clarification of complaints procedures.

Example

Patients in a private hospital were unhappy about the standard of cleaning and reception/telephone staff. Both had been sub-contracted. Patients constantly complained to nursing staff, judging them to be in some way responsible. Complaints were not made to administrative staff so there was considerable delay in rectifying the situation, resentment by nursing staff, and frustration by patients. A simple situation which would have been easily resolved by clearer information and preparation of all involved.

Preparing for YTS trainees

Having decided to enter the scheme, either as an Approved Training Organisation, or as a provider, decisions have to be made regarding the number and nature of the training placed on offer. Thereafter, much of the preparatory work is prescribed by the scheme itself, and failure to meet its standards and procedures will disentitle membership. The prescription also applies to monitoring. In effect, the enterprise has to be in a state of readiness and competence throughout. The scheme also directs attention to matters such as equal opportunities and health and safety, which may not have figured too prominently with regard to other areas of the workforce.

If an employer is applying simply to offer trainee placements the following checklist is used by the training body:

- Are the premises adequate?
- Is the training appropriate?
- Are the health and safety procedures adequate?
- Are the arrangements for off-site training adequate?

They apply to the organisation generally. A judgement is made of the competence of the employer to offer appropriate training within the correct framework. Details can be obtained from *The Managing Agents Handbook* published by the Training Agency (MSC) and more general information in the YTS *Action for Jobs* series of leaflets also published by the TA (MSC) and available at job centres.

Health and safety is a particularly high priority, and providers will have to consider whether certain areas of work should be prohibited to trainees because of the safety risks. Chapter 8 looks at health and safety more generally.

With regard to the training itself, the provider will have to demonstrate that it will ensure four interrelated outcomes. They are:

- Competence in job and/or a range of occupational skills
- Competence in a range of core skills, for example, communication, numeracy, computing and problem solving
- Ability to transfer skills and knowledge to new situations
- Personal effectiveness.

With regard to the individual scheme, the training process must contain four elements:

- Induction and initial assessment
- Participative learning
- Continuous assessment
- Guidance and review.

Each job should have competence objectives. The provider will have to demonstrate facilities for appraisal, supervision and support. The scheme has to be worked through in its entirety for the two-year period well in advance, and your training will have to integrate the off-the-job period of training, usually at a further education institution, and accommodate the required vocational award demands. Much discussion and liaison will be called for, both inside and outside the enterprise.

Management will have to be prepared and informed of the demands of trainees, and where the organisation employs other workers on new work patterns say, job-sharers, flexi-hours or the like, there will be additional matters to be considered to maintain adequate supervision of the standard thirty-nine hour week trainees. How much flexibility can be negotiated is debatable, although there has been wide use of the YTS scheme in work involving fluctuating or irregular hours, e.g. hotel and catering.

Many of the other issues relevant to preparation for YTS trainees are shared with other work patterns. The need for careful induction, effective communication and involvement of employees at all levels is vital.

SUMMARY POINTS

- Preparation for all new or atypical work patterns must involve *all* relevant groups of employees
- Preparation for some work patterns might require consultation or consideration of third parties
- Preparation for Category B and C workers is particularly crucial as it is harder to resolve difficulties or disputes later
- Preparation must include a welcome and the intention and ability to integrate *all* workers in the organisation
- New work patterns should be presented as being likely to achieve benefits, not apologised for as likely to cause problems

- Attention must be given to practical matters such as accommodation and social facilities, as well as more work-related issues and communications.

References
1 Leighton, P. and Winfield, M., *Does Job Sharing Work?*, Industrial Society and the Essex Institute of Higher Education, 1988.
2 Leighton and Winfield, ibid.

Source material
Competitive Tendering, Institute of Personnel Management, 1986
Kakabadse, A., *How to Use Consultants*, MCB Publications, 1986.
Leighton, P., *Subcontracting for Services*, A Report to the ILO, Essex Institute of Higher Education, 1985.
Preedy, J., 'What you should expect of consultants', *Personnel Management*, January 1987, p. 20.

Chapter 4

Redeployment and recruitment: the management of change

INTRODUCING CHANGE

Having identified the changes to work practices which match organisational objectives, whether on a corporate or a work unit level, employers need to consider how best to introduce these arrangements without falling foul of the law and existing cultural or management traditions.

The management of change when introducing new work practices is no different to change in any other aspect of employment. Changes which are to mutual benefit, or those in the furtherance of equal opportunities policies, are likely to cause few legal or industrial relations problems. Changes which are to the perceived disadvantage of employees or third parties may be problematic and need to be introduced lawfully and sensitively.

In recent years, schemes redeploying or changing the composition of workforces have attracted detailed attention. They included the much publicised introduction of networking arrangements and job-share policies, wider use of consultants and schemes to sub-contract skills and services which were previously in-house.

Where new work patterns have been directly linked to occupations or areas of work new to the organisation, there have been few problems. However, changes to the working conditions of *existing* employees is a different matter. Opportunities for secondment and job sharing, and other innovations benefiting employees, have been welcomed; others such as changes to hours of work or conditions demanding greater flexibility from employees have been resisted.

The three contrasting case studies below illustrate some of the issues and problems involved. All, to a greater or lesser extent, caused litigation, and the findings give a good indication of the law's likely attitude to the process of change.

Example 1 is drawn from a large private sector, unionised employment; 2 is from a number of public sector, unionised, employers, 3 is drawn from a smaller, private sector employer where trade unions were not involved in the changes. All dealt with attempts to achieve greater flexibility of hours. They concern both full-time, permanent staff, and Category A staff.

Example 1: The mail order company

One of the most widely reported package of changes in work patterns was that of Freemans plc, which was largely completed by 1986.[1] They were mainly motivated by the needs of the employer, but did try to accommodate significant levels of employee choice. The example therefore falls between the 'economic push' and the 'social pull' models. Freemans is one of the largest mail/telephone order organisations, employing approximately 5 500 workers in London, Sheffield and Peterborough. Traditionally, terms of work had been negotiated with ASTMS, ACTSS, TGWU, and EEPTU, though without a formal bargaining forum. Freeman's business is prone to fluctuations, some of which can be anticipated. They needed to cope with these fluctuations and with new technology without excessive overtime or expansion of the workforce. Flexitime had been in operation for many of the workers since the 1970s.

The strategy was to increase the range of flexible hours arrangements. The following were introduced in addition to flexitime itself:

- *Flexitime was based on 4 week (78 hours) periods*
- *Weekly hours, varying between 34¼–39¾ per week, dependent on individual choice*
- *Flexible holiday contracts of between 16 to 31 days a year (21 being 'standard'), dependent on individual choice*
- *Temporary voluntary transfers from part-time to full-time work to cover peak demand.*

The proposals gave considerable autonomy to departments to assess and reflect their own needs. Most of these changes were negotiated with trade unions used to flexible working arrangements. Where changes were agreed to by individuals, they went ahead even in the absence of a collective agreement. There were no redundancies, no industrial action and barely any resignations, largely because the proposals were carefully negotiated and were to deal with specific and understandable employer needs.

Freemans developed a checklist for effective change, some of which is reproduced below, and coincides with much of what was discussed in Chapter 3.

Before change

People

— Seek advice from Personnel and Training Division.
— Consult with unions and staff over intentions (refer to Security of Employment Agreement: PER 11, PER 12 and PER 13). In particular explain carefully why, and listen to other views or alternative proposals.
— Feed back reaction to their views and the results of these.
— Inform unions and staff of the 'final' proposals, and keep them informed of progress in the pre-change period.
— Assess training and assessment requirements.
— Plan the change, making sure adequate time is allowed for each stage; that manning levels can meet both work and any retraining requirements and that there is provision for lead times for supplying equipment, furniture, recruitment, etc. Try to involve unions and staff in planning, the working environment, and job design.

- Consider job designs which ensure that, as far as possible, repetitive, monotonous, uncomfortable or stressful activities are broken up by other more varied work.

Equipment
- Seek advice from the Premises Development Manager and/or Health and Safety Controller.
- Decide, with such advice, whether O and M should be involved.
- Consider:
  - environment
  - is existing light adequate?
  - are blinds required?
  - how high will noise levels be?
  - is acoustic screening required?

However, even this well-prepared package had stings in its tail. By 1987, evidence of increased strains caused by the pace and extent of change were becoming apparent. In 1988, one of Freeman's female packers asserted that she was of 'equal value' as a male checker who received more pay. A House of Lord's decision supported her claim.[2] This put further strain on carefully considered grading systems and provided strong evidence that even the best laid plans sometimes go wrong.

Example 2: The dinner ladies

Since 1946, terms of employment for schools meals staff in Hertfordshire had been established by negotiation at a National Joint Council. Due to expenditure cuts in 1981, many local authority employers sought to change the terms of work of dinner ladies. Specifically, the employer wanted to reduce the weekly part-time hours and initiate contracts on a more casual basis, reducing or eliminating summer 'retainers'. In 1983, after failing to achieve change by agreement, Hertfordshire County Council wrote to the employees giving twelve weeks 'detailed notice of the variation in your contract of service'.

The employees argued that this was an attempt to unilaterally change terms, an agreed change having proved impossible. The employers responded by saying that the letters simply terminated the original contract and offered new terms, which the employees had accepted by staying in employment. The High Court decided that the letter was clearly an attempt to force through a change and was a breach of contract. Damages were awarded to employees on the basis of wages due under the original contract.

Subsequently, Hertfordshire issued notices to the dinner ladies which clearly terminated their contracts and offered the new terms. The National Union of Public Employees (NUPE) applied to the courts for judicial review of the action. NUPE argued that Hertfordshire had acted ultra vires, *in that they had disregarded the possibility of effectively and collectively negotiating the changes. Hertfordshire had also neglected to consider the effects of ignoring national wage levels. This, NUPE argued, could lead to poaching of workers by neighbouring employers and 'the risk of industrial anarchy'. The case went to the Court of Appeal which decided against NUPE. The Court stated that decisions such as this which changed the employment conditions of a group of workers could only be challenged by this legal mechanism if they were so unreasonable that no reasonable local authority could have taken them. Hertfordshire's conduct was not that unreasonable.*

Almost coincidentally, dinner ladies in Birmingham successfully challenged changes in their working conditions using the same legal arguments. Decisions affecting dinner ladies were taken and implemented by the Chief Education Officer. Under the Local Government Act of 1972 they could only legally be taken by the Education Committee. As the decision affecting terms of work was taken by the 'wrong' person it was ultra vires *and unlawful.*

Dinner ladies in Kent and several other parts of the country reacted to changes by making claims for unfair dismissal and redundancy payments. They argued that the imposed changes amounted to constructive dismissal and that the employer's conduct was unreasonable and unjustifiable. Some of these claims were successful.

Overall, hundreds of cases involving areas of law were brought by employees and their unions, with much disruption to the service and continuing industrial relations difficulties.

Example 3: The chicken catcher

Mr Wilson was employed to catch chickens. His 'normal' hours of work were 4 a.m. to 12 noon. His employers were a medium-sized enterprise which had expanded rapidly in the fresh chicken business. Mr Wilson was not in a trade union and terms of work were not collectively agreed with unions. In March 1985, the company decided to introduce a new system of shift working, produced an explanatory memo for employees and called a staff meeting. The major proposal was that the shift would have variable hours and commence between 2 a.m and 10 a.m. Mr Wilson, apparently alone, objected to the change as it would cause disruption to his family life and prevent his wife going out to work. He was given seven days to think over his position. When his objections still continued, he was dismissed.

He made a claim for unfair dismissal, but lost. The 'employers had acted perfectly properly. They clearly took into consideration not only the pressure on them; they also took into account the interests of the employee. They came to the conclusion that it was the applicant who must suffer'. The employers were justified in dismissing him for 'some substantial reason' (EPCA, 1978, s. 57(1)(b)), despite having unilaterally varied his terms of work.[3]

These case studies illustrate that the process of changing working conditions must be carefully considered and negotiated. Attention has to be given to the individual's legal rights as well as collective agreement and the law has a range of procedures and remedies which must be borne in mind.

A checklist for change

Three major questions need consideration. How much attention is given to each will clearly depend on the scale and nature of the proposal, the type of enterprise, and the characteristics of the existing workforce.

- Are there any legal restraints on the introduction of change?
- Are there any legal requirements for consultation, negotiation or notification during the process of change?

- Has the law relating to variation or termination of the employment contract been complied with?

Change which involves termination of contracts will be considered in Chapter 10.

RESTRAINTS ON CHANGE

There are relatively few legal rules affecting the employment relationship generally. Indeed, there are far fewer now than in 1979 (see Chapter 1).

In 1983 the Fair Wages Resolution of the House of Commons was abandoned. This had required government contractors to offer wage levels at least commensurate with those generally in the relevant area of work. Perhaps the only significant statutory curb arises through the Wages Act 1986, which, although it considerably weakened wages councils has still left them with the ability to set minimum basic wages for over 2.5 million workers.

However, two recent statutory developments are worth noting. The Local Government Act 1988 will require vastly increased levels of sub-contracting by local authorities, especially for services. Managements' ability to introduce coherent redeployment and restructuring of *existing* employees' contracts may be considerably affected. The 1987 Teachers Pay and Conditions Act sets down terms of contract for teachers. The so-called '1265' annual hours format prescribes detailed responsibilities for teachers and is based on the norm of full-time work. It is difficult to apply to part-time workers or job-sharers. Thus, although this statute was apparently partly designed to promote greater flexibility on the part of core workers, its impact may well be highly restrictive and considerably inhibit changes in the workforce more generally.

Areas of law to bear in mind

- Anti-discrimination measures
- The law relating to health and safety at work
- Aspects of contract law and criminal law.

The first two are relatively well established areas of law and have relevance to a wide range of proposed changes: the third has particular bearing on a plan to change the contracts of employees to ones of self-employment.

Anti-discrimination laws

Anti-discrimination laws discussed elsewhere (see Chapters 1 and 7) have a direct impact on changes to the working practices of existing employees and the recruitment of new workers.

A plan to dismiss most or all of existing part-time staff and to replace them with a system based on a small full-time workforce with annual committed hours, supplemented by temporary staff, may be challenged as discriminatory if, say, all the part-timers are women or from a particular ethnic group. This can also apply to plans that offer new benefits or opportunities to some workers, but deny them for temporary or part-time staff.

A restructuring package which included a decision to dismiss only women would automatically constitute unfair dismissal. However, a decision to dismiss a part-time workforce which happens to be predominantly female, may also be unlawful. Relevant case law is confused. The decision in *Clarke v. Eley* [1983][4] was that dismissing the part-time workforce which was 100 per cent female, before applying the 'last-in-first-out' principle, was discriminatory against women. It was accepted that child-care responsibilities, which made full-time work difficult or impossible, fell disproportionately upon women.

A different approach was taken in *Kidd v. DRG (UK) Limited*, [1985].[5] On similar facts to the previous case, the Employment Appeal Tribunal (EAT) was unwilling to conclude that child-care responsibilities fell disproportionately on women and thus limit most women with children to part-time work. It was said that, 'Ours are times of far reaching changes ... [for] married fathers sometimes cared for the children'. Although there may well be signs of this change, it would be unwise to rely too heavily on this case. Evidence shows that more and more women who seek employment seek only part-time work.

Some examples
Moves from full-time to part-time work and vice versa can cause problems. Change can be initiated by the employer, for example, by wishing to increase the size of the full-time workforce, and introducing a policy which requires part-timers to opt for full-time work or leave. The policy might also include refusals to allow employees to reduce their weekly hours, perhaps to cope with illness or domestic responsibilities. Alternatively, a policy might aim to increase use of part-timers and possibly select certain types of work for part-timers only.

A 'full-time only' policy
A 'full-time only' policy is likely to run into problems. If an employer, during a restructuring exercise, demands that employees opt for full-time work or leave and/or automatically refuses requests to work part-time it may infringe the law.

The leading case is that of *Holmes v. The Home Office*, [1984].[6] Here, a previous full-timer applied to return to work part-time after maternity leave. The refusal by the employer was held to be unlawful. The EAT accepted that the full-time only policy was a 'detriment' to some employees. This could be either because you then gave up your job, and with it seniority and accrued occupational and statutory entitlements, or because you would be forced into full-time employment, with the consequent effect on the costs and complexities of combining child-care with full-time work.

Can an employer ever justify a full-time only policy? Possibly, providing the reasons are genuine and are related to costs and efficiency. A need for continuity of work, policy development or managerial co-ordinating responsibilites may suffice. However, the recent decision in *Guthrie* v. *Royal Bank of Scotland*, [1987][7] provides evidence of an unconvincing argument. Here an employee in a systems development department wanted to work three days a week after maternity leave. The employers argued that 'the size and structure of the department is not conducive to such arrangements'. The industrial tribunal was unimpressed, and took the view on the facts that only a minor adjustment would have been required to accommodate her. The employers were merely being inflexible!

Job sharing
Justifying a refusal to accommodate an employee's wish to move from full-time employment to a job-share arrangement has proved more controversial and problematic. A useful example is that of the well-publicised decision in *Robertson and Griffith* v. *Strathclyde Regional Council*, [1986].[8] A scheme to job-share a careers officer post was worked out and supported by line managers, but objected to by senior management. The refusal was held to be discriminatory against women. The tribunal accepted evidence that considerably higher numbers of qualified male careers officer than female in the region were in employment, a factor explained by the demand to work full-time. It was also accepted that, given the nature of career officers' work and the managerial support, there was no valid justification for rejecting the proposal.

Later decisions have viewed employers' arguments more favourably.

Examples
1 *An application to job-share in the finance department of a university could be lawfully rejected, because the job had significant supervisory responsibilities and the employee had been offered what was thought to be appropriate part-time work in another section of the department.*[9]
2 *An application to job-share a health visitor's post could be rejected because the Scottish EAT accepted senior management's view that job sharing would not provide the required level of continuity of patient care: tribunals must consider 'efficiency as a critical factor'.*[10]

In addition to arguments based on the need to maintain efficiency levels, it would also be relevant that the employer already had made an offer to women, such as generous flexihours schemes, career breaks or secure part-time work which allowed retention of accrued rights and benefits.

Two factors need to be borne in mind:

- It will be more difficult to resist job sharing in a climate of growing recognition in both the public and private sectors. It will be seen less and less as an oddity, or impossible to manage
- It will be particularly difficult to resist in a workforce which already has

flexible work patterns or, for example management and work structures based on teamwork.

Change in hours
Anti-discrimination may bring about less dramatic changes in the hours of both full and part-timers. An annual hours contract may disproportionately and adversely affect women or ethnic groups, if it requires up to fifteen hours a week above the mean to cope with peak demands or seasonal changes, or changes in shifts to involve more weekend working.

Example
The recent case of Fluss v. Grant Thornton Chartered Accountants [1987][11] illustrates the point well. A requirement to work 9.30 a.m. to 5.30 p.m. Mondays to Fridays, which allowed virtually no flexibility, was held to be potentially discriminatory against Jewish people. Although the tribunal accepted that the nature of work here did require attendance on Friday afternoons, the underlying proposition could have relevance to other planned changes.

When considering a change in terms of work it is vital to keep in mind the three key questions of anti-discrimination law:

- Will the proposed change in hours, or the requirement to work full-time, or the rejection of proposal to change terms of contract by an employee cause that employee a detriment?
- Does that detriment disproportionately affect one gender, or an ethnic group or groups
- Can the conduct or condition imposed by the employer be justified?

Detriment can be defined in terms of intrusion to family life, pressure, a child-care arrangement, etc., as well as loss of pay, loss of job and interruption to career and work experience.

Claims covering discriminatory practices are growing. There is also the possibility of investigations by the EOC and the CRE.

The law of health and safety at work

Until recently the introduction of changes to working hours might have run counter to protective legislation affecting especially women and young workers. However, the Sex Discrimination Act 1986, and the Employment Act 1989 have removed virtually every restriction on hours for women. Additionally, the European Community has recently issued a Communication regarding protective legislation, which calls on member states to ensure such legislation is consistent across sexes and across occupational areas.

Measures needed to protect the special biological condition of women are excepted (though this affects new processes rather than working patterns), as where there are special occupational hazards. However, when developing proposals to move in-house work to homework it should be borne in mind that the appropriate occupation's safety regulations still apply to the home.

Contract and criminal law

The process of changing contract terms of employees, especially hours of work will be discussed in the next section. At this stage, the major topic is change of contract status of current workers from direct to self-employment. Sales staff may be renamed 'agents', and management personnel called 'consultants'. The term 'contractor' or 'freelancer' may apply to a whole range of workers in, say, driving instruction, delivery and installation work and financial occupations. Many regular workers in service industries might be re-titled 'casual' and have tax and national insurance arrangements altered accordingly.

If the change is merely cosmetic and leaves the employment relationship much as before (for example, arrangements to save on tax and social security liabilities), the law can declare the contract null and void as being for an illegal purpose. All rights and duties are thus extinguished. The arrangement may also constitute a fraud, and potentially both the employer and the worker can be guilty of criminal offences.

Government departments and the courts are increasingly willing to confront the issue of the genuineness or otherwise of the contractual arrangement. Quite apart from the special provisions affecting the building industry since 1974, there have been a series of investigations into specific occupations. The Inland Revenue and the DSS are employing more investigators and issuing more comprehensive and updated guidance leaflets on employment status. Although both have operated prescribed procedures and 'tests' of contractual relationships there is evidence that, as the decisions are localised or even individualised, many inconsistencies can occur. The law courts and tribunals have regularly reaffirmed their ultimate right to determine the 'legal realities' of a situation, even overruling the clear intention of the parties or, indeed, previous assessments by government departments. Much hinges on the attitude of courts and tribunals. Unfortunately, the record of courts in providing clear and coherent tests is not impressive and this whole area of law must be approached with caution.

Tests of employment status

Until recently, the level of control or supervision over the worker was the deciding factor. If you could tell the worker not only what to do but also how to do it, the worker was an employee.

With the growing complexity of work and the development of larger and probably more impersonal working relationships, the law has tried to evolve more flexible and realistic approaches. The courts now scrutinise the whole of the working relationship. They consider mode of payment, hours of work, occupational benefits, arrangements for tax and social security, restrictions (if any) on working for others, provision of equipment, application of disciplinary rules, as well as the declared intention of the parties.

In considering these factors, they have tried to identify an overriding or ultimate question to be applied to the facts. Once the popular approach had been to pose the question, 'Was the worker in business on his or her own account?'. This test was useful for many types of worker. It places emphasis on the financial aspects of the contract, such as payment ('fee' or contract price, for example), provision of equipment and facilities, and opportunities for profit and loss.

The current position has been heavily influenced by a 1983 Court of Appeal decision which posed the correct question, 'Was there mutuality of obligation between the parties?'. Specifically, was there an obligation on the part of the employer to provide work and the worker to accept it?

This approach led to a 'regular casual' waiter employed by Trusthouse Forte being viewed as self-employed. Technically, when called to serve at banquets or functions he could refuse to go.[12] Despite the fact that this ignores the realities of many work situations, the legal test has been widely used, especially where work fluctuates.

Sometimes fluctuation arises from the nature of the occupation, such as fishing, catering, entertainment, and some areas of manufacturing industry where fluctuations are endemic. However, temporary secretarial staff on the books of an agency have also been considered self-employed. They lack the necessary obligation to work when offered work for a client.[13] Recently, the test has been refined so as to pose the question, 'Did the parties have a *sufficient* mutuality of obligation?'. But there remains a question mark over what this phrase means.

The overall position remains confused for an employer who wishes to change the status of existing workers (or, indeed, recruit new ones).

A suggested approach:

- If the change in question will involve workers continuing to work on a regular basis, as an 'agent', 'consultant' or the like, to comply with the law that person should be acting 'in business on their own account'.
- If the change is to move workers to a temporary/casual self-employed basis, where they will be used on an irregular basis, the 'mutuality of obligation' test may well be the appropriate one.

Examples

A company engaged workers under contracts of employment for the manufacture and delivery of building materials. Until 1959 the delivery aspect had been carried out by sub-contractors when the company decided to end the agreement and to offer self-employment contracts to drivers, many of whom were previous employees. The self-employment status was challenged by the Ministry of Pensions and National Insurance. It appeared that the contract between the company and the drivers stated that the delivery lorries were to be bought on credit terms by the drivers, but would carry the company's logo. Drivers were required to wear the company's uniform and had a limited right to delegate work or carry out deliveries for other employers. They collected materials from the company's depot according to a prescribed procedure, though had some discretion as to when and how long they worked.

It was decided that the arrangement was one of self-employment, despite the level of supervision by the company. The judge said, 'He is free to decide whether he will maintain the vehicle by his own labour or another, he is free to choose who he will employ [to assist him] and on what terms ... he is free in his choice of competent driver ... free to chose where he will buy his fuel ...'. The supervision was, he thought, merely to make sure the business was run efficiently. The overall position was that an owner/driver was 'a small business man, not a servant'.[14]

An insurance company had employed a worker (J. Massey) as manager of a branch office and had a general agency agreement with him. For the period 1971 to 1973 he was regarded as an employee. In 1973 he requested that he became self-employed for tax purposes, though continuing as a manager. In 1975 he was dismissed and claimed compensation as an employee. The courts accepted that the 1973 agreement simply implied that he was 'just the same man under another name' (John L. Massey and Associates). They confirmed that he was self-employed. It was accepted that the agreement of 1983 was genuine and not 'tainted with illegality', not least because the court felt that in reality he had been self-employed from the outset. It was thought that he worked for commission and could take on other business, all of which confirmed his self-employed status.[15]

When he joined a company, a skilled sheet metal worker was given the option of being an employee or self-employed. He chose the latter. He was directed as to the work he should do, worked regular hours, and alongside workers classed as employees. He was taxed on a Schedule D basis. This arrangement was accepted by the Inland Revenue.

When he was dismissed he made a claim for unfair dismissal. He said he was 'in reality' an employee. He was successful, because he was subject to control as to how he did his work, and as he invested no capital or equipment could not be considered a 'small businessman'[16]

The outcome of individual cases may be influenced by the nature of the claim being made – a dense difficulty in assessing this area of law. Courts and tribunals have been reluctant to allow employees to seek protection from employment legislation having previously had the tax and other advantages of self-employed status. In cases such as industrial injuries claims, the courts may adopt a more sympathetic attitude to the worker where to do otherwise would leave them penniless. It is impossible to be precise.

Suggested guidelines:

- A change which is merely cosmetic and which leaves the working arrangements largely as before will be ineffective
- A change which changes 'labels', even though agreed to by the former employee will be ineffective
- Changes of status affecting skilled, professional and managerial staff may be effective, providing the previous employee has increased economic freedom, and personal responsibility
- Changes of status for manual, semi-skilled and similar workers, if they are not closely supervised by the employer and are free to refuse work or work for other employers, may be effective.

Following these guidelines, it is possible that a change from in-house to homework will change the status to self-employment, but perhaps only where the move involves increased financial independence, provision of equipment and a lessening or removal of occupational benefits. Change of workplace will not, of itself, change employment status.

Similar comments apply to moves from employee status to freelance or consultant. Financial and disciplinary matters are dominant and the business test is therefore appropriate. Employers need to 'distance' themselves from consultants to lessen inter-dependence. Whatever policy is being considered, it is vital to consider the long term as well as immediate implications.

CONSULTATION, NEGOTIATION AND NOTIFICATION OF CHANGE

Here again, there are relatively few legal demands relating to the process of change, other than those affecting the individual employment contract. These will be discussed in the next section.

Legislation, insofar as it requires employers contemplating changes to negotiate or provide information, generally does so in a context of recognised trade unions. The Employment Act, 1982, requires companies with more than 250 employees to insert in their director's reports a description of 'employee involvement' in the company. This does not impose an obligation to actually 'involve' employees in discussions or proposals for the company. It is limited to the private sector.

Providing information

Section 17(1) of the Employment Protection Act, 1975, requires employers to disclose information to authorised representatives of a recognised union 'for the purposes of all stages of collective bargaining'. Disputes can be referred to the Central Arbitration Committee (CAC) for settlement.

Note:

- Only recognised unions are entitled to the information and in the private sector
- Unions have, if necessary, to demonstrate that non-disclosure would impede negotiations 'to a material extent'
- There are specific exceptions to the need to disclose. These include information damaging to national security, in contravention of a statute or confidential information
- There is no obligation to provide information when the work involved would be 'out of reasonable proportion' to its value in collective bargaining.

Example
It was decided that a recognised trade union, wanting to devise and negotiate an in-house tender when cleaning services at the Ministry of Defence were to be sub-contracted, could not have information about outside firms' tenders.

The requirements on employers have been interpreted fairly narrowly, and have given rise to relatively few complaints to the CAC. This is despite ACAS's view that the provisions would have meant that employers disclose information about manpower planning if applied in the spirit rather than to the letter. Clearly, employers who do not recognise trade unions for bargaining purposes, or for only limited reasons, will not be affected by these provisions.

Consultation

The rules about obligatory consultation about changes in the workforce only apply when the change involves fairly large-scale redundancies, or redundancies which are planned to take place rapidly. Where an employer plans to dismiss at least one hundred employees within ninety days or less, or ten or more within thirty days or less the consultation should begin 'at the earliest opportunity'. Information must be provided for representatives of the recognised trade unions, including the reasons for the redundancies, the number involved, time-scale and the proposed method of selection. The employer must consider representations from the union(s) regarding the proposal and, if they are rejected, explain why. The Secretary of State for Employment must also be informed.

There are difficulties in fixing the date where the thirty or ninety day periods run from, especially when the proposals affect workers in sequence. However, it is clear that the law demands a realistic period of time for some genuine consultation (half-an-hour was not enough!), although it does not require the employer to comply with the union's view. The period of consultation is clearly distinguishable from the period of notice by statute or contract which must be given to individual workers. If an employer does not provide information or allow for consultation, the employees affected can apply to an industrial tirbunal for a 'protective award' of compensation, referable to the period of consultation which the law required. The sum will be 'just and equitable', having regard to the employer's default, and will be based on the employee's individual weekly rate of pay.

Where redundancies are part of a manpower restructuring policy, such as one involving sub-contracting, employing workers on a self-employed basis, or reducing the number of part-timers, the law may well require proper periods for consultation. Redundancies forced upon an employer, due to chronic financial difficulties, would be viewed less stringently.

An EC Draft Directive *('Vredeling')*

In the near future, the above Draft Directive may be approved by the Council of Ministers and may be binding on the UK. If implemented this would require employers to inform and consult with recognised unions, not only about the employer's intentions but those of parent or associated companies perhaps even those based in other countries. The Draft Directive recognises the influence of multi-national organisations, especially in the area of manpower planning. However, it should be said that there has been considerable opposition to its provisions, especially from the USA and UK governments.

Collective bargaining

Although statutory provisions are very limited, proposed changes in the composition and utilisation of the workforce will often have implications for collective agreements. As the Freemans case study showed (see p. 84), major changes can be successfully negotiated in the usual way, as can voluntary or compulsory redundancy schemes.

There can be legal implications if a change is made without reference to collective bargaining, or is introduced despite the opposition of the other parties to a collective agreement.

Breakdown in bargaining

It is always open to trade unions or employees to resort to industrial action. Some changes in the workforce involve job losses, for example decisions by health authorities to sub-contract for cleaning, catering and laundry service. Unless agreed to by the unions, industrial action can follow. However, trade unions will not have the option of suing for breach of a collective agreement as, at the time of writing, collective agreements are not assumed to be legally binding.

A legal challenge to change?

Some proposals have been fought through law courts, though not often with success.

Public law remedies

Case Study B (the dinner ladies) illustrated that there are circumstances where the manner, as opposed to the outcome, of decision making can contravene legal rules. Employers who operate within statutory powers, as do local and health authorities, various 'quangos' and other organisations established by statute, or employ workers on an office-holder basis, are subject to public law. The decision making process is reviewed by courts.

Courts will examine whether the employer acted unlawfully in reducing wages or benefits, or declaring redundancies. The concept has two dimensions:

- That the decision was one which they were not empowered to take
- That the decision was unlawful in some other way or was so unreasonable that no reasonable authority could have taken it.

Opportunities for courts to intervene are wide. If a statute or regulation requires specific notification, publication or consultation, a change in the workforce can be declared null and void by a court if not carried out accordingly. If a decision is taken by an unauthorised person, if material considerations are ignored, or irrelevant considerations taken into account, then they can be set aside. If a change to the workforce implied that the statutory requirements regarding, say, disabled or minority workers or health and safety could not be complied with, the decision could be similarly challenged.

Example: the Liverpool cases

The local authority had been locked in dispute with central government for financial aid and rates. A series of protests were organised and the relevant committees decided that pay would be withheld from employees who did not work on a 'day of action'. Teachers had their pay deducted when they could not work in the schools because the caretakers were engaged in protest action. A court held this response to be 'wholly unreasonable'. Subsequently, the authority issued redundancy notices to teachers as part of the same campaign to highlight its financial difficulties and bring pressure on central government. This, too, was successfully challenged, as closing schools would cause the authority, as an LEA, to be in breach of its duties under S.8 of the 1944 Education Act to 'provide schools sufficient for the ages, abilities and aptitudes' of pupils. Had it been required to do so, the court would have also held that the council's conduct was 'wholly unreasonable'.[17]

This decision notwithstanding, courts will not easily rush in to curb change, especially where it is introduced to improve efficiency, or part of a politically backed policy.

Variation or termination of the individual contract of employment

Law operates across all employee work patterns and, in common with the public law development discussed previously, is an area of growing importance and development.

The legal regulation of changes to contracts of employment remains a difficult area. Most of the standard texts on employment law devote relatively little attention to the process of variation to contract terms. Change to contract terms from the employee perspective can be positive, for example, pay rises or shorter working hours. They can also be less attractive, such as those requiring increased adaptability, mobility or skills.

More cases have come to court or tribunal because employees have considered changes introduced by employers will have a detrimental effect on them. This may be one consequence of the rapid changes to work patterns, and of decline in the impact of traditional trade unions and bargaining (see Chapter 9). More and more workers do not belong to unions or, as new entrants to the labour market, have not joined one. Until very recently, it could have been argued that a change to flexi-hours from standard hours, or the move to homework from factory based work, would have been legally effective if agreed to by the appropriate trade union, providing the relevant workers remained at work. The combination of these factors would have been viewed by law as acceptance of the changes. The simple rules of the law of contract which in theory require an offer of changed terms to be agreed to by the individual employee had been sidestepped. However, the last ten years or so have seen significant legal developments.

The Court of Appeal, in particular, has gone out of its way to restate the legal rules about individual consent to variation of terms. Current case law suggests:

- A change to working practices will be valid if *either* it was already authorised by the contract, or was agreed to by the employee
- Agreement will have taken place if the employee *expressly* agrees to the change, or, if the change was negotiated with a trade union or equivalent, by remaining at work and acquiescing in the change.

The starting-point is obviously the existing employment contract. If the employer wishes to introduce split shifts, homework, work at a different location or institute a different method of doing work, this may be already in the contract. Hours of work might be 'at the discretion of the employer, but not to exceed a thirty eight hour week'. Job location may be 'anywhere in England and Wales' or 'within a fifty mile radius of Birmingham'. The employer is then simply 'activating' the contract terms. In addition, the courts may be willing to imply certain additional obligations to the contract. For example, a change in workplace can be made so long as it is within daily travelling distance.

If the change is not already authorised by contract, the variation will have to be agreed to in some other way. Changes which materially affect the whole basis of the employment relationship will have to be particularly carefully negotiated, such as a move from full-time work to a job-share arrangement, or a weekly hours contract to an annual hours or committed hours arrangement and may well require the issue of a new employment contract. Arrangements such as job sharing ought to be individually agreed to. The fact that a job-share policy has been collectively negotiated would not be adequate. However, these changes will tend to be less problematic because the initiative often comes from the employee and is to their advantage.

Where a change is proposed it can either be put to employees, by letter, notice or memo, and then accepted or not. Written consent to change will clearly be effective, but what if the change is agreed to by a trade union? As mentioned earlier, this does not have any impact, unless it had been previously agreed by individual employees that contract change could come about by collective agreement. This is the 'carte blanche' approach, and is widely used in some occupations and increasingly in the public sector.

In the absence of such a clause, and on the assumption that the collectively agreed changes are communicated to employees, what then is the position? Again, the employees could signify individual agreement. But what if they say nothing or they protest? The legal position appears to be this. The courts have reiterated on many and recent occasions that a collective agreement achieves legal reality in the individual contract. Hence, change has obviously to be made to the contract. However, employees who remain in work, continue to draw pay and go along with the change will be deemed to have accepted the change. If they work flexi-hours, if they go along with the changed shifts, then agreement can normally be implied.

What if they stay at work and signify their disagreement. Can they insist on operating the contract as before the original? The general answer is 'yes', following the long standing decision in *Marriott* v. *Oxford and District Cooperative Society*, [1968].[18] Here a reduction in pay and status was considered a breach of contract by the Court of Appeal despite the employee remaining at work. The recent decision in *Rigby* v. *Ferodo Limited*, [1986][19] has confirmed an entitlement to sue for breach of contract when wages were reduced unilaterally. Simply sending letters or memos in an attempt to 'legitimise' a change will not work. Ultimately, the individual can resist a change and allege that the employer is in breach of contract.

The possible legal outcomes of unagreed to changes

On the assumption that the change is not already authorised by contract the situation appears to be this:

(a) The employee can remain at work, insist on the original contract but if the employer implements the change, sue for breach of contract.
(b) The employee can consider the enforced change as a repudiation of the contract, i.e. it goes to the heart of the employment relationship; they can accept the repudiation by giving in their notice and making a claim for either wrongful or unfair dismissal, or redundancy.
(c) The employee could ask the court for an injunction to restrain an employer from implementing the change if, in the view of the court, the integrity of the employment contract remained.
(d) If covered by public law, the worker could ask for judicial review of the process of change, or protection from the rules of natural justice.

Effective change requires consultation and support at all levels in the organisation, and with both unions and individual employees. Agreed procedures must be followed and decisions made in the appropriate manner. This process will not only avoid legal action but will gain the support of employees. Despite employer's efforts not all employees will want to go along with the changes. They may have to be declared redundant or dismissed, which itself may lead to legal action. Some of the relevant issues are discussed in Chapter 10.

RECRUITMENT

The process of change may not be confined to redeploying existing staff. Circumstances may require that entirely new personnel are recruited. The two basic circumstances covered by this section are:

(a) Where new work patterns are made available to and established for existing staff.
(b) Where new workers are recruited.

A number of important general points apply to the recruitment of Category A and B workers:

- The sources of potential applicants will be in many cases, different than those used for full-time staff. The recruitment methods and terms of employment organisations use will need to reflect this
- Selection criteria should place a greater emphasis on *how* the job is undertaken as well as *what* is being undertaken. In the case of job-sharers and distance workers, such as networkers, teleworkers and consultants, this will mean that each applicant's ability to self-start and manage his/her own workload will be a crucial factor
- For both these reasons, the job specification will need to be clearly defined. Managers responsible for drawing these up will require good analytical skills and training in appropriate job analysis and work specification skills.

Sources of labour

The pool of potential labour is far wider and more diverse than that available for full-time positions. In cases where flexible working has been introduced to cope with skill shortages, accessing the talents of this 'alternative' workforce will be the main reason for the initiative.

Some of the main categories include:

- Women, with or without children, who are seeking to find a practical outlet for their skills or to supplement the family income. Traditionally, they have been attracted to classical day-time part-time positions and shift work. If they are mothers, they will tend to want work patterns with fixed hours allowing them to drop off and pick up their children from school (for example, between 10 a.m. and 3 p.m.), or self-managed work which they can build around their domestic commitments
- Women already in employment seeking to combine professional work

REDEPLOYMENT AND RECRUITMENT   101

with starting a family. Whilst their needs may correspond to the category above, a key feature will be the *continuity* that the work scheme brings to their careers. They will therefore be attracted to schemes such as job sharing, extended maternity provision, networking and teleworking, involving responsibilities which will enable them to pick up and maintain their career development. These schemes should ideally be linked to some form of continuing training provision (see Chapter 1)

- Retired, or semi-retired people of both sexes, who are once again seeking a practical outlet for their skills, to supplement their pension or to maintain some form of career development involving a reduced commitment. Networking, consultancy and traditional part-time work, as well as job sharing, are all strong options
- Students in post-school education who are seeking to supplement their grant. They will obviously be interested in work which will fit in well with their study time. At a higher and more professional level, there are also growing numbers of full-time staff wishing to take on a reduced working commitment to undertake continuing education or training to keep their skills up to date or to make a career change
- Disabled people, frequently overlooked by equal opportunity policies, often require a flexible working commitment for physical or psychiatric reasons.

Self-employed people

The use of consultancy and contracted services in their own right will be considered later in this chapter. However, self-employed people are also often attracted to temporary and part-time positions with fixed hours which they can combine with their 'Schedule D' activities. This may be because they wish to secure their income or because the 'employed' work complements their consultancy (see example of the Stock Exchange below).

Secondments

Secondments in the UK are becoming more common. For example, valued staff are seconded by organisations to community schemes as part of a corporate social policy. Skilled manual and professional workers are lent for a specific period or specific task to another enterprise. In addition, staff are also seconded either between departments, subsidiary companies or individual organisations, for purposes of their own career development or enterprise needed.

Example: The Stock Exchange
Examples of how differing categories of flexible workers can be used to service the same scheme is illustrated by the job-share operated by the Stock Exchange, in the case of a senior training post. The position was initially requested by the existing full-time occupant of the post because she wished to work part-time in order to start a

family. Examples of workers brought in to act as sharers included:
- *a lecturer in management studies seconded from the Slough College of Higher Education. He divided his working week equally between his educational and managerial activities and found the bridge the scheme provided 'invaluable' to his career.*
- *two training consultants who divided their time equally between their employed and self-employed activities. One, Jean Lammiman, commented, 'There is certainly a good deal of similarity between what we are doing internally and what we both do as consultants. It's certainly helpful for us to have the Stock Exchange as our major source of work and to encourage that being known. On the other hand, the Stock Exchange gains from what we do outside. The fact that we are solving a variety of problems helps us to keep up to date in our "employed" work'. It is worth mentioning that Jean Lammiman was subsequently seconded to the City University Business School as Deputy Director of their consortium MBA programme, thereby giving the Stock Exchange another valuable contact with the education world directly linked to their management development needs.*

Recruitment methods

Internal recruitment

As with the selection of full-time staff, before advertising the post outside, it is important to identify existing staff within the organisation who may be interested in working on a new basis.

Many staff might welcome the opportunity. They will include many of the categories listed above: those wishing to reduce their hours for domestic reasons, to engage in further or higher education, to engage in some form of self-employed activity, to reduce their commitment for medical reasons, or to stagger their hours in preparation for retirement.

Few firms have evolved effective means of identifying staff interested in new work patterns. If the option to work flexible hours is to be made widely available, then an internal 'register' of candidates should be built up which can then be matched to specific vacancies as they occur.

Staff can be made aware of the opportunity to work on a flexible basis through any or all of the following methods:

- Voluntary redundancy schemes
- Career or performance reviews
- Notices and articles in house journals
- Announcements on staff noticeboards
- Notices in salary slips
- Leaflets in canteens, staff social venues
- Special exhibitions

In each case, the specific types of flexible work the candidate would be able to undertake should be noted in terms of hours, location and commitment and effect on current employment record and benefits. Separate management assessments of their suitability to undertake the work should be added, particularly if the scheme requires the ability to self-start and management their own workload. If additional training is required, this should also be specified. Some of the communication and negotiation techniques evolved to develop voluntary redundancy or relocation schemes might be built upon.

External recruitment

If suitable candidates are not available among existing staff, the position should be advertised externally. Even if the advertisement is aimed principally at applicants who wish to work full-time, it may be useful to stress that the opportunity to work in a new pattern is a feature.

Example

> DOWNLAND COLLEGE OF FE
> **Principal**
> Group 6   £25,818 (award pending)
>
> A successor is sought for John Brown, who is retiring on the 31st August as Principal of the College.
>
> The successful candidate will be expected to demonstrate a flexible management style and significant leadership skills.
>
> We pursue a policy of equality of opportunity. Applications are particularly welcome from people with disabilities.
>
> Further details and application forms may be obtained from the Further Education (Resources) Section, Downland County Council, Town Hall, Marlcoombe Road, Downsford, Downshire, SO4 8JZ. Applications must be made by 4th March 1988.

Many of the conventional outlets for recruiting full-time staff are also suitable for finding workers wishing to work atypically. However, additional outlets may be necessary to reach potential workers not currently looking for work, on the assumption that no positions in their skill areas are available on a flexible basis. The categories of workers most likely to respond to the type of needs should be reflected in the wording of any advertisement and/or briefings given to external recruitment consultants or agencies. The more common outlets include any or all of the following:

- recruitment advertising
- job centres
- employment agencies and recruitment consultancies

Recruitment advertising

To date, positions offering flexible working hours have been advertised most usually in the case of part-time positions (usually in the local press) and job-shares (often advertised additionally in the national and/or trade press).

There is no reason why most forms of Category A and B schemes cannot be recruited from press or radio advertising. However, the choice of media and the copy used should be carefully considered in the light of both the terms of employment and the category of worker most likely to respond. Particular attention should be paid to:

The location where the work will be undertaken and the level of commuting required – Will the worker need to work on the organisation's premises or off-site? If off-site, how often will the worker need to commute into the organisation for briefing and routine liaison? Will the salary and travelling time make the position only economically viable for local applicants?

Whether potential applicants are likely to be looking for work at the time of advertising – Potential applicants with technical, professional or managerial skills may have given up looking for work on the assumption that work in their skill areas is not available on a flexible basis. Radio advertising or advertising in women's or leisure magazines might be more appropriate than ads in the recruitment pages of newspapers or professional magazines. New methods of advertising may, for example, be necessary to attract distance workers such as women computer programmers, nurses or accountants who have moved with their husband's jobs and lost contact not only with their former employers but also their professional journals.

These considerations should also be taken into account when composing advertising copy. Copy should lay particular emphasis on:

The working hours and/or location – The fact that the work is being offered on a flexible basis should be heavily emphasised in print and broadcast at the beginning of any radio messages (eg., 'Job Sharing Teachers Needed!' or, 'Calling All Temporary Accountants'). If this is not made clear or the fact is hidden in the text, browsing readers may overlook the advertisement.

The salary scale or position's grade – particularly if these are pro rata to the equivalent full-time post. This may be critical in attracting response from applicants who assume that flexible working is invariably low-status and low paid.

The need for applicants to manage their own workload – if this is required. An applicant's personal competence to deal with independent working should be flagged clearly if this is an essential prerequisite for the job. Any special requirements dictated by the working arrangement should also be stressed, for example, the need to travel into the organisation for regular briefing in the case of networking or distance working schemes.

Examples

(a)

THINKING OF RETURNING TO TEACHING?

We now have several day-to-day Supply Teaching posts available in this Outer London Borough. These posts provide a good opportunity to continue, or re-start, your teaching career whilst allowing you the maximum professional and domestic flexibility.

You will earn between £45–£67 (depending on your experience and qualifications) and if you have been out of teaching for a while, it is a good way to re-start your career. There are even opportunities for staff willing to work on a job-share basis. These posts are, however, not suitable for probationers.

If you are looking for a more permanent appointment on a full or part-time basis, then please consult the Educational Press for posts advertised by Kenham, or contact us directly for details of what is available. We will always welcome your interest.

Kenham is particularly keen to ensure that members of ethnic minority groups are well represented in our teaching force. **We therefore would particularly welcome your application if you are from such a background**.

Application forms (s.a.e. please) available from the Director of Education, to whom completed forms should be returned as soon as possible.

2 Hockaby Road
London E14 7UX

London Borough of Kenham

(b)

BARNSWELL

Part-time
Project Manager
Circa £8,000 (from 4/88–3/89 inclusive)

The Authority has successfully bid for funds to carry out a year-long project to investigate the management information requirements of its further education sector. We are looking for a part-time Project Manager to do the following:

- Devise methods of identifying management information systems (MIS) requirements.
- Evaluate computerised MIS.
- Appoint, manage and train part-time researchers.
- Write reports.

The successful candidate may choose to be appointed as a consultant or on a part-time secondment from his/her present post.

For further details please contact;

**Ann Iwon, Education Department,
Civic Centre, 41 Tappison Way,
Barnswell TW4 5QD**
Closing date: 4.3.88
WE ARE AN EQUAL OPPORTUNITY EMPLOYER

Above are two recent examples of local authority advertising. Example (a) was placed by an employer experiencing considerable labour shortages. It was targeted to attract returners on a flexible and attractive basis. The headline catches the eye and is written in an encouraging style, making explicit the options on offer. Example (b), on the other hand, is a part-time fixed-term post in housing management which is not especially attractive initially. It fails to explain the hours of work (essential for some potential applicants) and only sets out a potentially strong inducement at the end. The opportunity to work on a consultant basis as a part-time/fixed-term employee could be a draw for some candidates who may be work from home, are studying or have other self-employed earnings.

If a recruitment advertising agency is being used, all these considerations should be included in any briefing or specification.

Examples

JOB-SHARE
District Estates Officer
S01. £5,646–£5,977 p.a. inclusive (18 hours a week) plus essential user car allowance

We are looking for a capable person with good communication skills to share the leadership of a group of three Estate Officers, advising and guiding them in their work as the prime contact between the Council and its tenants.

Your team covers approximately 2,000 tenancies in this busy inner London Borough. You will be expected to deal with a wide range of issues and problems, including liaison with active Tenants and Residents Associations. Occasional attendance at evening meetings will be required.

The post is at present based in an Area Housing Office in Pricketts Road, SW4 although you must be willing to work anywhere else within the Borough if necessary.

You should have a least five years Housing Management experience or be professionally qualified. The ability to be flexible and to work in harmony with your job-share partner is essential.

For further information please contact the present job-share postholder – Jean Allthing or John Mynott on 01–123 4567. REf.SFMH 4.

Wemford & Malham An Equal Opportunity Employer

Generally speaking any advert for flexible work should make explicit the demands of the post, in addition to information about job content. This is particularly important where the post is for a limited period. Simple phrases like 'holiday season', 'to cover holidays', etc., are inadequate. 'While post-holder on maternity leave', may be slightly clearer. The following is an example of where the phrasing of the advert may deter applicants.

GLENSIDE SUB-REGION SOCIAL WORK DEPARTMENT
Adult Education Tutor
Resource Centre, Queen Street, Glentown
Salary: APIII/IV £9,255–£11,700

This is temporary for duration of project.

This is a key post within the Project which will provide social and educational programmes for adult offenders. The successful applicant will be expected to make a positive contribution to the development of these programmes.

Applicants should possess a relevant teaching qualification or Diploma in Youth Community Work, they should also have a commitment towards working with adult offenders.

Application forms can be obtained from the Assistant Director of Personnel Services, Glenside Sub-Region, Regional Offices, Fletchers Green, Glentown G15 7LT and should be returned quoting reference number G 84763, by 7 March, 1988.

An equal opportunities authority **Glenside Regional Council**

Some applicants may view the job as very short-lived or precarious. Others, perhaps more legally aware, may view the advert as evidence that the post is a 'task' contract, which denotes disqualification from statutory provisions relating to fixed-term contracts and redundancy.

The next advert seems marginally more specific and might attract a wider range of candidates. It is a good example of using flexible work as a 'probationary' device, and by the use of capitals stresses that key aspect.

ESSEX
Columbine High School
63 Munro Grove, Ilford, Essex, IG6 3JJ
Tel. 01–321 5432
Head: Miss P. Cleverone, B.A. Hons
Roll: 423, Sixth Form: 103
Required from 13th April 1988 a suitably qualified and experienced teacher to take responsibility for Geography to G.C.S.E. and A level for this 11–18 independent grammar school for girls.

This could be a TEMPORARY post for one term or a PERMANENT post for the right candidate.

Salary: Baker Main Scale + Outer London Allowance for the right applicant. Closing date 8th March 1988.

Job sharing has to be advertised more carefully, though job-share policies may well have determined some of the key issues. For example, if the policy is to have all jobs open to job sharing unless otherwise stated, then a general statement preceding a group of vacancies will be appropriate.

REDEPLOYMENT AND RECRUITMENT

* All posts open to job-sharing, unless indicated otherwise (NJS). A register for pairing potential job-sharers is maintained by EO/PER/PS7, Room 533, The County Hall, London SE1 7PB. Tel: 01–633 3814. (N.B. applications can NOT be dealt with on this number).

Headships

Please refer to separate advertisement also in this publication on page 67.

Secondary Education

All secondary schools in the ILEA area are organised along comprehensive lines.

Others

East End Green (SB), 15 Clyst Street, E1 8QY. Tel: 01–101 8971.
Roll:1100. Head: N. Bahon.
Required asap Main Scale teachers, subject specialists in Science, Humanities, English, CDT and Creative Arts, with an interest and/or experience in Language and Bilingualism to join a Language Support Team.

Primary Education

Deputy Headships

Where a group of posts are considered inappropriate, this must also be explicit.

REPLIES

*Headship posts are **not** suitable for job-sharing.*
Unless indicated otherwise please send foolscap sae for application form and further details to Education Officer, ER/PS4B; Room 262a, The County Hall, London SE1 7PB. Closing date for returned applications is 4th March 1988 unless indicated otherwise.

Inner London Education Authority

ILEA is an equal opportunity employer

Advertising for some types of flexible work may be more effective through less formal means. Where personal working relationships or qualities such as independence and self-reliance are required for job sharing and homeworking respectively, word of mouth may be useful or even necessary. This can be on a one-to-one basis or through groups based, say, on community or health centres. A simple poster in a children's clinic or playgroup, an adult education college or via various 'grapevines' may be useful. Research shows that job-shares are overwhelmingly recruited via the efforts of existing job-sharers.

Example: The medical unit manager

In 1986 a factory in Essex engaged in high technology equipment experienced difficulties in staffing its medical unit. The experienced manager of the unit had decided that the job was too onerous on a full-time basis and, at the age of 55, she wished to work part-time. Reluctantly, the employers agreed to this and placed an advert in local job centres for a part-time equivalent. After three months there were no serious applicants, not least because the factory is located in an area of relatively low unemployment, especially among skilled women. Adverts in local papers had been equally unproductive. The employers had almost decided that the manager should leave or go full-time. The manager spoke to her daughter who said, 'Why don't you come down to the school gate this afternoon and see if anyone with nursing qualifications is looking for work. If the job was done on a job-share basis it would be a bit more attractive'.

On the second visit she found a woman who subsequently became her job-share partner. She had been doing agency and casual work but wanted something with more security and prospects, but on a part-time basis.

Job centres

Up to a third of all vacancies offered by job centres are for part-time or temporary vacancies. Notices placed in job centres should be for the appropriate skill areas normally covered by these government-supported agencies (i.e. non-professional) and take into account the factors discussed above.

Employment agencies and recruitment consultancies

There is no reason why employment agencies and recruitment consultancies cannot be used to find applicants for flexible working schemes, provided the briefings supplied are based on properly tailored job specifications. More effective relationships as well as lower charge rates can be established by taking time to classify needs and develop longer-term arrangements with the right recruitment services.

A selected number of agencies specialise in the provision of part-time work. Most employment agencies have tended to specialise in the provision of temporary work. In most cases, the agency itself undertakes the administration, payrolling, recruitment and training of the staff they provide.

If reliance is placed on an agency to interview and supply suitable staff, then the effectiveness of the earliest contact and specification will be put to the test. Their selection and the internal controls designed to ensure their efficient use provide a useful model for the deployment of external recruitment consultants in other areas of flexible working.

A detailed outline of the management systems required can be found in the section 'Preparing for agency workers' in Chapter 3.

Recruitment of YTS trainees

Chapter 3 sets out the necessary steps to prepare for recruitment of YTS trainees, in terms of demonstrating the competence of an enterprise to provide a well-structured and integrated programme of training in an appropriate environment. Before a contract can be signed with an ATO or with the MSC (if you are an ATO), of necessity, tangible and detailed performance objectives will have been established. Recruitment is therefore largely a matter of simply matching those objectives to individuals.

Providers and ATOs can recruit directly, though more usually trainees are sent via the local careers office following a screening and consultation process. The extent to which an employer will wish to rely on the judgement of the careers officers will be a matter of choice, but in any event the employer will be required to go through the trainee agreement with the worker. An example of an agreement appears in Chapter 5. Employers will also want to decide whether to offer the trainee employee status, which at present, approximately 5 per cent of the providers do. This will probably act as an incentive to recruits. The standard trainee agreement does not provide contractual rights, and trainees are not covered by statutory employment measures. In skill shortage areas, offering employee status may be useful and providers can then also build in other contractual terms consistent with the rest of their workforce. Employers who view YTS as a probationary period may feel giving employee status is an appropriate response. In any case, given the length of the YTS programme, there is relatively little risk of employee/trainees being able to exercise major statutory rights, most of which depend on a two year minimum period of employment.

Choosing a consultant

Much depends on the nature of the work, but there are some useful sources of information to aid the process. If the area of work is management, it may be possible to ask around at local management colleges or check the list of the Association of Teachers of Management. If the area is, say, computing, the Computing Services Association or the British Computing Society are able to offer general advice and information. Some occupations are not so regulated, for example, advice regarding the skills and specialties of lawyers and accountants is not always readily available.

Asking colleagues in similar circumstances of their experiences of consultants is another option. If references are offered by consultants, follow them up. Question these colleagues about:

- Cost against estimate
- How they worked with internal workers
- Did they meet targets, deadlines?
- Would they use them again?
- Did they respond to the culture and needs of the client?
- Did they introduce or use inexperienced staff once the contract was 'landed'?

The choice regarding size of consultancy is often important. The larger organisation is not always the best. Small organisations may get overstretched. Big ones can be disinterested in your project or account, though this can be off-set by excellent basic strategies and procedures.

When looking at the match between the consultant and your organisation the following areas should be included:

- The personality, mannerisms and style of the consultant should be compatible and based on the consultant's experience of analysing the client and needs
- The ability of the consultant to have a strategic and general appreciation of the client
- The range of skills on offer, which is crucial if the consultant is not only to enter and evaluate the situation but is to implement proposals. Are there, for example, training and research skills available?
- The experience of the consultant in terms of dealing with client personnel. If the consultancy is financially or promotionally orientated, experience of working with middle and specialist management may be adequate. If the consultancy role will involve strategic and policy implementation, such as those to do with manpower planning, there ought to be experience of working with all levels of management

Setting the fee

Virtually every consultancy contract will require personal contact and negotiation. There are a few guidelines regarding the correct fee levels as market forces operate *par excellence*. In larger consultancies, the fees are generally set on a daily basis, with the status and seniority of the individual consultant being the crucial factor, rather than the task to be performed. This makes it all the more important to ensure that the individual you are paying for actually carries out the work. In smaller consultancies, or where the consultant operates alone, there may be no standard fee or daily rate and every contract will be individually priced.

Many consultants operate differential rates depending on the sector of work. For example, there is wide recognition that public sector employers, charitable organisations, trade unions and the like are under considerable financial constraints and fees are adjusted accordingly. It may well be that if the task or project has been carefully defined and the potential consultant fully aware of the culture and organisational structures of the client's organisation that the parties have similar views on fees. It is always possible to invite tenders for consultancies. Although this is regularly done in, for example, advertising, it is rare in most areas of work. If tenders are invited a judgement has to be made on the importance of cost as a factor, though if one of the tenders is widely under or over priced, this may raise doubts as to the experience and ability of the consultants.

If there is a wide discrepancy on fees, this may indicate markedly different views as to the nature of the project. The client may see the project as limited and short term; the potential consultant may perceive deep-seated problems in the whole enterprise which will need to be tackled to achieve improved performance. For example, using a consultant to change working practices may be seen by the client as being required to simply change employment contracts. The consultant may be aware of the need to make attitudinal changes, to deal with industrial relations, and equal opportunities training. If there are widely differing expectations, the consultancy is unlikely to succeed.

Efficient selection of consultants is of paramount importance. Although a carefully worded contract which contains provisions for termination and/or penalties, the 'arm's length' nature of the relationship may make informal adjustments very difficult. When problems occur, as with sub-contracting, they are often resolved by a complete re-negotiation which is time consuming and costly or by ending the arrangement prematurely. Planning and selection can reap large dividends especially where consultants are employed on a long-term project or for diagnostic purposes.

Choosing a sub-contractor

Much of what has been discussed regarding the choice of consultant has relevance here. Specific factors will depend on the type of sub-contract arrangement and whether or not there was a tendering process. Important too, will be the weight to be given to cost.

If an organisation has a policy to accept the lowest tender, providing the costing is considered realistic and accurate, the decision is a simple one.

In other situations, an organisation might consider the following questions before making a choice:

- Does the sub-contractor have a reputation for reliability and efficiency? Have informal enquiries been carried out? Do you have confidence in their financial procedures?
- Has the contractor adequate knowledge of the organisation's workforce, premises, management structures and culture?
- Are you satisfied that the contractor is fully aware of the characteristics of the organisation so that they can relate and integrate with it?
- Are you satisfied regarding the skill, quality and stability of the contractor's workforce? Are there adequate training, safety and induction procedures in operation?
- Are the arrangements for monitoring and supervision of the work adequate?
- Are the procedures for dealing with complaints and changes in work performance adequate? Can you have confidence in them?
- Are there characteristics of the sub-contractor's workforce which make them seem likely to harmonise with the organisation's workforce?

There will be suspicions if the cost of the contract varies markedly from another, especially where a contractor is relatively inexperienced. Another possible problem is comparing the quality and likely performance of a DLO against an outside bid. Decisions have to be taken objectively, although it is likely that the shortcomings of the in-house unit will be more obvious through familiarity.

SUMMARY POINTS

- Employers seeking to change the terms of employment of existing workers should ensure that they have taken into account:
  - any legal restraints on the introduction of change
  - any legal requirements for consultation, negotiation or notification
  - the law relating to variation of termination of employment contracts
- Areas of law to bear in mind include:
  - anti-discrimination measures
  - the law relating to health and safety at work
  - contractual law relating to any change in employment status
- When recruiting Category A and B workers, employers should bear in mind that:
  - the sources of potential applicants will be, in many cases, different from those used for full-time staff. Recruitment methods and terms of employment will need to reflect this
  - selection criteria should place a greater emphasis on how the job is undertaken as well as what is being undertaken. In many cases, this will mean that applicants' ability to 'self-start' and manage their own workload will be a crucial factor
  - for both these reasons, the job specification will need to be clearly

defined and drawn up by managers with the right analytical skills and training
- When choosing consultants and sub-contractors, employers should take into account:
  - their reputation and their experience of working with organisations using atypical workers
  - their awareness of the characteristics and procedures of the organisation
  - their own flexibility
  - their ability to be self-managing and responsive

References
1 'Freemans – variations on a theme', Industrial Relations Review and Report 389, 31 March 1989.
2 *Pickstore v. Freemans plc* [1988] IRLR 359.
3 *Wilson v. Faccenda Chickens Ltd* [1987] EAT/98/86.
4 *Clarke v. Eley IMI Kynoch Ltd* [1983] IRLR 482.
5 *Kidd v. DRG (UK) Ltd* [1985] IRLR 190.
6 *Holmes v. The Home Office* [1984] IRLR 299.
7 *Guthrie v. Royal Bank of Scotland*, COIT 31796/86.
8 *Robertson and Griffith v. Strathclyde Regional Council* [1986] S/3322/86 and S/3555/85.
9 *Prince v. University of Manchester*, IT 28161/86.
10 *Carey v. Greater Glasgow Health Board*, EAT 745/86. See also *Clymo v. LB Wandsworth* [1989] IRLR 122.
11 *Fluss v. Grant Thornton Chartered Accountants* [1987] COIT 1907/15.
12 *O'Kelly v. Trusthouse Forte plc* [1983] IRLR 369.
13 *Wickens v. Champion Employment* [1984] ICR 365. See now *Ironmonger v. Morefield Ltd t/a Deering Appointments*, EAT 67/88.
14 *Ready Mixed Concrete (South-East) Ltd v. Minister of Pensions and National Insurance* [1986] 2 QB 497.
15 *Massey v. Crown Life Insurance Ltd* [1978] IRLR 31.
16 *Young and Woods Ltd v. West* [1986] IRLR 201.
17 *R. v. Liverpool City Council, ex parte Ferguson* [1985] IRLR 501.
18 *Marriott v. Oxford & District Co-operative Society* [1970] 1 QB 29.
19 *Rigby v. Ferodo Limited* [1987] IRLR 61.

Source material
Consultative Document on Draft EC Directive (Vredeling), DE and DTI (1983).
Davies, P. and Friedland, M., *Labour Law: Text and Materials*, 2nd edn., Weidenfeld and Nicolson, 1984.
Ewing, K. and Grubb, A., 'The emergence of a new labour injunction', *Industrial Law Journal*, 1987, p. 145.
'Freemans – variations on a theme', Industrial Relations Review and Report, 389, 1987, p. 6.
Leighton, P., 'Contract law: new challenges to managerial prerogative, *Manpower Policy and Practice*, Vol. 3, No. 2, 1987, p. 14.
Leighton, P., *Sub-contracting for Services*, A Report to the ILO, Essex Institute of Higher Education, 1985.

Leighton, P. and Rayner, C., *Job Sharing in South-East Essex*, Essex Institute of Higher Education, 1986.
Lewis, R. (ed.) *Labour Law in Britain*, Blackwell, 1986.
Wedderburn, Lord, *The Worker and the Law*, 3rd edn., Penguin Books, 1987.

Chapter 5
Employment law and worker contracts

Over the past few years there has been a process of de-regulation in employment law which has left up to a half of workers outside major statutory protection. In particular, they lose out because of the two year qualifying period of continuous employment, the sixteen hours per week minimum and the growing tendency to see casual, agency and other staff as self-employed. Self-employed workers become regulated by commercial as opposed to employment contract law.

EMPLOYEE OR SELF-EMPLOYED?

The borderline between Category A and B can be blurred, especially in the case of freelance and casual workers. Employment documentation as well as more general work practices can help clarify the issue. Tribunals, despite strictures from appellate courts, still tend to attach considerable weight to the 'label' a job is given. However, as was discussed in Chapter 4, 'labels' must not be used to avoid tax or other legal liabilities. The attitude of courts and tribunals can be further illustrated by the following cases:

Examples
1 *The 'sessional' clerical staff[1]*
Four applicants claimed a redundancy payment in 1987 from the London Residuary Body. Each had worked for the respondent for between five and fifteen years. All were clerical workers. Their employment documents were headed 'Employment of Sessional Staff'. A session was defined as a period of work not exceeding eight hours, and stress was placed in the documents on the casual nature of the work. There was apparently no obligation to offer or undertake work, and the documents emphasised the 'non-permanent' nature of the jobs. In reality, all had 'as good an attendance record as the permanent part-time employees'. Nonetheless, the tribunal decided they had been self-employed, despite their having paid income tax and being subject to the employer's usual disciplines and grievance codes. The lack of 'mutuality of obligation' to offer or accept work was crucial and was evidenced by the label 'sessional'.

2 *The architect[2]*
An architect was described as 'part-time', though he worked at least thirty hours per week. He was labelled a 'consultant' and paid a 'fee' rather than salary. He worked regularly, was fully integrated in the business of a housing association, attended staff meetings and was provided with a mug for his tea like all the other staff. Nonetheless, as a skilled professional in theory able to market his skills, a court decided he was self-employed: the 'label' attached to him and along with the apparently part-time nature of his work tipped the balance to self-employment.

Many workers themselves exert pressure to be classified as self-employed, and employers have shown a growing tendency to accede to their wishes. Where self-employment is genuine rather than nominal the documentation must clearly reflect this. Courts and tribunals are not impressed by employers or workers who happily go along with one employment status, and then when something goes wrong – be it dismissal, an accident, damage to a third party – want to argue that the other status was the correct one. This apart, legal 'support' for self-employment has grown in recent years.

These self-employed workers can present management with problems, and confuse liabilities. They sometimes work alongside permanent employees, and are subject to the same or similar rules. They are often socially integrated and provided with some occupational benefits. Confusions also occur over their tax and national insurance situation, especially when earnings fall below relevant thresholds.

THE CONTRACT DOCUMENT

The drafting and management of the employment contract, be it of employment, self-employment, or one with a sub-contractor or supplier of labour, is of crucial importance if the objectives of using different work patterns are to be achieved. Category A employee contracts, especially if contrasted with those of the full-time permanent workforce, generally require greater planning. Matters normally taken for granted and usually needing little articulation will require attention. They will need to be unambiguously expressed.

Key issues:
- The identification of the major characteristics of the work pattern
- The identification of likely problem areas
- Consideration of the appropriate structure and content of contract documentation

Documentation of employment contracts is often considered the 'Cinderella' of employment law. However, changes to the make-up or deployment of the workforce provide the opportunity for a thorough review of contract document procedures at an organisation.

Employment law makes relatively few demands on the form and content of the employment document, beyond those required by the ordinary law of contract. There are virtually none on the contract of self-employment (Category B) or for the supply of labour and/or services.

The law

In most respects, Category A workers are subject to the same legal rules as core employees. There are a few general points:

- Outside occupations covered by wages councils, there are no requirements regarding minimum or prescribed wages
- Other than some specific occupations (usually where safety is a key issue) there are no restrictions on the number and distribution of *hours* to be worked
- Basic legal rules regarding illegal contracts, e.g. for a fraudulent purpose, or criminal activity, apply equally to all employment contracts
- Rules relating to restrictive covenants and restraint of trade apply equally to Category A workers. However, where work is performed on a part-time, temporary, or other limited basis, restriction on other work activities are less likely to be seen as reasonable compared with terms in full-timers' permanent contracts. It is unlikely that courts would enforce a contract banning a part-time computer operator or teacher from working similarly for another employer unless there was a risk to confidential information
- Absence of written material does not mean there is no legally binding relationship. The fact that work is part-time or of short duration may prevent statutory claims under the Employment Protection (Consolidation) Act, 1978 (EPCA) but common law rules and remedies, such as damages and injunctions are available.

Written material

For Category A workers, the law states that within thirteen weeks of employment commencing the employer must provide all full-time employees (sixteen plus hours per week) with a written statement or a written employment contract which conforms to Section 1, EPCA Act, 1978. Many casual and short-term staff do not need to be provided with written material, though practice suggests that many regular employers of temporary, casual and seasonal staff do provide appropriate material. When homeworking, job sharing or some other new work pattern is introduced, it is important to bear in mind if a relevant employee has already worked for upwards of five years for at least eight hours per week they also qualify to receive written material.

The content of the document

Employees must be provided with comprehensive information, or be able to find written information which is reasonably accessible. It might be in a handbook, collective agreement, code of discipline, or pension scheme booklet. Information must cover the following matters:

(a) Names of the parties to the contract.
(b) The date employment began, and is to end (if it is fixed term).
(c) Whether service with a previous employer is to count as part of continuous period of employment.
(d) The scale or rate of remuneration, or its method of calculation.
(e) The intervals at which it is paid.
(f) Any terms and conditions relating to hours of work.
(g) Holiday pay provisions, if any.
(h) Sick pay provisions, if any.
(i) Terms relating to pension and pension schemes, if any.
(j) The length of notice required to terminate the contract on either side.
(k) The title of the job the employee is employed to do.
(l) Disciplinary rules applicable to the employee.
(m) Details regarding the grievance procedure.
(n) Whether there is a contracting out certificate in force for the employment relating to the state pension scheme.

Failure to provide any or all of this information entitles employees to ask an industrial tribunal to specify the terms of work (S. 11 EPCA).

Other general points

- Letters, memoranda, as well as document 'headed' employment terms, will comply with the law and there need be no single document
- The employer has a choice of whether to provide a written statement of terms, or a written contract of employment. The latter will provide definitive evidence of terms, and be binding on both employer and employee. The former is evidential only and in some circumstances can be overridden by evidence of practice, or even verbal agreements. The choice facing employers is a real one. There has been much recent evidence of a growing tendency to use written, binding contracts so as to safeguard the increasing flexibility of the core workforce. This often covers such matters as mobility, hours of work, job content, and possible redeployment. However, care must be taken to ensure that the proposed document is, indeed, a written contract. For this it should have the following characteristics:
  - A heading which indicates it *is* a written contract.
  - Language which unambiguously stresses key obligations, and does not confuse descriptive with prescriptive issues.
  - The signature of both parties to clearly indicate agreement (not just understanding and receipt of the document).

If binding obligations are imposed upon an employee relevant obligations will be equally binding on the employer. This may give little room for manoeuvre or informal negotiation, a feature which may have proved useful in connection with some work patterns.

Whichever type of document is used, it is vital that it be carefully worded. In particular, care should be taken to ensure that it does not muddle legal matters with general information, such as details about personnel, size of organisation and social facilities.

It is important to separate out areas which are discretionary from those which are mandatory. For example, if overtime or bonuses are available, say, to part-time staff, it is crucial to clarify whether it is a legal entitlement for the employee, or is at the option of the employer. Words such as 'may', 'can', 'at discretion', 'opportunities', '*ex gratia*', must be used carefully and tested for possible ambiguity. Who makes decisions must also be clearly stated. Simple reliance on what has 'worked' in the past is best avoided, especially when dealing with workers who spend less time on the premises or who have short engagements. Many members of the new workforce have a lower level of integration in the organisation. A higher priority has to be given to effective communication of the basic contractual details, because many workers will have fewer opportunities to follow up information, raise queries or question colleagues.

INCORPORATING WORK CHARACTERISTICS

The forces and pressures which have led to the new workforce are not only varied but include some from employees. The document must provide balance and avoid confusion or possible abuse. This need is greatest in some types of contract, especially job sharing, flexi-hours, negotiated annual hours contracts and some types of homeworking. It is important to clearly define the parameters of obligation, management and employee discretion, and facilitate effective management and monitoring.

CONTRACTS FOR CATEGORY A WORKERS

Some preliminary questions need consideration, especially when introducing an entirely new work pattern:

- Is it possible or desirable to adapt current contract documentation used for existing full-time, permanent or part-time staff?
- Should an entirely new type of contract be devised?
- Is the aim of the document to be comprehensive in itself, or refer to a policy document which sets out the major objectives of the work pattern?
- Which aspects of the work pattern need to be specified in writing? How much can be left to informal or oral communication?
- What are the possible problem areas in the work pattern? How should the document respond to them?

- What aspects of general management policies, especially disciplinary and grievance procedures, need to be adapted/modified in relation to particular work patterns?
- What existing occupational/fringe benefit arrangements need to be considered and amended in the light of particular work patterns.

Although it is tempting to use 'off the peg' documents, or muddle through with existing full-time or part-time contracts, a review of personnel procedures and documents will be worthwhile. A study of job sharing in Essex during 1986[3] revealed that although there were many instances of job sharing there was not a single purpose-built job-share contract available. Employers simply used the existing part-time contract and sometimes retitled it. It is also assumed that if an aspect of a contract is changed (for example, job location is moved to the home) all you need to do is add that as a term or send a letter to that effect. In fact, there are often 'knock-on' effects, especially to procedural issues, which may make it necessary to reconsider the document overall.

Some employment relationships have one or two key characteristics. A good example is fixed term and temporary contracts, where the basis upon which work is to be performed and ended must be established. However, all work patterns have essential characteristics requiring attention. Suggestions are made on the basis of current managerial practices and research experience in the context of the relevant legal framework.

Work patterns have generally been considered in relation to three groups of workers according to:

- the time when work is performed
- the length of employment contract
- the place where work is done.

Time

The main types of contracts here are flexi-hours, part-timers, job-sharers, those with contracted core hours, and annual hours contracts. With regard to flexi and other forms of variable hours the major concerns are:

- To ensure that the arrangements are unambiguous
- To state clearly the forms and process of decision making
- To establish efficient systems of time recording
- To determine related matters of access to overtime, premium rates, time-off arrangements and the like.

All schemes require careful planning for the relevant time period. They can become complex and working them through can be very time consuming, as the Freeman's Case Study in Chapter 4 illustrates (see p. 84). It may also be necessary to build controls into the system so that individual choices do not distort the objectives of the department/unit/area of work. In the Freeman's contracted core hours arrangement, the vast majority of employees preferred longer holidays and less pay holidays than less holidays and then higher pay. This led to imbalance and shortages at certain periods.

Flexitime

Flexitime arrangements also require careful implementation to provide adequate coverage at peak times. It is vital to translate the objectives and characteristics of the scheme into appropriate legal structures. Ideally, a 'pilot' exercise should be undertaken to gauge employee response to options. To retain control over flexibility the legal structure must specify *who* is responsible, and their range of discretion.

Does all this require a different type of employment document? Is it possible for employers to evolve a standard or a series of standard form contracts when, untypically, the whole workforce is on flexi-hours or annual hours contracts?

Examples

1 A central government department
The scheme is set out in a separate document. Core time is expressed as 9.30 a.m.– 3.30 p.m. and the scheme has a four week 'period of account' requiring 144 hours attendance. Employees are required to complete daily time sheets and line managers control them through collection and sample checks. Time off is granted by line managers and is normally up to two and a half days in the 'period of account'. Four weeks' notice has to be given of five days of flexitime, with managers having discretion to refuse. Any abuse of flexitime can result in flexitime being withdrawn from offenders. They then return to standard time. The parameters and decision making process appear clear, with a 'coverall' phrase making the scheme dependent on 'the exigencies of the service'.

2 A large employer in the finance sector
The scheme forms part of the conditions of employment handbook. This, too, works over a four week 'accounting period', but here the flexi credit or debit is also related to the four weeks. A maximum of ten hours is allowed to be carried forward. The Head of Department has to give approval to half or whole day leave. The scheme is apparently highly controlled with a computerised clocking-in system and a two hour penalty on flexitime for failure to properly record. The scheme itemises matters such as credit for illness, study periods, holidays, business lunches and examinations.

The two schemes can be contrasted regarding the form of document, the control of scheme and nature of penalties. Example 1 probably relies on trust and goodwill but allows greater flexibility. However, the efficiency of a system without automated timing and a clear role for line management may be doubted.

Part-time contracts

These raise relatively few issues. The hours of work must, of course, be specified. If they are to vary, this too must be contractually expressed.

Employers may want to increase or reduce the input of part-timers at various stages. This can be done with prior agreement.

The opportunity and arrangements for overtime must also be considered and other circumstances, such as bank holiday work where pay may vary from the standard rate. The provision of sick and injury pay is also an important consideration – one which may be soon affected by the impact of the European Community. If left silent, the law does not provide clear guidance as to the situation when the employee is sick (see Chapter 7). This is best dealt with directly.

Job-share contracts

This is the most complex form of part-time work and presents a wide range of options regarding the form of the contract. A number of possible problem areas have emerged from existing practice. These must be anticipated in the contract. It is vital to prepare documents which not only deal with these but which are compatible with the documents and procedures used for other groups of workers at the workplace. Questions to consider are set out below.

Is there an actual or anticipated job-share policy?

There has been a tendency for public sector employers to develop written job-share policies, often by collective negotiation. This area has been discussed in Chapters 3 and 4, but a few points need reiteration. Often the existence of a policy will appear on job adverts and will reassure applicants for jobs that there is a coherent structure and attitude to job sharing. A policy will set out the basic objectives of the scheme and will have covered the following areas:

- General statements regarding the motivation(s) for the scheme
- The scope of the scheme: which jobs are available/excluded from the scheme. If appropriate, it should set out the decision making procedures
- Details regarding recruitment to job sharing: advertising procedures, selection, the distinction, if any, between procedures affecting applications from in-house staff and outsiders. It might make reference to in-house or external job-share registers
- Any special rules applying to job-sharers regarding supervision, discipline, grievances
- Any special rules regarding training appraisal and promotion
- Clarification of the situation when one or both job-sharers leave. Is the vacancy to be advertised, the remaining sharer to be offered a full-time post; redeployed or dealt with in some other way? Are there to be time limits or vetos to any of these procedures?
- A general statement regarding the position of job-sharers and occupational benefits, especially pensions.

Research shows that the penultimate issue is crucial. A policy may contain a clause committing the employer to find a replacement when one sharer leaves. If the employer decides to 'freeze' the half post for reasons of financial cutbacks or operational matters, this amounts to a breach of contract. It is possible that the employer can legally justify the decision (see Chapter 10). Nonetheless, it may be desirable to consider the position carefully before putting pen to paper. Of all the legal and managerial issues affecting job sharing, this is the one which causes most controversy and must therefore be given adequate attention.

Is the policy going to form a part of the employment contract?
A policy can be part of the contract by using a letter or memorandum referring to it. If this is the objective, the policy itself ought to be provided, or must be 'reasonably accessible'.

If the policy is used this way, it must have an appropriate language and style. To be contractual it must be unambiguous and prescriptive: it must not confuse descriptive matters, e.g. of the origins and expectations of the policy, with prescriptive matters.

What form is the documentation to take?
Documents must be compatible in style and content with other contractual documents at the workplace. For example, provisions dealing with incapacity, holidays, pensions, discipline and grievance matters must fit in with the procedures for other employees. The employee must also decide whether to devise a specific job-share contract, or adapt an existing contract document. Preparation of a specific job-share contract may be time consuming but the exercise will clarify issues and may well lead to better practices. If an existing document is to be adapted, the choice is usually between a full-time contract or part-time contract. Given the nature of job sharing it is preferable to use a full-time contract and then divide hours, benefits, etc., on a *pro rata* basis.

The employer must then decide whether to set down any additional requirements which job-sharing may give rise to. For example, is the contract going to incorporate a requirement for effective communication, provision of cover, or increased accountability for the 'product' of the job-share by the sharers themselves? This is rarely included, but often should be.

What aspects of the job-share ought to be a part of the contract document?
The following are some issues which job-share arrangements will probably need to address:

(a) Are there going to be any *contractual limitations* on job-sharers undertaking other paid employment outside the enterprise, or on job sharing another post at the same enterprise, or working there part-time? If so, a clause would operate as a restraint of trade clause and be subjected to the usual legal rules of reasonableness.
(b) Is the contract going to define precisely the *hours of work* or leave matters to individual/joint negotiation?

(c) Is the contract going to define the *work* to be carried out by the job-sharer? Are specific individual responsibilities going to be spelt out?
(d) How are job *performance* targets (if any) to be applied to the job-share?
(e) How is the job-share to be affected by any in-house arrangements regarding matters such as *bonuses*, merit payments, profit-related pay? Are the schemes to apply and, if so, do they apply to the job or the individuals? How are increments to apply?
(f) How are any in-house arrangements regarding *overtime* and other special payments, such as those for unsocial hours, to apply to job-sharers?
(g) Are the job-sharers going to be under any obligation to *cover* for the absent sharer? If so, to what extent? If one sharer is absent, does the other sharer have first refusal to cover the whole post?
(h) How is the enterprise's *job evaluation* scheme going to apply (if one exists)? Are the sharers to be evaluated individually, or as a team? Do you need to specify that an element of the evaluation will be their ability to work together as a team? Will promotion arrangements specify that the sharers display those qualities or will promotion be made solely on the basis of their individual qualities?
(i) Will the contract incorporate details of *training* opportunities? Is the training to apply to the post and the sharers or is the line manager to decide on how training is done; or is training to be on a purely individual basis?
(j) How will *occupational benefits*, especially sick pay and pension rights, apply to job-sharers? How will fringe or other benefits, such as cars, financial assistance for moving, health-care support apply?
(k) What will be the contractual position where one *sharer leaves*? Will the post be re-advertised as a job-share? Will the remaining sharer have the option of full-time employment?

Examples

1 *Local Authority A*
A metropolitan authority with a keen commitment to equal opportunities devised a job-share policy after a protracted period of negotiation, though full formal acceptance of the policy is still pending. In reality, departments within the authority do adhere to it. The normal part-time contracts are used as the basic documentation, and 'grafted on' to this are details from the job-share policy. Given the large numbers of job-sharers, consideration is currently being given to devising a special job-share contract.

2 *Local Authority B*
This employer has a coherent attitude to job sharing and employs considerable numbers, including senior management positions. The employer provides a general document for the purposes of S.1 EPCA. The technique is that clauses are ticked as appropriate regarding such matters as hours of work, pay and enhanced payments, holidays and sickness allowances and periods of notice. The main document refers to a guideline document on job sharing which is intended to have contractual status. Although rather complex, even repetitive in places, the employee is able to piece together the terms of the job-share contract from the documents.

3 Local Authority C

This authority spent a considerable period of time negotiating a policy with trade unions. The policy document deals with the general issues of availability of posts to job sharing, access to training, evaluation and occupational benefits, and the position when one sharer leaves. On this point, the authority adopted the fairly popular technique in the public sector of offering the rest of the post on a full-time basis to the remaining sharer. If not wanted, the vacant position was advertised. Individual sharers are provided with the normal full-time contract documentation. Hours of work and pay are expressed appropriately and reference is made to the policy document for further details.

Negotiated annual hours contracts

Experience of this form of contract is still very limited in the UK but several leading West German employers have developed well-publicised and influential schemes. The schemes present few legal problems, other than the need to be clear about the objectives and mechanics of each scheme. Hours of work should be subject to an annual individual negotiation. The likely format will set down the programme in a separate document – a sort of collateral contract. The section/statement/contract can make reference to the document in order to comply with EPCA 1978. The problematic areas here are the managerial ones of planning, balance, negotiation and monitoring. The legal ones fall into place fairly easily, though obvious areas of access to overtime pay, bonuses, and occupational benefits need careful spelling out.

Negotiated core and variable hours contracts

This is gaining support in the UK especially in occupations with fluctuating and seasonal demand. Many areas have allowed for increased or decreased hours of work on an informal basis, depending on time of year, weather and demand. The change has been regarding both the development of fluctuating hours contracts as a management strategy and as a process of formalisation. Occupations as disparate as teaching, leisure and mail-order businesses have introduced written contract terms to this effect.

Again, the legal formalities are not complex. The need is to express the base or minimum hours, to establish maximum hours and to identify any relevant circumstances which will set the parameters.

Examples

1 *A contract in the leisure industry*
'Your average weekly hours of work are thirty-seven and a half. During the months of October to March they will be thirty-five hours per week, to be worked between the hours of 9 a.m. and 5 p.m. with one hour for lunch. During April to September, they will be forty hours per week, to be worked between 9 a.m. and 6 p.m. with one hour for lunch'.

2 *Organisation in the catering industry*
'Your weekly hours of work shall be normally thirty-seven. Although a rota will be

posted one week in advance, management reserves the right to amend this by giving as much notice as possible. You can be required to work such extra hours as are reasonable. Time off in lieu will be given. In no event shall the weekly hours exceed forty-five'.

Other contracts will allow for evening or weekend working, depending on season, demand, etc. In areas such as education, the following formulae are currently in use.

3 *For school teachers*
'... a teacher employed full-time may be required to work on not more that 195 days in any year, of which 190 days shall be days on which he may be required to teach pupils in addition to carrying out other duties. . . .

'A teacher shall, in addition to the requirements set out in ... above, work such additional hours as may be needed to discharge effectively his professional duties. ... The amount of time required for this purpose beyond the 1265 hours ... shall not be defined by the employer but shall depend upon the work needed to discharge the duties'. (Regulation pursuant to Teachers Pay and Conditions Act, 1987)

The wording of this document has given rise to considerable dispute and industrial action. The intention of the document was to clarify duties. It was also to reflect the varying demands and characteristics of teaching, both regarding the mixture and distribution of hours of work. Debate has focused on the vagueness and lack of upper limits. For example, marking in connection with GCSE has caused upwards of twenty hours extra time per week. Is this included in the terms of contract? It would have been clearer to provide guidance and set maximum hours.

Some local agreements have been made which will limit the additional duties to fifty hours per year, giving a maximum of 1315 per year. Although some negotiations have achieved clarification, the issues surrounding teachers' contracts illustrate how difficult it can be to define and implement concepts of annual hours in professional and managerial occupations.

The agreement over lecturers' hours of work in further and higher education adopts a similar formulae. It recognises that in education there are peak demands, usually in the autumn and spring, with troughs at other times of the year depending on the type of student and courses.

Lecturers in further and higher education are required to teach twenty-one hours per week. Currently the national conditions of service state, '... in order to meet the exigencies of the service, a lecturer may be required to undertake class contact hours in excess ... such additional class contact hours shall be subject to a limit of 2.5 hours per week which in aggregate should not exceed 22½ hours in any term ... such additional class contact hours would have to be balanced by reductions in class contact time ... as soon as practicable'. This formulae is more precise, establishes upper limits and leaves discretion to management.

Length of contract

A range of contractual arrangements come under this heading. They are linked by the fact that at the outset of the contract both parties envisaged the work coming to an end upon an agreed event. This might be a predetermined date, the return to work of the employee the temporary worker was providing cover for, or the completion of a task. Training and apprenticeship contracts (but not YTS arrangements) also come under this heading but they will not be discussed in detail here.

Use of terminology is confusing here. Terms such as 'casual', 'short-term', 'project' workers, as well as temporary 'sessional' and 'seasonal' workers, are widely used. They are sometimes used in different ways in different areas of work. Some denote self-employment. On the assumption that the temporary worker is an *employee* their legal position can be stated as follows:

- Those not continuously employed for thirteen weeks or more do not qualify for certain employment protection benefits such as the right to written particulars, guaranteed pay and SSP (see Chapter 7)
- Those not continuously employed for two years or more do not usually qualify for unfair dismissal or redundancy payment claims
- Those employed on a 'fixed-term contract' of two years or more are protected under S.55 EPCA from unfair dismissal if the contract is not renewed, unless the employee has agreed to waive that right
- Those employed specifically to provide cover for maternity leave can be fairly dismissed providing it was agreed that this is the basis to the contract
- Those employed on a 'task' contract have no statutory or common rights to compensation when the task comes to an end (see Chapter 10).

Contractual considerations for temporary work

There are *two* major areas to consider:

– Clarification of the temporary nature of the contract itself.
– Consideration of other aspects of the employment contract, and of occupational facilities.

The nature of the contract

In principle this is not a difficult area. The documentation ought to confirm any oral agreement that the work duration is limited. It is preferable to use 'fixed term' or 'temporary' rather than casual. In some cases it is possible to identify precisely the starting and completion dates, especially where the work is seasonal. Some areas of the leisure industry, retailing (particularly 'sales staff'), and teaching, have devised effective temporary contracts. It is tempting to use the terms 'casual/temporary' to leave it open-ended and keep options open. This can be very unsettling for employees. Other possibilities exist. In retailing, it is a common practice to establish a fixed-term contract, but allow for renewal.

130 NEW WORK PATTERNS

Examples

1 *July sales*
'V Ltd' is a large and well-known department store. The conditions of employment read as follows:
'TEMPORARY STAFF
CONDITIONS OF EMPLOYMENT – SUMMER SALE PERIOD 198-
(i) Duration of employment and hours of work
Temporary staff are engaged on a fixed-term contract, terminating on Saturday 2 July. It may be possible to extend this contract to Saturday 9 July, or beyond, and this will be reveiwed on Friday of each week.
  Please indicate on the attached form whether you would like to extend your employment.
June 24 198-'

This approach clearly specifies the nature of engagement, and allows for extension. The 'review' mentioned in paragraph two is in the hands of the employer and the employee has agreed to be available for further work. The document does not commit the employer to any additional responsibility, but both parties are aware of the implications of the arrangement.

2 *The English language summer school*
This was a more problematic contractual arrangement, which led to a number of individual disputes and considerable uncertainties, albeit in a complex area of work. 'A–S Ltd' ran vacation courses for teenagers from Italy, mostly during the summer. As well as having language teaching during the mornings, students went on a number of cultural and sporting trips. Each course was described as lasting for three weeks. The number of teenagers attending was left vague as was their date and time of arrival. Teachers were recruited to a 'short-term ESL teaching post'.
  The documentation contained the following information:
'APPOINTMENT OF COURSE TEACHER
Course dates 28.6.198- – 18.7.198-.'
Then followed information about pay, teaching and other duties.
'(iii)(c) Termination of employment
Should student numbers fall below those anticipated A–S Ltd may be obliged to cancel a teacher's contract. Regrettably, no compensation can be paid. . . .'

This aspect gave rise to considerable dispute. Employers understood it was a 'short-term' appointment, and even accepted that the engagement might have to be cancelled. But, in reality, the employer used the clause to extend or shorten courses, alter days of work and make other adjustments. Although it was unlikely that aggrieved employees would resort to law when disputes arose out of short-term engagements, the ill-will generated and the development of a generally 'easy come, easy go' atmosphere was unproductive and caused resentment. If there are variable factors or uncertainties, firms can spell them *all* out, or provide for payment regardless and attempt to provide for protection as an employer to cover these costs.

A series of 'fixed-term' contracts?

A popular though criticised device is to employ workers on a series of end-to-end contracts reviewable after, for example, six weeks, six months, or a year. Where the period of employment is unbroken, the suspicion might arise that there is nothing truly temporary about the work. Fixed-term and temporary contracts, if subject to breaks, will theoretically deny the employee a continuous period of employment for employment law and some other purposes. There are a few circumstances where the law sees these arrangements as creating so-called 'global', and thus continuing, contracts. Case law establishes that where the pattern has developed over a period of time, and there is a mutual understanding that the contract is of a continuing though variable or intermittent nature, such a 'global' contract can exist.[4]

The courts have been reluctant to support this approach (see Chapter 10), preferring to use the provisions of EPCA 1978 which see the 'gaps' between periods of work as a 'temporary cessation of work' thus preserving continuity through those non-work periods.

Where a series of fixed-term contracts have run back to back there may be little merit in using phrases and headings in documents to support the apparent fixed-term nature of the arrangements. However, the following might suggest 'genuine' fixed-term contracts, and prevent continuity of employment arising:

- Factors in the work itself indicating uncertainties which could not be easily anticipated
- A formal process of re-evaluation prior to the expiry of the term
- Possibilities of re-negotiation at that time regarding terms and nature of work.

The presence or absence of a 'gap' between work is less significant than the attitude of expectations of the parties. Courts and tribunals appear to be influenced by the nature and demands of the particular occupation. Formal declarations by the employer, e.g. regarding their temporary needs, can be influential.

Other aspects of the contract documentation
The characteristics of temporary work require consideration of other matters. Some of the major ones might be the following:

– *Whether to issue a purpose-built temporary contract?*
Many employers with fluctuating demands have devised such documents. These generally stress the non-permanent nature of the contract; tend to have a determinedly different style and content from the documents used for permanent staff; and appear to overtly distance the workers from the enterprise and from other groups of workers. Some contracts expressly require the temporary worker to remain available for work even during gaps in work; others reserve the employer's entitlement not to be under any duty to provide work at all. The legality of these devices is debatable, either because the alleged agreement to terms by workers are not supported by consideration (money) and are therefore not legally binding; or because the terms are so unreasonable so as to fall foul of the Unfair Contract Terms Act, 1977.

Example: a South Wales manufacturer
'The company is not bound to assign you to a contract at any time.... You are paid only for the hours actually worked.... You are not normally paid for illness or injury.... You agree to be available for work. If you are not available, the company will assume you have resigned.'

This may not be enforceable (or advisable). However, it is likely that using a purpose-built temporary contract will be sensible.

– How to deal with keeping options open to admit a temporary worker to a permanent position?
Many employers use temporary status as a probationary device, and this is well understood in certain occupations or specific organisations. These intentions need clarification at the outset, not so much to avoid legal repercussions but to minimise resentment from the employee. Decisions not to extend temporary contracts rarely fall foul of law, especially if the contract documentation makes the situation absolutely clear.

Examples
1 'B' was a temporary employee with a health authority. She applied for a permanent post advertised internally in accordance with a union agreement. She was not appointed but a tribunal decided that the employers' obligation was simply to consider her impartially for the post.

2 'W' was recruited as a temporary shorthand typist to replace a permanent secretary on leave. The temporary worker was dismissed when another permanent employee was appointed. It was decided that the employers had no obligation to 'W' and they were entitled to impose different standards for permanent as opposed to temporary posts.

Some temporary staff will not want a more secure position along with the other benefits which usually accrue. Others will. It is well to be clear about what is likely to happen at the end of the engagement. This should be communicated in writing to the employee.

– How to express the pay and pay related aspects of temporary work?
Considerable confusions can arise over the precise entitlement of temporary workers to pay. In traditional areas of casual work, such as catering, agriculture, building and even computing, employers will generally have a clear view of the appropriate basis of payment. In other cases, especially with short- and fixed-term contracts, a number of issues need to be defined from the outset:

(a) To clarify whether pay is earned on a daily or weekly basis, or is only payable when the short-term engagement is completed.
(b) To clarify what happens when the employee is ill or doesn't turn up to work.
(c) To clarify what happens if the employer cannot provide work during the period or wishes to limit or extend the contract.

Example: the English language summer school
The organisation had recruited teachers on the basis that the engagement was expressed to last 'usually ... three weeks'. Pay was stated to be:
  £90 per week (out of London)
  £95 per week (in London).
This was for the period 28.6.198- – 18.7.198-. At the end of the engagement, which turned out to be different from that specified, the employer stated that pay was on a daily basis and clearly only for days actually worked. Practice indicated that the three week period was the crucial matter; payment was only made at the end of the short-term contract and all other matters, such as PAYE and NI contributions were based on that period. This demonstrated the employer's confusion about basic features of the temporary contract.

The employees were very puzzled and annoyed, though did not resort to legal action. This was probably due to the relatively short engagement and small sums of cash involved.

Place of work
Approximately three-quarters of a million employees work at or from home and their numbers are probably growing. Traditions regarding employment contracts and their documentation have varied considerably, though the 'newer' homeworker contracts have tended to be more clearly articulated. 'Place of work' is not strictly an item which has to be specified under EPCA. Ideally it should be, though perhaps in a manner which allows the employer to move, or consider an employee's request to move in-house.

The following aspects might be considered:

- Hours of work
  Strict monitoring of hours of work is unlikely to be possible, or even desirable. Hours might be expressed broadly, in monthly or annual terms. Or, as has often been the case, pay related directly to output. In any case, many homeworkers are paid by task. Where work requires availability for visits or phone calls or other mechanical communication systems, it might be necessary to specify those hours. A reporting and monitoring system might be attached to the contract
- The method and level of payment will need clarification, especially where work is *not* based on task or piecework. If employees are using their own equipment as well as premises, it is vital to reflect this in pay scales, and to consider the loss and liability insurance aspects. If the employers' equipment and materials are being used, similar questions of cost and insurance arise. The responsibility and costs of transportation of goods and materials must also be specified. Travel expenses must be considered, especially for travel to headquarters, as should telephone costs
- Sick pay and procedures must be considered and specified
- Provision for attendance at an office or headquarters will need to be set out
- Disciplinary rules and grievance procedures may need adaptation, especially regarding the identification of the appropriate manager.

Disciplinary rules will need to reflect the primary concern of quality of work rather than personal behaviour, with clear criteria indicated
- Access to occupational benefits must be clarified and appropriately modified, to compensate the homeworkers for the inaccessibility of traditional in-house benefits, such as canteen and social club facilities. It may be that this can be balanced by more direct help with the homeworker's own premises, such as a redecoration allowance or help with community charges and other outgoings
- If the enterprise has a formal appraisal system, this will have to be modified and specified for the homeworkers, especially if homeworking is an option on a temporary basis for in-house staff
- Some contractual matters dealt with informally for in-house staff may have to be spelt out for homeworkers. This covers confidential information, fidelity, and restraint of trade terms. Where the homeworker has a franchise to sell or repair a product the exact scope or responsibilities will need to be specified and monitored. The contract may need to clarify the situation regarding working for another organisation.

More generally, the contract documentation needs to be informative and comprehensive on communication procedures and for personnel matters. This can help prevent the isolation felt by many homeworkers a factor which is discussed in greater detail in Chapter 6.

CONTRACTS FOR CATEGORY B WORKERS

The major groups here are consultants, freelance and casual workers who have a direct contractual relationship with you but on a self-employed basis. There is no obligation to provide specific contract documentation. But the same professional approach is always desirable. Contracts should be in writing. Many Category B workers will be working alongside your employees and there will be a general need to harmonise aspects of contractual arrangements, such as disciplinary rules and safety procedures. However where the worker is performing a self-contained task, perhaps off-site, this need will be less pressing.

With the exception of self-employed casual staff, it is likely that many contract terms will have been previously negotiated (see Chapters 3 and 4). This strategy should have eliminated uncertainties and likely flashpoints. It should have established:

- The objectives of the contract
- Basis of payment
- Criteria to determine successful completion
- Procedures for monitoring
- Procedures for handling disputes.

Other matters may have to be considered, though much will depend on the type of work. Many derive from the fact that the consultant/freelancer (be it management consultant, computing staff, trainer or 'session musician') will be integrated in the organisation.

Issues to consider:

- What is the contractual position when the consultant, etc. is ill or unable to work? Do they lose pay, can the time be made up or can they provide a substitute?
- Can the consultant delegate some or all of the work?
- Where and with what facilities, including secretarial support, is the work to be carried out?
- Are there to be any restrictions on the consultant taking on other work during the continuation of the contract?
- What is the label or title to be attached to the consultant? Is the employer to be able to 'exploit' their name, and vice versa?
- Whose is the copyright or other rights in materials produced by the consultant, especially when done jointly with in-house staff?
- What are to be the arrangements for expenses, use of facilities, etc?
- Who has the responsibility for insurance?
- Is the employer to provide any indemnity for the consultant?
- What are the precise provisions for dealing with complaints about work and conduct of the consultant? Can the contract be terminated immediately or can cash deductions be made? Are there to be provisions for arbitration to resolve disputes?

Examples

1 The training organisation

This organisation had used consultant trainers for a number of years, most on a regular and long-standing basis. Goodwill had built up. But with the expansion of the organisation's training and advice service, previously informal and unwritten arrangements needed to be 'tightened up'. Specific problems had emerged. For example, if a consultant was recruited, but then the training course did not run, what was the position? Similarly, if the course ran but the trainer could not attend, what happened then? The objective was to be fair to both sides, but also reflect the sometimes variable and imprecise nature of engagements. The following document aimed to deal with these issues, and took the form of a letter with a tear-off slip to signify agreement to the terms.

'Dear ...

We are pleased to offer you appointment as a trainer for a course concerned with ... on ... at a fee of £ ... This will cover provision of training materials, but reasonable travel expenses will be provided, plus subsistence and accommodation where this has been previously agreed.

Should the course not run for whatever reason we undertake to provide as much notice as possible. Expenses reasonably and necessarily incurred in connection with the course will be reimbursed.

Save in an emergency, if you are unable to participate in the course you will undertake to provide a substitute trainer who is acceptable to the organisation.

Materials provided for the course remain your copyright and should be your own or acknowledged work. Information provided by ourselves or which becomes available during training should not be used by you without our express permission ...'

Consultancy contracts rarely reserve the right to withhold payment if the consultant's work is of a very low standard. However, insofar as the consultancy contract impliedly carries with it a warranty of competence, payment can be withheld for breach of contract on normal legal principles.

Although consultancy arrangements require goodwill and trust in order to thrive, frequent disputes arise over abuse of information gleaned during the consultancy, lack of clarity about individual responsibilities and over satisfactory completion of the work.

2 The financial adviser
A.S. Associates entered a consultancy contract with a large commercial undertaking. They became aware of serious financial irregularities which subsequently became the subject of police investigations. They, too, became involved in the legal proceedings. There was nothing in the consultancy contract to provide indemnity or immunity or to cover legal costs. Although they did not face court action they did suffer losses and considerable inconvenience over matters which they were wholly unaware of originally, and which probably affected their reputation. Where contracts involve access to sensitive confidential matters, the contract should clarify the situation and deal with indemnities and costs.

Other Category B workers

Many seasonal, sessional and casual staff have been held to be self-employed. They generally perform less skilled or critical roles in an enterprise and are often thought of as requiring little or no contract documentation other than that required for tax purposes. Ignorance or confusions can lead to disputes regarding, for example, precise hours of work, rates of pay, entitlement to enhanced pay, and application of disciplinary rules and grounds for ending the contract. Although these workers are outside more statutory employment protections, other than anti-discrimination and equal pay measures, they *are* covered by normal rules of contract. Courts are willing to imply terms which are reasonable and relevant to an occupation. Where there are identifiable customs in an occupation, regarding method of payment for example, courts are willing to enforce them as an implied obligation. An oral agreement such as 'casual, cash in hand' does not, therefore, mean that there are no binding contractual terms.

Contract documents define these responsibilities but may have to tread a fine line of providing sufficient control without leading to a conclusion of employee status, if that is the objective. Contracts should deal with similar issues to those for consultants.

This might include:

- Responsibility for tax, national insurance and personal loss and liability insurance, as appropriate
- Situations involving injury to the worker or if a worker injures someone else or damages property
- Clarification regarding sensitive, confidential and copyright material (the

law will not normally *imply* obligations of loyalty on self-employed workers but *will* protect confidential matters)
• Discipline, monitoring and appraisal procedures, including the circumstances justifying termination, or payment of liquidated damages.

CONTRACTS FOR CATEGORY C WORKERS

This group of workers do not have a direct contractual link with the enterprise. They are clearly the legal responsibility of their own employer on an employee or self-employed basis. The contractual link is with the sub-contractor, agency or seconding employer. Two areas require consideration:

• The commercial contract to provide worker(s) to the enterprise
• Provision in that contract, if relevant for the terms of work, job relating to either the employment contracts of the sub-contractor's own workers, or to conditions or matters relevant to the 'host' enterprise.

Commercial contracts

Many of the key issues will have been the subject of negotiation through the process of designing specifications, recruiting an employment agency or reaching agreement for the secondment of staff. Many sub-contractors belong to trade or professional associations which have codes of practice setting out standard terms of contract. Cleaning, computing, catering, engineering, as well as 'artistic' occupations, such as music and design, have such rules or guidelines. Although the codes deal with broad issues of integrity, some general contract terms can also be extracted. Many provide for arbitration in case of disputes. The most sophisticated are probably the standard contracts in the construction industry, which provide some useful material.

The Computing Services Association issues a range of 'Briefing Notes', one of which is 'Contract Staff Guidelines'. This is intended to be a guide for all users of contract staff and contractors themselves and should be distributed 'at the time the contract is negotiated'. Its terms can be expressly incorporated in contracts. Sample terms include undertakings by contractors 'not knowingly to give misleading information' about work, to supply only workers who 'as far as it can be reasonably ascertained, have relevant experience', to 'keep all information regarding the client's business completely confidential', and not to 'exploit such information for commercial gain'. There should be 'no attempt to recruit staff from the client company during the period of the contract'.

Many terms attempt to deal with the possible abuses of the sub-contract relationship and to build in certain guarantees. Other contract terms have to be specific to the engagement. They largely hinge on matters of complaint, damage and liability. These should include:

- Tasks and mode of payment
- Length of contract
- Terms relating to renewal and renegotiation
- Arrangements for monitoring
- Arrangements for dealing with delay, shortfalls or other alleged breaches
- Any specific terms relating to use of premises, equipment, responsibility for insurance, access and use of confidential information and other restrictive or sensitive matters
- Mode of communication and accountability *vis-à-vis* in-house staff.

Agency contracts and secondments

The importance of careful negotiation for secondment arrangements has been discussed in Chapter 3. But it is also important that the contract between host and seconding organisation is clear and reflects the intentions of the parties. Some of the issues are the same as for agency contracts, though geared to a longer time-scale. Assuming the host and seconding organisation are agreed on the purposes of secondment and the acceptability of the employee, the contract must develop mechanisms to monitor the secondment itself. It is preferable to spell out too much than too little, not least because although the worker will be subject to day-to-day control by the host organisation technically he or she remains the employee of another. It is vital to establish performance targets or criteria and to agree on the supervision and discipline of the worker. Matters of pay and working conditions can usually be easily set out, it is the legal expression of quality control which is more problematic.

Suggested areas for consideration include:

Agency contracts
- Task, rate and mode of payment for workers
- Hours of attendance at the client's premises
- Name or title of client's employee to whom agency worker is responsible
- Arrangement when worker is not satisfactory to client
- Arrangement when the worker is dissatisfied by client
- Arrangements where allegations of loss, damage, caused *by* worker
- Arrangement when loss, damage caused *to* worker
- Responsibilities for insurance, if not dealt with already regarding damage
- Provision of conciliation mechanisms to deal with disputes

Secondment contracts
- Arrangements for pay, increments, pension and related matters
- Length of agreement, option for renewal or permanent transfer, if appropriate
- Procedure if secondment is unsatisfactory
- Grounds and procedures for termination and compensation
- Liability for loss and damage inflicted by seconded worker, and insurance matters
- Provisions for a satisfactory work environment.

The last point is crucial. English law considers any losses inflicted by the seconded worker as normally the responsibility of the seconding employer. Similarly, in contractual terms, losses caused *to* the seconded worker remain generally the responsibility of the original employer. This is an unclear area of law so it is best dealt with by the parties to contracts.

YTS contracts

There is no real problem here in that contracts are set out in handbooks produced by the Training Commission and its successors. It is possible to include additional terms, but not to modify existing terms.

Terms of work of workers covered by the contract

In general, there is nothing to preclude employers and clients agreeing on terms of work to be offered to workers covered by the contract. It may be that rates of pay should be broadly comparable with in-house staff for industrial relations or other reasons. In many cases this is a sensitive area because agency staff, e.g. nurses and computing staff, often appear to earn higher sums than comparable in-house employees. Contracts can determine the skills, qualifications, wages, matters of discipline, adherence to in-house safety rules, trade unions affecting the workers.

Some areas have become subject to legislation or formal agreement:

- Under the Local Government Act 1988, it is unlawful for client local authorities to insist that particular terms of work be applied to workers of a sub-contractor. This does not apply to other employers.
- 'Contract compliance' has developed as a feature of some public sector clients. It requires sub-contractors and agencies to comply with equal opportunities and related policies. It may be difficult to enforce by local authorities in view of the 1988 Act
- Many employers who belong to professional trade associations voluntarily agree to apply certain terms of work to their employees. This forms part of the sub-contract itself.

Devising contracts for the use of Category B and C staff is a detailed and technical process. But a number of underlying themes emerge. Unlike contracts for employees, the precise purpose of the contract has to be defined and structures and strategies developed distinctive from the usual supervisory rules to monitor its performance. Using non-employees, especially combining them with your own staff, leads often to tensions, practical difficulties and inconsistencies which have to be anticipated and regulated. There are no simple answers. The essential thing is to sit down and envisage the working through of the contract, not necessarily in an ideal way!

SUMMARY POINTS

- Over the past few years, deregulation in employment law has left up to half of workers outside major statutory protection. As a response, many workers affected have turned to traditional courts of law which places a greater emphasis on the strict contractual rights of the parties.
- The borderline between employed and self-employed workers can be extremely blurred. Tribunals will judge the worker's status on the basis of the individual circumstances of the relationship between the organisation and the individual rather than the classification used in the contractual documentation. Key factors, depending on the nature of the arrangement, include:
  - degree of self-dependance and financial autonomy
  - the ability to refuse offers of work, and to work for others
  - level of supervision by the organisation
- Employers should avoid using standard form contracts or hastily adapted versions of documents used for full-time staff. Contractual documentation should take into account the particular needs of the work pattern and express aspects of the work relationship which may not be necessary for full-time workers. Legal clauses should express clearly the obligation and intentions of the parties and cover aspects of the relationship going beyond those required by statutory provisions

References
1 *Scarle, Brodie, Banks and Alsop* v. *London Residuary Body* [1987] IT 12907, 13128, 13150, 13151/87 LN/C.
2 *W.H.P.T. Housing Association* v. *Secretary of State for Social Services* [1981], ICR 737.
3 Leighton, P. and Rayner, C., *Job Sharing in South-East Essex*, Essex Institute of Higher Education, 1986.
4 *Nethermere (St. Neots) Ltd* v. *Tavener and Gardiner* [1984] IRLR 240.

Source material
Leighton, P., 'Observing employment contracts', *Industrial Law Journal*, 1984, p. 84.
Leighton, P., *Contractual Arrangements in Selected Industries*, Research Paper No. 39, Department of Employment, 1983.
Leighton, P. and Doyle, B., *Making and Varying Contracts of Employment*, Department of Law Research Paper No. 1, The Polytechnic of North London, 1982.
Wallington, P., *Butterworths Employment Law Handbook* 4th edn., Butterworth, 1987.
Wedderburn, Lord, *The Worker and the Law* 3rd edn., Penguin Books, 1987.

Chapter 6

Management and development

It is not surprising that of all the interest groups traditionally blocking the introduction of new work patterns, line management is often the most vociferous.

New ways of working inevitably need underpinning by new management systems to cope with the particular logistical problems the reforms will place on communication and control, appraisal, discipline and relationships with both internal and external colleagues. These may often bring with them significant changes to the function of line management and potential training or re-training.

A further issue is the extent to which Category A and B workers are integrated into the organisation. As new work patterns are introduced at increasingly senior positions, it is becoming possible for people to develop their careers while remaining in working arrangements traditionally excluded from access to continuous training and promotion. More and more organisations are finding that in order to recruit and retain key staff they are having to adapt their organisational structure and systems to take into account the personal needs of employees. Once again, the implications require careful consideration before the work patterns are introduced.

The key areas most affected by the introduction of new work patterns are summarised in Figure 6.1 below.

CENTRAL ADMINISTRATION VERSUS LOCAL DISCRETION

Like many other management of change exercises, the introduction of new work patterns requires acceptance at the bottom and middle layers of the organisation as well as commitment at the top. Policies encouraging job sharing, secondment, homeworking, formal career breaks, re-recruitment, and other working arrangements designed to meet the changing social needs of the workforce, will become worthless scraps of paper if local managers fail to implement them. This is particularly true in de-centralised

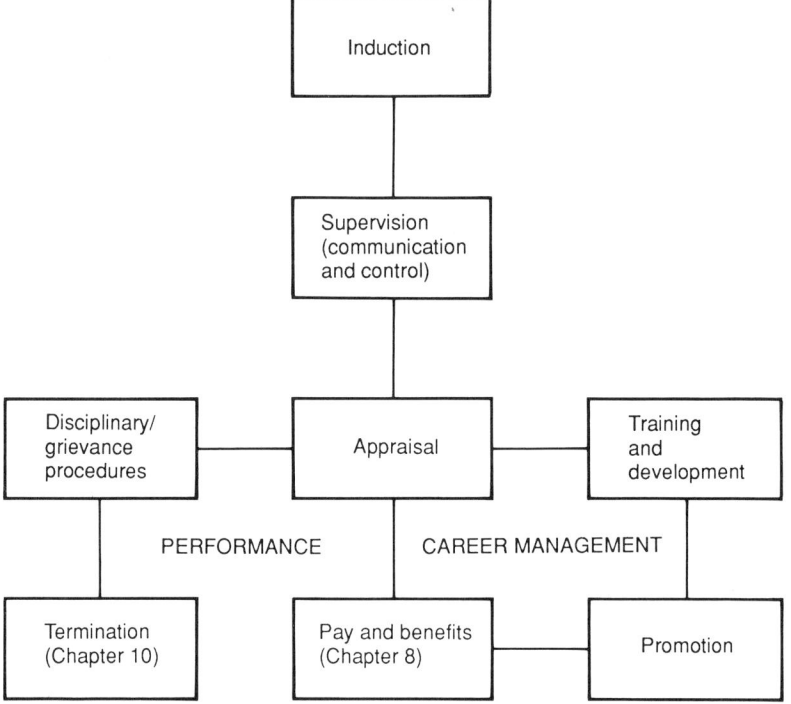

Fig. 6.1 Management of new work patterns: key issues

organisations where local managers have considerable discretion in decision-making and fulfil many of the functions previously undertaken by personnel departments.

Many public sector organisations are experiencing problems in fully implementing equal opportunities programmes negotiated throughout the mid-1980s. In 1986, Joyce Epstein, Administrator at the Royal Institute of Public Administration commented:[1]

'The foundations for achieving real equality of opportunity have been laid in many public authorities in the form of equal opportunities policy statements and staff whose specific and often sole responsibility is the implementation of these policies. While there has been progress because of such steps, progress is painfully and unacceptably slow ... the picture that emerges is one of discouraging resistance to change, at both the human and organisational level.'

Because so many new work patterns are linked (formally or informally) to equal opportunities programmes, it is not surprising this resistance to change directly affects their take up. In Chapter 2, we saw that formal career break schemes guaranteeing re-entry and run from the centre of the organisation were more likely to succeed in their purpose than discretionary schemes more dependent on the assent of local managers, some of whom may have private reservations about women combining work with child-care. Similarly, research by the Essex Institute of Higher Education shows that organisations with job sharing policies do not necessarily have a high take-up of applicants; whereas firms who do not have policies and whose managers approach new working arrangements *ad hoc* often have a far higher proportional rate of active schemes.

In Chapter 3, we stressed the need for any major initiative to be negotiated with key interest groups (including local managers and trade union representatives) and launched with an education or publicity programme designed to gain the acceptance of other workers.

This process often requires the subsequent support of a monitoring programme, conducted by the personnel function, to assess the take-up of the scheme and pinpoint whether a low response is due to poor awareness of the benefits among potential applicants or a resistance to implement it among line management.

If the scheme is linked to an equal opportunities programme this responsibility could be attached to EO officers; if not, it could be delegated to an appropriate personnel function such as those responsible for management development, career management and the better use of internal labour markets.

COMMUNICATION AND CONTROL

Radical changes to *when* and *where* staff work pose a number of important issues surrounding day-to-day communication and control. In particular:

- How and when they are briefed and allocated work
- How they will liaise and communicate with colleagues inside the organisation
- How decisions taken by staff working new patterns will affect other people's work
- How they will liaise and communicate with people outside the organisation (customers, clients, suppliers, etc.)
- How their work will be monitored and assessed
- How office space and facilities will be allocated.

Induction and integration

Good communications start at the beginning. Routine induction systems which apply to permanent full-time staff should be extended to ensure that all Category A and the more important Category B and C workers receive the same start-up information. This should include:

- General information about the organisation – its principal activities, history, culture and geographical locations
- Information about regulations covering:
  – health and safety

- fire drill
- smoking
- dress regulations
- use of telephone for personal calls
- time-keeping
• Information about the benefits and facilities open to the particular category of worker, including:
  - holiday leave
  - sick leave
  - maternity leave
  - career break schemes
  - pension schemes
  - career counselling
  - training facilities
  - staff discounts
  - sports and social facilities
  - season ticket loans, etc.
• Specific information about the role of the department and the key people they will be supporting or working with
• Talks by senior managers or chief executives.

All of this information will have a direct bearing on the worker's efficiency and performance. Equally important, it will make the worker feel part of the organisation. This second point is worth stressing. As we saw in Chapter 1, many Category A and B workers and those Category C workers who work regularly for the organisation often feel isolated and excluded from both its culture and day-to-day activities. Key factors that will make them more committed include:

• Whether they are represented in staff associations (and also by trade unions – see Chapter 9)
• Whether staff facilities available to full-timers are also extended to them – sports facilities, staff outings, competitions, social events (e.g. Christmas parties) as well as financial perks such as luncheon vouchers, staff discounts, etc.
• Whether their activities, achievements and interests are reported in in-house employee communication literature such as house journals.

All of these factors will have the psychological effect of making them feel accepted as *full* members of the organisation even if they are not working full-time or on-site. The professional and social contact they will gain with other employees will enable them to build good personal networks and break down much of the traditional hostility they might encounter from colleagues. The conventional complaint that part-time staff lack motivation and leave early is frequently caused by their complete failure to identify with the organisation. Too often, this is the organisation's fault rather than any inherent flaw in the adopted work pattern.

Reporting and monitoring

The introduction of new work patterns will increase the need for effective reporting. This is particularly true for workers outside the office (networkers, teleworkers, homeworkers, etc.) but also for any form of working arrangement where employees are expected to take greater responsibility for supervising their day-to-day workload (such as job-sharers, professional part-timers, consultants, etc.)

Systems to monitor a worker's output could include all or any of the following, where appropriate:

- Fixed meetings on a regular basis to:
  - set objectives
  - negotiate success criteria
  - monitor progress
  - adjust deadlines

  These meetings can be one-to-one involving other members of the department or team, depending on the nature of the work
- Daily telephone reporting at fixed hours of the day and the more imaginative use of electronic mail
- Regular days on which workers are expected to work on-site

In certain circumstances, the requirement for off-site workers to keep in regular contact with their supervisors or managers should be built into the contract. Meetings or briefings should be fixed well in advance and take into account workers' domestic and personal circumstances. For example, early morning and late afternoon meetings are often inconvenient for working mothers who will have to fetch and deliver their children to school. For similar reasons, open-ended meetings are usually unpopular.

When allocating work, duties should be broken up into easily defined and measurable tasks, projects or objectives. Achievements of these responsibilities should be broken into set deadlines according to an agreed timetable. Regular review dates should be incorporated to identify problems early on and adjust deadlines if appropriate.

The balance between on-site and off-site working should be carefully reviewed to ensure that workers keep in touch with essential colleagues; have access to professional facilities (libraries, data bases, copying equipment, etc.); and do not become isolated and therefore demotivated. A key factor in the early success of the Rank Xerox networking scheme was the regular visits by off-site workers to their local offices, to regularly review their work but also to keep in touch with the organisation's mainstream activities.

Formal systems of reporting should also be supported by the better use of standing sources of information. The constant flow of people off and on-site means that company and work unit *noticeboards* are likely to become more important sources of routine information – in much the same way as those in college and educational institutions. Changes in company regulations, new developments affecting individual work units and other vital information that permanent on-site workers have easier access to should be posted on the board. Part-time, temporary and home-based workers should be encouraged to refer to the board regularly to keep themselves updated. Better use of office memos, the publication of important information in house journals and the dissemination of weekly or monthly work unit bulletins will all help to keep outplaced, off-site workers in touch with their department.

It is also worth stressing that this kind of reporting system is equally valid for Category B workers. Consultants, in particular, draw much of their professional strength from the variety of organisational cultures they have worked in. Being closely linked and integrated with the organisation will be an important motivator and a key factor in the business's ability to attract the right external expertise.

Allocation of office space and facilities

Another major implication of having a more diverse workforce to achieve the same objectives is that office accommodation and facilities will need to be more widely shared and allocated, using carefully designed rostering. Examples include:

- Individual or shared office space
- Conference facilities
- Staff facilities: canteens, leisure rooms, sports facilities
- Equipment – word processors, instruments and tools, recording equipment, etc.
- Personal transport.

In a situation where full-time staff, part-timers, homeworkers and on-site visits and consultants working on the premises are all competing for the same resources, the allocation of facilities will need to be governed by a strict order of priorities linked to key organisational objectives.

Clearly, problems are bound to occur with facilities or resources which are usually individual to certain members of staff and carry a psychological status. Two obvious examples are:

Company cars: which in the UK have been often allocated as a perquisite rather than a pre-requisite to the job.

Individual offices or office space: which carry a sense of personal space over which the individual has total control – the invasion of this personal territory often produces a similar psychological reaction as if the individual's home was under threat!

The obvious solution is to allocate these kind of facilities strictly according to the level of their use. A three-tier system would operate as follows:

Individual allocation: where the facility is likely to be permanently or constantly used by a single member of staff.

Shared allocation: where the facility is likely to be used regularly by a fixed and specified number of individuals – as in the case of job-sharers and professional part-timers. This allows for some degree of personalisation and joint status.

Random allocation from an organisational pool: in the case of consultants, temporary workers, homeworkers on routine visits and agency or sub-contracted staff.

Office space, equipment and personal transport should be divided into these three categories according to a ratio based on the particular balance of the organisation's workforce. External and off-site workers using office space equipment or transport from an organisational pool should be encouraged to give adequate notice of their requirements to allow for effective rostering.

Certain items of equipment or facilities will be individual to one employee, regardless of the hours worked or the location. Examples include:

- Clothing and overalls, particularly if they are marked with the employee's name and title for security reasons
- Security passes
- Special equipment or adaptations to equipment to take into account a physical or mental disability.

Example

At the Financial Times, *for example, a member of the paper's editorial staff employed under the organisation's job sharing scheme required an orthopaedic chair – a piece of equipment worth in excess of £1000. Although the paper would have had no hesitation in underwriting the cost of the chair in the case of a full-time member of staff, the request raised the issue of whether grants of this nature were open to part-time employees. The union argued successfully that the concept of job sharing would be prejudiced if the request was turned down on these grounds.*

CHANGES TO INTERNAL RELATIONSHIPS

The introduction of new working patterns is bound to affect the nature and pattern of working relationships. The problems divide into two main categories:

Psychological

As we saw earlier in Chapter 3 reaction to new work patterns among existing staff tend to be schizophrenic. On the one hand, they tend to regard staff working these patterns as uncommitted, inefficient and unreliable; on the other, they see them as better paid (in the case of consultants, agency workers and contractors) or enjoying life-style benefits that they are denied (in the case of job-sharers, secondees, professional part-timers). Above all they see them as *different* and therefore outside the system.

A number of actions will help to remove this inherent distrust:

- A comprehensive education programme explaining the implications of the new working arrangement (see Chapter 3)
- Encouraging new categories of workers to play an active role in the social life of the organisation to break down personal barriers
- Extending the availability of new working patterns to all employees to remove the sense of a confined privilege
- Ensuring that communication and liaison between the various categories of worker is sufficiently practical to avoid tensions during working hours.

Practical

Badly designed communication and control systems can add to the problem. Complaints will occur that employees working part-time or off-site are difficult to get hold of; cannot respond as quickly; are not available for meetings called at short notice and further problems are caused if permanent full-time staff are required to cover for newer types of worker due to expected or unexpected absence.

Example

The practical difficulties of working alongside staff whose attendance and continuity of employment failed to fit in with existing procedures was highlighted most vividly in a recent study of job-sharers. The study highlighted a number of perceived disadvantages in using job-sharers:

The 'two Mondays' syndrome: *Both job-sharers and managers commented on the difficulties which faced individual sharers after changeover – one job-sharer's manager commented (when asked about the sharers' productivity), 'I have heard comments when they come in on Wednesday mornings, "You know what it's like on a Monday morning, it usually takes a few hours to get in the swing of things"' .... A job-sharer corroborated this by saying, 'When you come in at twelve o'clock you might find circulars ... piled up on your desk before you start'.*

Unresponsive to crises or peak demands: *If problems or pressure arose suddenly, as in social work, journalism or in a managerial capacity, job-sharers could not always respond quickly in these cases. The burden fell on their full-time colleagues, causing particular resentment where work units or teams were small and under-resourced. In one case-study full-time team workers expressed 'Negative feelings towards part-timers and had voted not to split another job in the team'. The type of work or situations often required regular or ad hoc meetings. Some managers spoke of difficulties in arranging such meetings so that the whole team or unit could be presented. Where meetings could be scheduled most organisations settled the change-over day or time so that both sharers could be there.*

These comments applied specifically to the greater use of job-sharers. But most referred to issues of continuity and effective teamwork which apply, to a greater or lesser extent, to other Category A and B workers whose participation in the day-to-day work of the unit or team is likely to be sporadic – particularly part-time and temporary staff, consultants, and part-time secondees.

Once again, the problems may be overcome through:

- Proper reporting systems and regular meetings, not only between flexible workers and their managers but with other members of the department.
- Clear lines of accountability, so that if more than one flexible worker is responsible for another department member's work the division of responsibility is practical and understood by both the flexible workers and the supervised member of staff.

One area that can bring about both psychological and practical barriers is that of social habits which can offend individual colleagues and house regulations. The most common problem area is clothes being worn which do not suit the organisation's culture or dress regulations (a diminishing problem) and smoking (a growing problem).

Certain categories of part-time or temporary staff may not be covered contractually by dress or smoking regulations and this will certainly be the case for external workers such as sub-contractors and consultants. Organisations should therefore decide whether to make compliance with these regulations a contractual term or come to a special arrangement where this is likely to cause friction.

Finally, there is the question of culture: consultants, agency temps, sub-contracted staff, secondees, and other fixed-term workers, may not share the collective 'values' of the organisation, work unit or team.

The problem was most vividly illustrated in the findings of the report on secondment published by the Centre for Employment Initiatives (CEI) (see Chapter 2). The report commented, 'Whether the secondees themselves are conscripted into secondment, volunteer for it or find themselves involved for other reasons, seems to have less effect on the eventual benefit than the manner in which both host and company treat them . . . . Because they work in one organisation, and yet remain employees of another, they have at best the role of ambassador and at worst the status of refugee!'

The secondment manager of one of the organisations profiled in the study, Project Fullemploy, stressed that their secondees are assessed as much on their character and mentality as the skills they have to offer, 'We need people who can adapt well to a different culture', she said, 'Attitude is paramount. Many people from the private sector approach secondments as a charitable exercise and this can often lead to a patronising manner that can severely prejudice their relationship with staff and course participants. Our secondees will need a commitment to equal opportunities and a strong awareness of racism and sexism'.

This issue also applies to many other Category B and C workers. We have already seen in Chapter 1 that sub-contracting and the use of external consultants has caused least problems in organisations with a long tradition and experience of how to manage the process. Cultural issues also apply. A consultant visiting organisations sporadically will fit in far better to a work unit used to 'permanent' staff being regularly off-site (such as a research unit) than one where day-to-day social contact is the norm.

The most valued agency temps are also those who can adapt quickly to the social as well as the working fabric of the organisation. A successful fit in all these cases is usually due to sensitive recruitment techniques which build 'cultural' issue into the criteria for selection. As Fullemploy's secondment manager concluded 'Sometimes our interview process results in a recommendation that the candidate would make a good secondee – but not in our organisation!'

CHANGES TO EXTERNAL RELATIONSHIPS

Another perceived problem attributed to new work patterns is the effect they will have on external relationships – with clients, customers, suppliers, visitors, the press and general enquirers.

Concern is regularly expressed in many organisations that customers, be they clients (in a commercial company), patients (in a medical care unit), students (in an educational establishment) or buyers (in a retail outlet), will find it difficult to build up a good relationship with more than one person; may find it difficult to communicate with someone working from more than one site; and may not receive the continuity of service they require.

Like so many others highlighted in this chapter, these are practical problems rather than insurmountable barriers. Possible solutions include:

- The education of external parties to expect to be dealing with more than one person or with a person from more than one site – in the case of two account executives handling one client's account on a job-shared basis, for example, the client should be introduced to both and given the opportunity to assess their joint suitability
- The design of a sufficiently effective communications system to ensure that enquiries reach off-site workers, or the right part-time member of staff, in time for them to be dealt with effectively
- The proper rostering of work to ensure that:
  – decisions made by one flexible worker which affect the external liaison of another are passed on and communicated accurately
  – continuity of service and contact with external bodies and the general public is maintained
- Where a one-to-one relationship is important or essential to an outside body or individual, responsibilities are divided by project or client as well as working time.

The impact of new working patterns on external relationships is often exaggerated. Provided the work is properly organised, outside bodies are used to dealing with more than one person in more than one location at a time when project management and teamworking is used extensively in many organisations.

The study on job sharing (see example above) found instances where lack of continuous contact with a specific individual was a distinct problem. A manager in the Civil Service commented, 'Some people do expect the same person to answer the phone whenever they ring up. In international negotiations our person had to be seen as the British representative of "X" and you build up a relationship with the other side ... these contacts will feel puzzled if it is rather "hit and miss" with two different people!'

A social work job-sharer was also conscious of the length of gaps between family visits which remained a problem despite her smaller caseload. Meetings and visits were generally more difficult to arrange, not least because 'they [the clients] are not there the day you are there!'

Yet the report found little guidance that, in the majority of cases, the lack of consistent contact generated resentment, dissatisfaction or complaint on the part of third parties: as we saw earlier, the complaints are far more likely to come from internal colleagues who may have to field additional communication in the absence of the right sharer.

Using handbooks or codes of practice

The use of handbooks or printed codes of practice to summarise and specify the regulations and standards governing the work of flexible workers has been a popular measure, particularly in organisations employing travelling sales staff and home-based researchers. These provide a useful benchmark against which managers can assess the worker's output and provide the basis for systematic performance appraisal.

APPRAISALS, PROMOTION AND TRAINING

These issues are critical. The appraisal, promotion and training of atypical workers, and the extent to which organisations are prepared to invest time, money and effort into making sure it is undertaken effectively, will help them either feel genuinely integrated or not. This certainly applies to all Category A workers and in certain instances to Category B workers where their role is long standing or central to the organisation. The issue is less relevant to Category C workers who will normally turn to their own employers for training and appraisal, and on rarer occasions for promotion.

Appraisal, promotion and training are also key issues because, as we shall see in Chapter 7, they are directly linked to the design and administration of pay systems and related occupations benefits. More and more organisations are introducing performance-related pay, including a growing minority in the public sector. By implication, this requires accurate and wide-ranging appraisal systems supported by personnel and line managers who will apply them sensitively and objectively.

Finally, these policies and procedures are central to effective career management. More and more 'social pull' working arrangements – job sharing, sabbaticals, part-time working, networking, formal career break schemes – will be requested and taken up by existing full-time staff. In many cases, these arrangements will have been introduced by the organisations specifically to retain key staff and facilitate their career management. Proper appraisal to identify future intentions and plan for them, are critical to the ability of these policies to meet their objectives.

Appraisal

Key questions here are:

- How can career appraisal be used to pinpoint future demands for new working arrangements amongst existing full-time workers and be extended to existing and future atypical staff?
- How should performance appraisal systems be adapted to take into account the changes in job design required by individual work patterns?
- How can performance appraisal of Category A workers and Category B workers be linked to their method of remuneration?
- How can both performance and career appraisal be linked to the promotion and training needs of atypical staff?
- Should performance and career appraisal apply to Category B as well as Category A workers?

Performance appraisal

If accurate performance appraisal is to be extended to all categories of worker, it must take into account the context and circumstances in which the job is being performed. This is particularly important in the case of work patterns where the workers have a high degree of discretion over how and where they perform their tasks (such as homeworking) or where the success of the arrangement is dependent on close collaboration with one or more colleagues (such as job sharing).

In many types of new work pattern, it is often difficult to pinpoint whether a failure to reach agreed or accepted standards of performance is due to the shortcomings of the individual worker, the poor design of the working arrangement or (as can often be the case) the prejudice of line management and/or fellow workers.

It is therefore important that performance appraisal systems:

- are adapted to take into account:
  - the quality of the work unit's communication and control systems
  - the physical circumstances in which the job is being performed, particularly if this differs markedly from those in which the job has been previously undertaken
- are based, wherever possible, on agreed targets, leaving individual workers maximum discretion on how they achieve these targets.
- as a consequence, allow individual ownership of the process, enabling

them to suggest and assess feasible targets which they believe they can achieve
- allow supervisors and line managers ownership of the process, ensuring that they accept the *practicality* of the work methods in the context of the work unit as a whole; and (more importantly) the *principle* of flexible working in the context of the work being performed
- ensure that the appraisal systems are relatively simple to understand, operate and monitor – and that managers have been trained in the processes of performance management and understand the importance of making consistent and defensible judgements on their subordinates.

Career appraisal

If anything, accurate career appraisal is even more important to the effective use of new work patterns, particularly if they are being used to retain key staff and aid career management.

We have already argued that, in a labour market where the demand for skilled labour greatly exceeds the supply, able and valued 'core' employees may decide that they do not wish 'upward development' linked to a conventional career structure. They may wish, at certain times of their lives, to work at home or on a part-time basis. They may wish to spend some or all of their time working self-employed or engage in some kind of further education or continuous training. At other times in their careers, they may wish to return to a full-time career. To retain their skills, organisations will need to adapt existing career structures to meet individual requirements.

At the same time, there may be existing 'peripheral' workers who would be interested in pursuing a long-term career with the organisation. Many of these individuals may possess skills knowledge and experience which are in short supply. Consultants, in particular, may be open to offers of full-time employment.

Effective career appraisal is therefore important:

- to anticipate the future career needs of existing 'core' workers and link these to new or already established flexible working schemes
- to appraise the potential of existing 'peripheral' workers and, where appropriate, link them more closely to the organisation

Any existing or future career appraisal system should ensure that the future career needs of employees which are likely to warrant flexible working arrangements are pinpointed well in advance. This is particularly important in the case of female employees who may wish to start a family in mid-career and who may welcome the availability of a formal career break scheme and/or working arrangements such as job sharing, professional part-time working or homeworking. But it also applies to workers of both sexes who may want or need the opportunity to widen their professional or personal experience through study leave, sabbaticals, secondments and networking.

Two factors are particularly important:

The openness with which the appraisal is conducted: participants should be encouraged to be frank about their future career aspirations. They should not be made to feel that their desire for more flexibility will act as an automatic barrier to promotion and further training. This is particularly important in the case of female employees who often feel reluctant to reveal any indication of their plans to start a family until the last moment. In many cases, this is with good reason. A large civil service department recently investigated why so few of their promising female managers were reaching senior positions. The personnel department discovered that many line managers were not recommending female members of their department for promotion on the grounds that they were married and 'would therefore not be interested'.

The accuracy and continuity of personnel data: many career records fail to take into account periods when key workers are employed in new work patterns or in leave of absence under a career break scheme. A recent study into career break schemes by the Institute of Manpower Studies[2] found that continuity of personnel data was only maintained if:

- Maternity leave(rs) was recorded as a separate special category
- Records were kept of those leavers who did not return
- Maternity leave and employment under new work patterns (part-time work, homeworking, networking, etc.) were incorporated into career histories
- Periods of full-time and part-time work were properly integrated
- Separate periods of service were recorded on one career record.

Training

Two aspects of training are important to the effective introduction of new work patterns:

- Job-specific training
- Training as part of a long-term career plan

Job-specific training

Periods of training may be necessary to enable individual workers to undertake new forms of employment. This could include:

- Skills training to operate new kinds of machinery or equipment (for example, a computer terminal link in the case of homeworkers)
- Training in self-management (for example the ability to work to defined targets, identified objectives or set deadlines)
- Training in client liaison, interpersonal skills and networking, if the new

work pattern places the worker in regular contact with the organisation's customers for the first time
- Basic financial training, if the new work pattern involves periods of self-employment (e.g. networking as operated by Rank Xerox).

Access to long-term training

Many Category A workers (particularly job sharers, homeworkers and part-time staff) and some Category B workers may also welcome access to further training, possibly linked to an agreed career progression. Depending on the individual's circumstances this could include:

- Formal training courses, run internally or by an external training provider
- Distance learning packages, computer learning programmes and correspondence learning, all linked to some form of regular face-to-face tuition
- The opportunity to attend professional or company-specific conferences, seminars and discussion groups.

Two factors are particularly important

Timing and method of delivery: training should be provided, wherever possible, at times which enable part-timers and homeworkers to attend. If company-based learning is impractical, new methods of computer-aided or distance learning should be employed, provided it is linked to some form of face-to-face tuition.

Delivery on company time: employers also need to decide whether training is to take place on or off company time. This is likely to be a key issue in the case of part-timers, job sharers and homeworkers who may not be able to undertake training outside their normal working hours.

Example: Training at F International

A major study of telecommuting in 1987[3] examined the training provided by F International to their home-based teleworkers.

The majority of homeworkers at F International are self-employed and to maintain this status, the company has had to keep 'at arm's length' over the matter of training. Much of the training has been undertaken by means of distance learning. Most homeworkers and their line managers stress, however, that while distance learning is useful, people learned more quickly face to face and any form of group training has an important additional 'bonding function'.

People undergoing distance learning commented that they missed out on the sharing of problems and successes and on assimilating knowledge by comparing notes. As one homeworker put it: 'Some subjects are suitable for distance learning but one doesn't find out things as one goes along as in conventional work.'

Although some of F International's workers felt they were left to acquire their own skills 'on the hoof', others stressed that there were training facilities available on request. 'If there is a project which requires knowledge of some new technology, they will train me', another respondent commented, 'F pays for the time if they endorse it but you pay for your own time if you decide to train yourself.'

The homeworkers interviewed in the study were paid for their mileage to attend company-endorsed training sessions plus a retainer of £25 per day (in 1987). This helped homeworkers release the time to attend the course but as one stressed: 'It is not directly cost-effective since I have to take care of my domestic situation and pay a childminder.'

The report stressed, however, that F International recognised that training was essential for keeping their homeworkers up to date in a rapidly moving industry and had an important secondary role in overcoming isolation.

A final category of flexible worker for whom training is essential is the returner from a formal career break scheme or secondment. If either arrangement commits the organisation to re-integrate the individual into the same level of responsibility from which they originally left, knowledge of skill updating will probably be essential and should be undertaken either during or immediately following their period outside full-time employment.

Established career break schemes use a variety of means to achieve this. At Barclays Bank, participants receive monthly information packs to help keep in touch with organisation changes. BP encourages the employee to keep in regular contact with their manager and make frequent visits to the office to discuss updating skills. At British Gas, employees are sent the house journal and annual report. They are also encouraged to attend training courses and briefing sessions, with their expenses paid.

Leicester City Council places particular emphasis on up-dating skills and knowledge. They provide participants with a 2½-day refresher course to establish training needs for an annual 10-day programme. On their return, they book participants on the next available re-induction programme which lasts six weeks.

A growing number of organisations also provide 'return-ticket' secondees with training to up-date their skills and knowledge. At Barclays, for example, over 50 per cent of secondments are now for career development purposes. Many involve high-flying managers from Barclays management development programme. Secondees are kept in touch with each other through a regularly up-dated bulletin and regular contact maintained with the departmental manager who nominated the individual for the project.

'We ensure that throughout the secondment, secondees know that they are not forgotten and that, while it is not possible at the start of the assignment to specify exactly what position they will return to, their regional department is actively engaged in planning their future.', commented the manager of Barclays' secondment programme in a recent article[3].

Promotion

Many surveys of flexible workers find that access to promotion is perceived as the most important 'acid test' of the organisation's commitment to the individual. Lack of promotion prospects is often seen as the factor which most distinguishes 'core' from 'peripheral' workers.

Clearly, many categories of flexible worker may not be interested in promotion. Those most likely to be interested in developing their careers with the organisation are Category A workers such as permanent part-timers, job-sharers and homeworkers. But less obvious candidates may also nurse career aspirations which the organisation is often quick to overlook. Agency workers are often open to offers of full-time employment. Indeed, regular research by Alfred Marks indicates that up to 15 per cent of their clients use agency assignments specifically as a recruitment aid. Freelancers, consultants and contract workers – while often disinterested in permanent employment – may be attracted to an offer of full-time work if the post gives them access to better training and enhances their careers.

In most cases, offers of promotion will entail necessarily a return to full-time employment. In some, it may be possible to promote individuals who wish to continue employment in their existing work pattern.

The most obvious example is job sharing, a concept designed partially to extend part-time working to more responsible and professional areas of work. Job sharing teams have been promoted as a unit in some organisations. At London's Stock Exchange, for example, two sharers performing the role of training officer were promoted jointly to the more senior position of training manager as their role in the department expanded.

A recent study of job sharing, however, found that promoting job-sharers in this fashion was subject to a number of problems.[4] One manager in the study referred to regrading and promotion problems when 'one post holder is believed to be performing better than the other'. The same manager drew attention to an apparent anomaly arising from the fact that in some organisations, employees are able to share more than one post. He described a situation where a section head decided she wanted to job-share. Her subordinate applied for and obtained the other 'half'. He retained half his original job and a third person was appointed to fill the other half. Their manager somewhat ruefully said 'I find it difficult to get my head around that part of the week he is supervisor to the other part of the week'.

Overall, the study found that promoting job-sharers was a complex area. For job sharing to be successful at the workplace, job-sharers have to see promotion as a tangible possibility. In larger organisations the issue of promotion can probably be accommodated so long as more senior posts are available and managers are prepared to take on board the additional personnel and administrative burdens. A highly competent job-sharer ought to be able to gain promotion, as indeed should flexible workers of all types, provided the system of appraisal and training is sufficiently flexible in itself to accommodate individual needs and constraints.

THE MANAGER'S ROLE: CHANGES, TRAINING AND PREPARATION

One aspect of co-ordinating new work patterns is common to all issues discussed in this chapter: they affect the traditional role of the manager as much as the conventional position of the worker.

The abilities required to motivate, monitor, supervise and communicate with workers employed under widely differing working hours, and in various sites or locations, are often very distinct from those needed in the case of on-site permanently employed full-timers.

Particular skills required include any or all of the following:

Project management

In a situation where workers have a greater degree of control over their day-to-day working methods, departmental and individual objectives will often be task-orientated, based around fixed objectives. Managers will therefore need the ability to:

- Define targets and identify objectives
- Build these into a realistic schedule with fixed deadlines
- Balance individual objectives against departmental targets
- Monitor the progress of both through the introduction of staged 'milestones' and effective reporting systems.

Teamworking

A key element of this process is effective teamworking. The characteristics of managing distance workers and distance workers are remarkably similar to those involved in supervising the work of full-time teamworkers. Managers require the ability to:

- Act as the link between the work of individual workers
- Ensure that there is effective and regular communication between them
- Motivate and encourage them, particularly when they are working off-site and lack the energy generated by contact with colleagues or workmates.

Counselling

A manager's traditional role as a counsellor and supporter is strengthened by the introduction of new work patterns. Managers will need to:

- Ensure that workers are happy with new working arrangements and that the design meets their needs as well as those of the organisation
- Act as a vital link to the mainstream of the organisation, ensuring that individual workers do not feel isolated or cut off in a culture still shaped by full-time staff

MANAGEMENT AND DEVELOPMENT 159

- Take into account individual workers' domestic and personal circumstances when assessing performance and productivity – particularly in the case of distance working where the environment in which the work takes place is not the same as in a conventional office or factory.

As we saw at the start of the chapter, the changes new work patterns impose on managers' and supervisors' responsibilities can be threatening, particularly if they lack the necessary preparation. It is therefore important that:

- The changes to the individual workers, the department and the manager are clearly identified and defined
- The issues raised are discussed in detail with supervisors and managers and their support and co-operation obtained *before* the new arrangements are introduced
- Managers and supervisors are properly prepared, if necessary by formal training, to ensure they have the correct skills.

Example: Teleworking at ICL

In 1987 ICL employed 280 teleworkers in its computer programming and product maintenance divisions. The supervisory role in these departments is an essential factor in the scheme's success. Among other things, managers are expected to:

– arrange regular pep-talks and exchanges between the homeworkers in their teams both on a project and a regional basis
– re-brief the programmers when clients fail to provide them with adequate information
– provide individual briefings once a month to set targets for the following weeks and monitor progress on previous projects.

Although these seem, on the face of it, straightforward talks, the particular needs of the homeworkers make the role of the managers far more subtle than might first meet the eye.

Managers have far more discretion over the levels of supervision they impose. A minimum contact of once a week or so is needed to check on whether people are maintaining standards and keeping to schedule. Thereafter, quality, rather than quantity, is their stated aim. Those homeworkers who feel they needed only a little supervision only get a little, while juniors just joining have all they require.

A guiding hand is always available if staff have problems but as homeworkers they are allowed much more autonomy in managing their work than on-site workers.

This approach makes formal reporting systems all the more important. As the general manager of Computer Programming Services, comments, 'You expect people to manage themselves but within a well-defined framework, they have to know what is expected of them and where the boundaries lie'.

SUPERVISION AND DISCIPLINE

The regulation of employees can take various forms, but they must be effective and legally correct. Permanent full-time staff can be disciplined by indirect means, such as withdrawal of bonuses, lack of promotion and the unavailability of training programmes geared to career development. These fall within the scope of managerial discretion. However, the working arrangements of many Category A workers are inappropriate for these measures. Lateness, misconduct and inefficiencies will normally be dealt with by direct means.

Typical problems might be:

- Persistent absenteeism by temporary/casual staff
- Regular friction between and disruption caused by job-sharers
- Abuse of the flexi-hours arrangement by poor reporting and 'stoppage' of hours of work
- Poor time recording and quality of work by homeworkers
- Informal 'swapping' of hours by part-timers.

Some, though by no means all of these problems derive from the higher level of autonomy which the new work pattern gives to employees themselves. Greater responsibility for the management of their own work implies that supervision arises through the quality of work, rather than through more tangible performance indicators, such as time input and involvement in the general workload of a unit, department or shop. Supervisory and disciplinary measures have to be appropriate to counteract these problems.

Responses by management can be divided into procedures and practical measures.

(a) *Procedures*
Examples:
– Oral warnings
– Written warnings
– Entries on personal records
– Loss of promotion.

(b) *Practical* (direct effect on employee)
Examples:
– Suspension on pay
– Suspension without pay
– Re-deployment
– Withholding pay
– Deducting pay
– Deletion from register
– Lock-out
– Removal of occupational benefit
– Relocation.

The ultimate sanction of dismissal will be considered in Chapter 10.

The legal framework

The law will allow an employer wide discretion on the imposition of procedural penalties, so long as they are not imposed in a racially or sexually discriminatory way. There is no reason to think that application to new work patterns should be any different, although due to the frequently short-term engagement the impact of measures on career development is likely to be less dramatic.

Practical measures are subject to legal regulation, primarily through the operation of the employment contract. Most employees are entitled to information regarding the disciplinary rules and procedures affecting them. Disciplinary codes are considered contractually binding, therefore conduct by an employer in breach of them will also involve breach of contract. The courts have recently tightened up on the standards expected of employers and the current position can be expressed as follows:

- The response by the employer has generally to be authorised by contract, or consented to by the employee. Thus, the right to withhold pay, suspend or relocate employees should be specified in the contract or code. The only exceptions will be where there is gross misconduct amounting to repudiation by the employee, or where the courts allow for an 'equitable set-off' to compensate for loss inflicted by them. The fact that the employee is temporary or part-time does not allow greater latitude to the employer
- Deductions or withholding of pay have also to conform to the Wages Act, 1986. This applies to all employees and requires that deductions be authorised by contract, or by consent in writing. Deductions where an employee has contact with the public, such as in catering, the leisure industry, retailing and transport (all areas where Category A workers are prominent) must be limited to 10 per cent of gross pay in any pay period. Deductions can be made for any reason – lateness, rudeness, poor performance, as well as to deal with cash or stock shortages, and, other than the special area of 'public contact' workers, there is no legal demand that deductions be reasonable. Failure to conform to the Act entitles an employee to make a complaint to an industrial tribunal. Deducting pay is clearly an attractive option for employers of short-term and less skilled labour. Although, at the time of writing, experience of the 1986 Act is limited, it would be advisable to ensure that rules regarding deductions are specific, unambiguous, effectively communicated to employees, especially new ones, and fairly and rigorously enforced
- Disciplinary procedures must be adhered to and operated fairly. Most disciplinary codes allow employees opportunities to explain, appeal against and be represented before disciplinary measures, especially serious ones, are imposed. The absence of codes does not mean that employers can behave as they wish–the law will imply reasonable procedures. The Court of Appeal in *Dietmann* v. *Brent London Borough*

Council[5] (the summary dismissal of a social worker following an inquiry into the Jasmine Beckford child abuse case) has confirmed the need for disciplinary procedures to be fair and fairly administered, regardless of the alleged seriousness of the 'offence'. The case of *Polkey* v. *A. E. Dayton Services*[6] has confirmed that only in extreme cases will an employee be allowed to argue that use of procedures would have made no difference to the disciplinary outcome. A temporary waiter accused of theft or shortchanging, a homeworker accused of making a secret profit on materials, or a job-sharer thought to be undermining the position of their partner, are entitled to use procedures however 'open and shut' the employer considers the allegation.

The implications are that managers should examine whether disciplinary rules are appropriate to *all* types of employees and whether procedures need adjustment. Is it clear, for example, who is responsible for the discipline of homebased workers? Who do they appeal to? Is the appeal committee or panel accessible and appropriately composed so as to deal with disputes? Are the rules adequately explained to all employees? Are there aspects which are esoteric and so 'firm specific' that casual and off-site workers might not understand them?

Has responsibility for discipline been accorded to the most appropriate manager? If responsibility for part-time and temporary staff is given to a line manager, is there adequate monitoring of the manager's record and performance. Is there, for example, a 'hire and fire' or cash withholding mentality which might repeat badly on the reputation of the enterprise?

Overall, it must be remembered that Category A workers are entitled to the same basic legal protections as 'core' workers. The fact that traditionally casual, temporary, part-time and homeworkers have often been treated in a somewhat cavalier manner by some employers should not allow for complacency. As new work patterns become more regularised and recognised, greater care will have to be taken over disciplinary rules and their application. This is especially so in one area where courts and tribunals are becoming more demanding on all employers.

The legal framework relating to Category B and C workers

Self-employed workers and consultants are clearly not covered by the same legal framework as employees. However, they are often integrated into the workforce and their conduct and work performance have influences at the workplace. The central dilemma regarding these workers is exemplified by the problems of discipline and control. Too much control and the law might view the workers as employees 'in reality'. Too little, and the quality of work will be adversely affected.

Discipline will have to be imposed through effective monitoring, in a context of clear explanation of the expectation and ethos of the enterprise. An effectively negotiated contract will have identified not only likely problem areas but also dispute mechanisms. Problems should not be allowed to 'fester'. However, the law does allow for the imposition of penalties, providing they have been properly negotiated. Sums of money can be deducted, and this in the form of liquidated damages. This may have been negotiated for consultant contracts, but is not likely regarding casual workers. More usually, the contract is simply terminated if performance is unsatisfactory. It is more effective (or it will avoid disputes) if the contract specifies a dispute resolution mechanism, including arbitration.

It must be remembered though that if a contract is ended, the 'dismissed' worker may have a claim for breach of contract. This is *not* an easy or well-developed area of law. Unfortunately, many self-employed contracts end in acrimony, with feelings of resentment and dissatisfaction on both sides. Only rarely do the parties resort to law and so the end of the relationships is characterised by loss of goodwill and/or resentment rather than the litigation in law courts or tribunals involving employees.

Category C workers, especially agency, seconded and sub-contracted workers, frequently carry out their duties on the employer's premises alongside the host workforce. Supervision and discipline should have been anticipated by the contract so as to ensure consistency and effective communication. It is essential to ensure that complaints about the performance of Category C workers are communicated in the agreed manner. Usually this will entitle the employer to call for the withdrawal of the worker(s) in question. At an extreme level the employer can lawfully claim that the contract has been broken through the conduct of workers and it can be ended.

This is a sensitive area. The contract should have:

- Specified managerial and supervisory responsibility
- Allowed for regular monitoring by the host enterprise
- Dealt with breaches of discipline by Category C workers. Category C employers should apply their disciplinary procedures which are responsive to the fact that the workers are working for another employer. It should not be possible for the Category C employers to 'wash their hands' if their employee commits an act of indiscipline.

Research indicates that many employers have devised effective supervisory procedures for both Category B and C workers. They vary considerably depending on the nature of work. The recognised need is to anticipate problems and plan for them.

SUMMARY POINTS

- Radical changes to when and where staff work pose a number of important issues surrounding day-to-day communication and control. In particular:
  - how and when they are briefed and allocated work

- o how they will liaise and communicate with colleagues inside the organisation
- o how decisions taken by staff working new patterns will affect other people's work
- o how they will liaise and communicate with people outside the organisation (customers, clients, suppliers, etc)
- o how their work will be monitored and assessed
- o how office space and facilities will be allocated
- Organisations should ensure that routine work systems take these issues into account and are properly designed to ensure the effective day-to-day management of the work unit. The implications of the arrangement on the work of other employees in the unit, supervisors and line managers, and their attitudes to the 'new' workers, should also be carefully considered
- A key factor in the success of management systems is the extent to which atypical workers are, and perceive themselves to be, properly integrated into the organisation. This also applies to opportunities for atypical workers to develop their careers in the organisation. Category A workers, and in certain circumstances Category B and C workers, should therefore be given access to:
  - o opportunities for promotion
  - o tailored performance and career appraisal
  - o training provision which enables them to perform their present responsibilities effectively and develop their careers in the organisation.

References

1 Epstein, J., 'A more demanding scale', *Manpower Policy and Practice*, Vol. 4, Summer 1986.
2 Hirsh, W., Hutt, R. and Atkinson, J., *Women, Career Breaks and Re-entry*, Institute of Manpower Studies Report No. 105, 1985.
3 Kinsman, F., *The TeleCommuters*, John Wiley and Sons, 1987.
4 Leighton, P. and Winfield, M. *Does Job Sharing Work?* The Industrial Society, 1988.
5 *Dietmann* v. *Brent LBC* [1987] 1 CR 737.
6 *Polkey* v. *A E Dayton Services Ltd* [1987] IRLR 503.

Chapter 7
Pay and benefits

In Chapter 1 we discussed the fact that the new workforce has evolved for a variety of reasons, some of which have led to traditional work patterns, such as homeworking, freelancing and sub-contracting, being revamped or used more extensively. Methods and rates of pay have often also evolved on traditional lines. For some workers, this has meant insecurity of income and low pay. Sometimes it has been explained in terms of the autonomy and entrepreneurism of some workers. In others it was simply a reflection of perceived lack of commitment. Part-timers and casual staff have been generally worse-off even when highly skilled.

Changes in work patterns and demographic foresight have played a greater emphasis on the retention of key staff (see Chapter 1) and some traditional attitudes have been challenged. There may need to be a major overhaul of presumption and practices (see Chapter 2). If pay levels and occupational benefits are sacrificed to a greater or lesser extent, it may not be effective to offer a previous full-timer the opportunity to work part-time or to have a short-term contract, or be based at home after maternity leave. Similarly, one of the major reservations job-sharers have about the work pattern is that they are frequently unable to move up salary/incremental scales or are jointly placed at a point in the scale of the 'lowest' sharer.[1]

Access to training and promotion is therefore a key related issue. Similar comments are voiced by temporary and fixed-term staff. However, perhaps their main concern is that they do not have the same access as core staff to occupational benefits. Benefits such as occupational pensions, enhanced sick pay and profit-sharing schemes have traditionally been dependent on significant periods of service and full-time work. The treatment of many non-core workers regarding occupational benefits often reflects long-standing attitudes to them. This vital area of management policy should be subject to reappraisal. The introduction of some work patterns, especially job sharing, networking, and secondments, has been accompanied by a conscious evaluation of the pay and benefits package. This has not occurred in other types of work.

When such an exercise does take place, it will be essential to link matters of pay and benefits to:

- The nature and form of the contractual arrangement and its documentation (see Chapter 5)
- The management, appraisal and promotion and training facilities of the individual worker (see Chapter 6)
- Discussions on any sabbaticals, career break, 'keep in touch' or retainer policies applicable to non-work periods.

TOPICS FOR CONSIDERATION

Earnings can be divided into two categories:

(a) *Work or performance related benefits*
Wages/salaries   Performance
including increments   related pay:
and grading   1 of worker
                             2 of enterprise

(b) *Non-work/performance related benefits*
Subsidies, benefits   Occupational
in kind, 'fringe'   welfare payments
benefits

Some of these areas are regulated or reinforced by law, such as occupational sick pay, pensions and maternity provision. They have also an established place in most management policies and practices. Additionally, many topics have been subject to recent and major statutory reform, such as the form of payment (cash, cheques, etc.), security of earnings, and occupational pensions. More and more employers in the public as well as private sector have sought new ways to recruit, retain and motivate workers, as well as to improve efficiency and output. Initiatives such as share option schemes have excited interest and publicity.

The sections below focus on Category A workers, such as part-time, temporary, and homeworking staff. Category B workers will not receive much attention because their 'fee' will have been negotiated and occupational benefits will not generally be provided, as to do so might suggest employee status (see Chapter 4). Consultants, freelance workers, many casual workers, and some homeworkers, will therefore fall outside most of the discussion in this chapter, as will Category C workers. They are the responsibility of their own employer.

THE APPROACH AND DEMANDS OF LAW

Law and practice in this area can be divided into two broad categories:

- Where there are special provisions for particular work patterns
- Where the workforce can be treated similarly.

PAY AND BENEFITS 167

SPECIAL PROVISIONS

Pay

Since 1975, employers have been required to provide details of pay and deductions. The statutory provisions set out in S.8 EPCA are specific and are enforceable.

Part-timers (up to sixteen hours per week) and many temporary workers are not covered by this provision. It is difficult to see the reason behind the law's exclusion. Most employers provide some information. They recognise that temporary staff, for example, have a particular need for information, because they may not have time to become familiar with the practices of an organisation, ignorance and anxiety breeding resentment and alienation.[2]

Pay in non-work periods

This is a crucial area. Flexibility often implies employing workers only when you have numerical or functional needs. It also implies that employers do not want to pay wages when work is not available. Any legal rules which impose major obligations upon employers might be resisted as a result.

An employer is theoretically liable to pay the agreed wages even when work is not available, if the employee remains 'ready and willing to work'. Unless an employer makes clear to casual or temporary workers that their relationship is based on 'no work – no pay', wages would continue to be due.

Courts and tribunals have not taken this legal rule too literally; they are often willing to interpret casual work as not requiring the employer to keep on paying. That said, it is best to clarify the situation, preferably in writing, especially for 'regular' casual staff. The problem of pay does not arise where there is no continuing contact during non-work periods.

Example
In the Hull fishing industry, the trawler companies traditionally paid wages for the period at sea, but the men drew unemployment benefit when on shore. Many fishermen were long-standing 'company men' with up to thirty years service with one organisation. The rapid decline in the industry had left only a handful of ships sailing out of Hull by 1982. Men not taken on again when fishing ended claimed a redundancy payment, arguing that over the years they had established a 'global' contract of employment with their employers, regardless of the intermittent nature of the work. They lost. The Court of Appeal decided that they had had a series of short-term engagements, which ended everytime the ship arrived in port.[3]

For wages to remain payable for periods when work is not available or performed, the following must exist:

- The workers must be employees
- They must have a continuing or 'global' contractual relationship linking work with workless periods

- The legal obligation to pay wages during workless periods has not been rebutted by contract.

Statutory guaranteed pay

Provisions regarding payment for employees during workless days are contained in SS. 12–18 EPCA. They require employers to pay a prescribed sum of money to cover workless days (i.e. days when you were *contractually* bound to work), unless the employee has unreasonably refused alternative available work, or 'worklessness' has been caused by an industrial dispute at the workplace. The statutory demands are not onerous – £13.20 per day for up to five days in a three month period – though they do give rise to over a thousand complaints to ACAS each year.

Example
B had been recently engaged by RHM Ltd, a small East Anglian manufacturing company. The factory closed for five days over Christmas. It was accepted that it was a term of B's contract that there would be no work over the holiday period. They were not 'workless' days, therefore he received no benefit.

Protections are only provided for certain staff. The following are excluded from the law:

- Part-timers (up to sixteen hours per week)
- Those who have not worked continuously for four weeks before the 'workless' day
- Employees on fixed-term contracts of twelve weeks or less
- Employees engaged for a 'specific task' to be completed in twelve weeks or less.

Thus, law makes relatively few inroads in the area. But with more and more evidence of labour shortages, attention may have to be given to devices to attract and retain temporary staff. In some cases, this will mean considerable attention will have to be given to the periods 'between' work. Decisions will therefore be based not so much on legal demands but on expediency.

Pay during sickness or injury

This is a complex area, especially regarding the application of the Statutory Sick Pay Scheme (SSP). Although SSP is not strictly within the managerial ambit of employers and the key decisions are made by the DHSS, there is generally an interplay between SSP, occupational sick pay (OSP) and the basic contractual position. The detailed workings of SSP are beyond the scope of this book but it must be noted that the structures and application of the scheme leave many workers with no state sick pay during illness. For example, the scheme excludes workers on fixed-term contracts of three months or less. The requirement that an employee has four or more consecutive workless days due to incapacity before qualifying for benefit also leaves many part-time and temporary staff facing delays before claiming. Does an employer have to continue to pay all or part of pay during illness? Until recently it was thought that he did unless the contract expressly rebutted it. It appears that the obligation to pay during illness will be implied by law. Case law is lacking on the point but it seems less likely to be 'reasonable' to imply an obligation to pay casual and temporary staff than, say, job-sharers. Few contracts are silent on the matter. It is therefore an area which can be easily dealt with.

Occupational sick pay: current practices

Payment of all or a part of salary during illness has been a growing practice. The most effective provision is concentrated on traditional employees. Only carefully negotiated work patterns such as networking and job sharing provide comparable safeguards. There is a clear gradation in entitlement, with temporary and casual staff at the bottom of the pile (see Chapter 1).

Table 7.1 Employees receiving OSP

Type of employee	% receiving OSP
Full-time permanent	94
Part-time	78
Temporary	48*

* Estimate   (*Source:* Department of Employment (1989) *Research Paper* 63)

The proportion of part-time employee receiving OSP is fairly high, though it is concentrated on 'regular' part-time staff in white-collar and public sector employment. Temporary staff who receive OSP tend to be employees on fixed-term contracts, generally in white-collar occupations. Research shows considerable variety in practices by employers, with length of service proving a key factor.

Examples: provision of OSP for some work patterns[4]
– *Rowntree Mackintosh provide OSP for all process workers from the day they begin.*
– *Selfridge plc, the London store, provides the same scale of benefit for part-timers as full-timers.*
– *Midland Bank plc employs job-share and hourly paid part-time staff. Some of the hourly paid are recruited locally on temporary contracts. Their terms of work are determined by the individual branch manager, although the part-timers are treated exactly as full-timers for OSP purposes. Temporary hourly paid do not receive OSP.*
– *Ford (UK) Ltd: OSP is available depending on length of service, including part-timers. For example:*
  up to 3 months' service: 3 months basic salary and 9 months ½ salary
  *   6 months' service: 6 months basic salary and 6 months ½ salary*
  after 12 months' service: 12 months at basic salary.
– *Access: all full and part-time staff eligible but with variations,*
  up to 3 years' service   : 2 months full pay
  *   5–15 years' service: 6 months full pay*
  over 20 years'   : 12 months full pay.

– British Airways: OSP is only payable after 13 weeks service, though the airline does not differentiate between full and part-time workers.

These examples illustrate that in some areas of employment part-timers qualify, but temporary staff are worse off.

Should OSP be provided?

In terms of total labour costs, the provisions of sick pay is a minor element (1.2 per cent of total labour costs in production industries). Experience indicates that it is the area of work, rather than status of worker, which is the prime motivating factor to pay or not during sickness and incapacity. For example, voluntary social welfare payments, occupational pensions, sick pay, marriage gratuities and the like, account for approximately 15 per cent of wage costs in the finance sector of employment, but only 4.3 per cent in the distributive trades. However, over 35 per cent of employees in the latter group are part-time, but only 8 per cent in the finance area.

Temporary staff are the least likely to receive OSP. Many temporary staff are perceived as less committed and less motivated than permanent staff. Anything which encourages their absenteeism is seen by some employees as worsening the situation. Indeed, many employers accept that absenteeism is inevitable, see it as a 'right' to have the option to work or not. These include regular employers of large numbers of casual and seasonal staff, especially in catering and leisure industries, who see absenteeism as a useful indicator of a welcome lack of commitment on the part of both sides of the employment relationship relieving them of the obligation to provide benefits.

Key questions:

- Are you operating in an area of employment where there are strong expectations that OSP is paid?
- Are there industrial relations and/or equal opportunities issues which indicate that OSP should be available to workers?
- Is there, or should there be, a policy which aims to cement employment relations between the organisation and staff?
- Are there employment needs which suggest that unless there is an attractive employment package workers will not be recruitable?
- Will provision of OSP help or hinder any problems with absenteeism?
- Is your provision of OSP in any way discriminatory? (It must be noted that the 1988 Social Security Act will require employers not to differentiate in arrangements for OSP between men and women.

Many of these questions require that attention be paid to data on areas such as recruitment, commitment/motivation of workers, and absenteeism.

A review of current practice, may lead to a new policy which differentiates between various categories of workers. Job-sharers and home-workers may well be receiving OSP but in part because they have tended to be previous full-timers, or have contracts derived from carefully negotiated policies.

Should the policy be extended to fixed-term and temporary staff, if currently excluded? Given that providing sick pay is not likely to be a major expense, apart from administrative costs, the key questions turn on what it symbolises, and whether providing payments during illness or incapacity will aid other employment policies at the workplace. It connotes mutual commitment which some will want to encourage more than others.

Pregnancy, childbirth and entitlements to pay

Given that women figure prominently in the new workforce, maternity pay, as well as job security through pregnancy and childbirth, are important issues. As with SSP there is a statutory scheme which is both complex and geared to the needs of 'core' workers. There has to be a period of at least twenty-six weeks continuous employment before maternity leave, at a rate of pay at least as high as the minimum of National Insurance contributions. Effectively, therefore, many casual, temporary and/or part-time employees are excluded from the basic scheme.

Higher rate SMP is payable by employers (though, as with SSP recouped from the employer's NI contributions) to employees who have been continuously employed for two years or more and who work at least sixteen (eight) hours per week. It is nine-tenths of normal weekly earnings for six weeks. There are complicated rules to determine normal weekly earnings when they are irregular or fluctuating, though they are fairly receptive to the needs of the employees covered.

Many workers lose out more heavily in the provision of occupational maternity pay to 'top up' statutory provision. Not all employers provide such a benefit. Amongst those who do, the practice is variable both as to amounts of cash and periods for which it is paid. Temporary or fixed-term employees only receive this benefit in exceptional circumstances.

Part-time workers sometimes qualify. Many job-share schemes have made a particular feature of safeguarding maternity benefits. A study of fifty-one maternity agreements in the public and private sector in 1984 found that twenty-eight placed no additional service requirements on part-timers than full-timers.[5]

Examples
– *Enterprise A (a private sector professional organisation) undertakes 'that ... part-time female employees will qualify for ... maternity pay ... if they have been employed for at least one year'.*
– *Enterprise B (an urban local authority) provides that maternity leave and pay 'shall be made on a proportional basis according to the number of hours worked'.*
– *Enterprise C (education establishment) will provide maternity pay 'if part-timers work an equivalent of one year's full-time service'.*
– *Enterprise D (a public utility in the private sector) requires sixteen hours per week part-time employment to qualify.*

Current practice indicates that job-sharers and homeworkers will be covered so long as they conform to the appropriate formulae.

Should an employer provide occupational maternity pay?

A decision to extend maternity pay to part-time staff may depend on various factors. For example:

- Commitment to equal opportunities policies
- Maternity rights issues in collective bargaining
- Issues of labour turnover, skill retention and recruitment difficulty
- Relative cost.

At the very least, it would be well to consider or reconsider the basis upon which a maternity scheme has been developed. Specifically, should the number of weekly hours, length of service, level and nature of the job be the key factors for entitlement and extent of benefit? Would the cost of extending maternity pay to all female employees be significant, especially if linked in with contractual and personnel arrangements for returners to employment after childbirth? Perhaps the appropriate question might be, 'Are there valid reasons for denying maternity pay' rather than 'ought we to extend the benefit to flexible workers?' It may be worthwhile to check the 'return' rates after maternity leave between full-time and part-time or other atypical workers. There is nothing to stop an employer making return to work a condition of receiving a generous benefit so long as the scheme were not 'unreasonable'. The analogy here would be relocation packages, which contain 'claw-back' terms. It is necessary also to conform to the provisions of the Wages Act, 1986.

Occupational pensions

Recent changes in the law open up a whole new range of possibilities for both employers and employees. Occupational pension schemes are now accepted as 'deferred pay' – pension benefits should be both contractually funded and actually paid out. Particular problems surround this concept. There is not necessarily a clear relationship between amount of contribution and amount of benefit. Most schemes base entitlement on salary or wage at time of retirement, which may be lower than at other periods.

Illustrative problems:

- A highly paid employee with regular contributions, who job-shares, i.e. earns half pay at time of retirement.
- A female employee who has participated in a career break scheme which interrupts the contribution period or prevents minimum years service for full pension benefit
- A worker who, after fifteen years service in the public sector finds his area of work sub-contracted, moves to work for a private sector employer which does not operate a pension scheme
- Temporary staff who are unable to join an occupational scheme until the completion of five years continuous service.

Atypical workers have traditionally been faced with highly inflexible pensions, designed not only for core workers but for long-serving employees whose earnings peak at time of retirement. Schemes are often highly complex, making their application to workers with intermittent or fluctuating work almost impossible. Pension schemes have often been drawn up according to type and area of employment rather than the needs of individual workers.

Occupational pensions are by far the most expensive benefit for employers. It is likely to be seriously debated when an organisation is considering moves to more flexible and varied work patterns. Increasingly, trade unions are giving occupational pensions a higher priority in negotiations. The European Community and organisations concerned to promote equal opportunities at work, as well as a growing body of case law, have all given recent attention to occupational pensions, especially for new standard employees.

The current situation

Approximately half the workforce is covered by occupational schemes. Of those not covered, 7.5 million work in areas where schemes exist but they are ineligible to join. Many schemes exclude part-timers. A study by APEX showed only nine out of a sample of fifty-one schemes in engineering extended to part-timers; 57 per cent of the schemes in food and drink excluded part-timers. The electricity supply industry requires twenty hours a week to enter, the AA sixteen, and Imperial Tobacco at least 30 per cent of the normal working week. Studies by IMS and IDS show that temporary and casual staff, even those on high grade fixed-term contracts are almost invariably excluded, with some notable exceptions in the public sector.

The two basic and interrelated issues are:

1 Whether an enterprise should enter or develop occupational pension facilities to more staff? If only some are to gain access, what criteria should be used to differentiate them?
2 What options are there to accommodate the needs of mobile, fluctuating or intermittent workers? Are there schemes being developed more appropriate to the needs of the new workforce?

It is necessary to consider both the new statutory framework dealing with pensions themselves, and the anti-discrimination measures referred to previously (see Chapter 1).

The new pension law

The relevant provisions are contained in the Social Security Act, 1986 and the second 1987 Finance Act. Their major intention has been to make occupational, especially personal pensions, more attractive and popular, and thereby to reduce dependence on SERPS. This will be achieved by reducing SERPS pension entitlements and, most significantly, by removing the 'best twenty years' rule which overcame the problem of career breaks and periods of lower earning perhaps due to moving at particular stages to part-time or casual work.

The law aims to encourage contracted out personal pensions in a situation where it is no longer lawful to require occupational scheme membership by employees. In 1987, 84 per cent of pension schemes were compulsory. Now employers are not able to demand that employees take out personal pensions either. Therefore, there is greater choice on an individual basis, including the continuing option of joining SERPS. At the same time, employees can opt out of SERPS, not only by joining a defined occupational scheme but on a personal pension, basis. Alternatively, workers can make no provision at all.

Another option open to employees, especially atypical workers, will be to remain in an occupational scheme but to make Additional Voluntary Contributions (AVCs) either to the main scheme or, more likely, to a free-standing scheme. Employers have to inform employees of these possibilities.

Implications for the new workforce

Casual, temporary and intermittent workers will probably find the best option (if any) to be the 'portable pension'. It is probable that occupational schemes would never have become appropriate to these types of workers who have more affinity with the self-employed. The position regarding part-time staff, job-sharers and homeworkers, is less clear cut. Many job-sharers and average part-timers may still want to remain in or gain access to occupational schemes, especially in the public sector where there is a measure of inter-changeability. Pressure will come from such workers to 'hedge their bets', by joining an occupational scheme in a low level way but also make AVC's to a free-standing scheme. The general response of trade unions is unclear. Many, for example NALGO and MSF, had made considerable efforts to gain access for groups of non-core workers to many occupational schemes.

This is a very problematic and unpredictable area. Logically, the outcome of the new legislation will be to ease many problems of employers regarding atypical workers, and give the workers themselves better opportunities. Logically, also, employers will want to retain occupational schemes for their traditional workforce. Whether employees will see matters in the same way is questionable. There is the possibility that the 'opting out' provision will leave many traditional schemes devoid of cash and members.

High pressure selling and their attractiveness to younger workers will probably make private pensions a viable option – particularly for workers who anticipate job mobility, or periods working as an employee interspersed with periods of self-employment or non-employment. From an employer's perspective, access and encouragement to workers to join their occupational scheme may well depend on the following factors:

- The viability of the scheme itself, given the balance of the workforce between core and non-core workers, and possible opting out by core staff
- An analysis of 'the track record' of workers to determine their likely continuity of employment with the employer. This may lead to different categories of workers being treated differently
- The need to clarify the criteria which suggest opportunities for membership of the scheme
- The need to explore whether the occupational scheme could be more flexible and effective.

Anti-discrimination law and occupational benefits

In Chapter 1, we set out some of the wider issues and trends concerning anti-discrimination law, especially the role of the European Community and the impact of decisions of the European Court of Justice. These developments have relevance not only for basic pay and benefits (because they include the equal pay provisions), but also for a wide range of other occupational issues.

It has long been established that pension rights, as opposed to matters concerned with age of retirement, form part of the working package which must not discriminate between men and women or between various ethnic groups.

It was established in *Worringham* v. *Lloyds Bank* in 1981[6] that a pension scheme which applied different conditions to men and women and (thus affected their earnings) contravened Article 119 of the Treaty of Rome, which requires equal pay for equal work. A scheme which applies different age limits for entry, different contribution periods and different benefits, amounts to direct discrimination.

Article 119 is enforceable through UK courts. However, it does not deal with the issue of greater relevance to many workers – that of entry to schemes themselves. The situation is most starkly presented in relation to part-time workers, especially those with long service. This issue was considered in the West German case of *Bilka-Kaufhaus GmbH* v. *Weber von Hartz* [1986].[7] The complainant was a part-time employee in a department store, which operated an occupational scheme for full-time employees. It was possible to join the scheme as a part-timer but only after a very long period of service. As virtually all the part-timers were female, the operation of the scheme was held to be discriminatory under Article 119.

Even if a scheme is indirectly discriminatory, it is possible that employers will nonetheless be able to provide justification for the way they operate it – for example, if the labour turnover rate of part-timers is very high, if the administrative costs of providing access are a burden, or studies had shown disinterest in the scheme. In the UK, the availability of personal pensions or schemes more receptive to the needs of various groups of workers may make the 'defence' more plausible, especially if employers provide their own research findings.

Of great significance is the Social Security Bill 1988 which implements Article 86/378 of the European Community. This will require equal treatment between men and women regardless of occupational pension arrangements. It will probably be effective in 1990. The non-discriminatory demands also apply to redundancy and retirement arrangements.

AREAS WHERE THE WORKFORCE CAN BE TREATED SIMILARLY

The Wages Act, 1986

This legislation, deals with the form in which payment is made and security of earnings. It applies to all employees, and to some self-employed workers. Since January 1987, it has been possible for employees to be paid in various manners, including cash and cheques. Any change must be agreed to by employees. The question which arises is should all workers be treated alike? More generally, should there be a move towards cashless pay for all? Traditionally, many part-time, casual and homebased staff have been paid in cash. The Wages Act now allows for reconsideration of practice in this area, and for harmonisation of personnel policies. Any contemplated change must be negotiated and agreed (see Chapter 4).

Security of earnings

Section 1 allows deductions from pay for any reason, be it for provision of an occupational benefit or for indiscipline, providing authority is provided by the employment contract or consent is given in writing. Note: notices and memos are inadequate. Many workers are employed on a seasonal or casual basis in areas such as retailing, catering and the leisure and travel industry, where they have contact with the public. The Act limits maximum deductions for such workers to 10 per cent of gross earnings in any pay period. Breaches of this law leads to complaints to industrial tribunals, the only means of enforcement. There are no other restrictions on employers. For example, there is no requirement that deductions be reasonable. Where deductions are made due to industrial action, they can be made on an equitable basis regardless of the statute. There is no reason, in principle, why workers in all work patterns cannot be partially disciplined through their wage packets providing the correct procedures are followed.

Care should be taken about 'deductions', as it can be interpreted as a failure to pay 100% of the wage. Many temporary staff suffer delays in payment – this now gives them a right to claim. Withholding fringe benefits, pay in lieu of notice, holiday pay and travel expenses are all covered by the Act, providing the sum was 'properly due'.

Work/performance related payments

The basic contractual rate

Traditional pay practices have applied to particular occupations or workers. For example:

- Homeworkers are often on piecework, consultants are paid a 'fee' or a lump sum, casual workers are sometimes paid for a task/product or receive 'cash in hand'
- Part-timers are generally hourly paid, freelance workers are paid for 'a session', a day, or according to output.

Workers involved in 'new' work patterns, for example, teleworkers, job-sharers and consultants, have challenged long established customs. They have sought to be treated as 'core' workers receiving comparable treatment or negotiating more advantageous conditions. Clearly, workers are not a heterogeneous group when it comes to pay, but often payment systems operate as a clear barrier to 'core' status or more formal recognition.

Broadly speaking, atypical workers receive less than core workers. The discrepancy is particularly marked when the full benefits package is taken into account. Yet not all workers experience lower basic pay than their 'core' counterparts. Indeed some of the workers involved in newer patterns, especially in rapidly developing sectors of employment (such as networkers, consultants and agency staff) often have higher rates of pay than their full-time equivalents. Freelance computer programmers expect to earn at least 30 per cent more on basic wages than in-house staff, agency 'temps' often have higher hourly pay, especially in medicine and specialist secretarial areas. Even some homeworkers involved in processing and manufacturing (especially in wages councils industries), can earn higher rates than factory based workers. This is particularly so when the homeworker is skilled and efficient, given that they are usually paid on piece rates.

Examples

1 *Rowntree Mackintosh (UK) Process workers, confectionery division.* Part-time work either fifteen or seventeen hours a week and received pro rata pay, many on 'twilight shifts'. They do not (unlike full-time staff) receive shift premiums for twilight shifts, though they do qualify for overtime at time and a half. Full-timers only receive the fixed weekly shift premiums for double day work, three shift working and for nights.
2 *Cheltenham and Gloucester Building Society Branch staff.* About 39 per cent of staff are part-time, working between fifteen and twenty hours per week. The same hourly rate is paid as to full-timers, though part-timers are concentrated in clerical grade 2, with some experienced part-timers being on grade 3. Full-timers are recruited to grade 3 regardless of previous experience. Only rarely do part-timers get asked to do overtime.[8]

Employers rarely state that lower wage costs are a major reason for employing atypical staff. They confirm that the main savings are on occupational benefits, especially in the case of temporary workers. Why do part-timers have lower overall earnings? The following factors provide some explanation:

- The high representation of women as part-time workers
- The concentration of part-timers in manual work, especially in service occupations, and 'women only' work
- Less participation in overtime
- The high proportion placed on basic rates
- Lack of opportunity to earn bonuses, receive incentive payments, etc.
- Relative lack of opportunities to train, especially on an enterprise specific basis
- The relatively few opportunities for promotion
- That almost 50 per cent who return after a break return to a lower paid post than they left.

Some of these factors are endemic to areas of work and occupations and give managers little room for manoeuvre. Many part-timers work in occupations such as cleaning, retailing and domestic work where pay is very low or is subject to wages councils' orders. Personnel policies therefore, have a lesser role to play. However, personnel policies can have a major impact in other areas, and can continue to restrain earnings.

Examples

1 A was a full-time primary teacher in an education authority located in eastern England. After maternity leave, she sought to return on a job-share basis, and this was agreed to by her employers. Her job-share partner, also a previous full-timer, had been on Scale 1, whereas A was on Scale 3, and thus paid at a higher rate. The LEA would only agree to the job-share if both were paid at Scale 1.

2 A large public sector employer with severe recruitment problems recently introduced new salary scales for staff employees and an incentive scheme, performance related. It was anticipated that this could add at least 10 per cent to basic pay. The scheme excluded both part-time and fixed contract employees.

3 A large building society with about 22 per cent of its workforce part-time and over 700 'casual' staff 'on its books' who could be called in when needed, introduced a major pay restructuring in 1985. Hours of full-timers were cut from 36¼ to 35 a week but part-time wages on an hourly rate remained at 1/36¼, though the minimum hourly rate was raised to that of the lowest clerical grade, part-timers (but not casual staff who are on a fixed hourly rate) are able to obtain merit payments and overtime premiums. From 1987, part-timers have participated in the profit sharing scheme.

The decision in Example 1 may be explicable in terms of preventing job-share arrangements leading to 'unwarranted' promotion, had they put both sharers on Scale 3. There was the option of leaving them on the different scales of 0·5 but this was not considered. The other two examples highlight the unwillingness of some employers to see the increasing contribution which some workers can provide. It is as if they had 'peaked' or have a finite work span, or have such a limited commitment to the enterprise that they do not permit higher earnings. Much depends on the attitude of individual managements but practices vary widely. Example 3 demonstrates that the position of part-timers in restructuring can attract detailed attention. Although they suffered a relative decline in terms of basic earnings, they were provided with a wide range of options for extra cash. Again, the temporary, even fixed-term worker was excluded.

Employers have often put considerable effort into revising pay and benefits in the case of new work patterns such as job sharing, consultancies, agency work, teleworking, annual hours contracts committed hours contracts. Other traditional types of work, such as casual, seasonal and part-time, have been less often reviewed unless prompted by trade unions or law. Can the relatively weak position of temporary staff (even if highly qualified personnel) be explained by tradition, cost, administrative burden, or by their own perceived lack of commitment? It is worth reviewing and could reduce unnecessary turnover and increase output.

The role of law: equal pay legislation

The notable exception to a lack of legal pay regulations is the equal pay legislation in the UK and the relevant provisions of the Treaty of Rome. This requires that where 'like work' has been 'rated as equivalent' or is of 'equal value' to that of a comparative worker of the opposite gender, the worker must be paid the same pay. Until the 'equal value' aspect was opened up in 1983, women could only make complaints when there was a man with which to compare themselves in the same employment and the same area of work.

A number of basic points:

- The legislation applies both to employees, and those who 'personally execute work' on a self-employed basis. Casual workers, homeworkers, consultants and freelance staff, though self-employed, are covered by the law
- The legislation covers other terms of work, such as occupational benefits, hours of work, and the application of disciplinary rules
- Decisions of the ECJ (European Court of Justice) and UK courts have widened the impact of our equal pay legislation. This trend is likely to continue
- The law has encouraged challenges to many collective agreements which have perpetuated 'unequal' pay.

The most significant aspect of equal pay legislation, is its 'equal value' provision which allow for claims to be made by women usually when they are employed on different kinds of work from men. This has prompted a major re-think on salary/wage scales and the abandonment of the lowest (female dominated) pay grades.

Examples
- In local government pay scales the bottom two grades were abolished in 1982.
- The NHS is in the process of abandoning a hierarchical structure in favour of pay scales based on an equal value approach. Hence, dining-room supervisors and deputy head porters would be on the same scale, as would domestics and porters.
- At Frayling Furniture, female sewing machinists achieved parity with male upholsterers in 1986.
- A Northern Ireland manufacturing company agreed in 1986 to abolish a differential between women sewing machinists and paint sprayers.
- Claims were made by secretarial staff at the Midland Bank for parity with bank messengers, who were paid £200 per annum more than the secretaries. Following the claim the Bank undertook a major re-assessment of job evaluation aimed to iron out these possible anomalies. The assessment was undertaken with full involvement of unions, it took advice from the Trade Union Research Unit at Ruskin College, and after a 'pilot' job evaluation of 600 benchmark posts using the Hay evaluation system, was extended to the full 35 000 workforce and a new grading scheme introduced in June 1987.

Virtually none of the reports of exercises have made explicit reference to part-timers, casual staff and other similar groups of workers. However, when pay is based on hourly rates, any regrading will inevitably be advantageous to part-timers. The abolition of basic grades will also usually help temporary staff.

Equal pay and the new workforce

Implementing this legislation has been complicated by the attitude of courts to the different contributions by atypical workers than core staff. Most of the case law has focused on core staff. However, the law does allow for differential payments to be made where there is a 'genuine material difference' between the situation of a man and a woman where jobs are broadly similar or have been evaluated as the same, because of a 'genuine material factor' when jobs are of equal value.

How does this leave women part-timers, homeworkers and other groups? An early decision on the legislation – *Jenkins* v. *Kingsgate Clothing*[9] found that paying hourly-paid part-timers less than hourly-paid full-timers was unlawful. However, it did leave open the possibility of management providing evidence that matters such as overheads, administrative costs or uneconomic use of equipment justified pay differentials. With more and more evidence of higher productivity pro rata by part-timers than full-timers this may be an increasingly difficult argument to sustain.

The legislation concentrates overwhelmingly on the job itself rather than the way it is performed. As a result, it does not effectively challenge underlying assumptions about various work patterns. For example, pay scales generally reflect length of service and, of course, promotion and/or recognition of experience and skill. Temporary, casual and part-time staff often remain on lowest grades, with only freelance and highly paid staff able to effectively negotiate higher pay levels than full-timers. The legislation has not really tackled these issues as yet. This aspect again throws into relief the issue of training, appraisal and promotion which was discussed in Chapter 6.

Equal pay claims by some female groups of workers may prove difficult to win. Unequal pay might be justified because of the limited commitment by temporary staff, and their 'untried' characteristics. In occupations as diverse as teaching, bar work, retailing and clerical work, temporary workers are generally put on the lowest rates. This situation is unlikely to change markedly.

Suggested guidelines:

- Paying female part-time, temporary and homeworkers less than equivalent full-time permanent male staff engaged in similar work, or work rated or valued as equal, will, *prima facie*, contravene the law
- Justification of these differentials will be possible if there is a genuine difference between her situation and the equivalent man. Apart from acceptable factors of seniority, skill, etc., it may be that employers can argue the relevance of market forces. For example, Mrs Rainey worked as a fitter of artificial limbs in Glasgow. Her male colleagues, who had been recruited into the NHS *en masse* from a higher paying company, were paid considerably more than her. It was accepted as grounds for the pay difference that the employer was faced with demands for higher pay from the men and in order to recruit them at all the NHS had to provide equivalent pay levels as the private sector.[10]
- If an employee wants to justify different payments the evidence must be carefully organised, objective and analytical. Even if, for example, an employer attempts to justify lower pay by saying that workers are, for example, less valuable, more subject to absenteeism, more difficult and costly to discipline and manage, it may be argued that the causes lie in poor management and the burden should not be carried by individual workers.
- A job evaluation exercise should be carried out fairly and not perpetuate gender bias. For example, undue consideration should not be given to muscular strength, or a downgrade of skills associated with clerical or domestic work. A recent ECJ decision in *Drummler* v. *Data-Druck GmbH*, [1987][11] confirmed that courts and tribunals can reassess job evaluation schemes for latent discrimination. It may be that even the popular Hay job evaluation process is guilty in this regard as it unduly stresses managerial skills more commonly still exercised by men.

An evaluation may innocently downgrade skills provided by part-timers or casual staff by stressing factors especially relevant to permanent and full-time staff. The law is not yet highly developed, but it would be wise to re-examine job evaluations to ensure that schemes are fair.

A policy on wages for the new workforce

Changes brought about by equal pay legislation are only effective because it happens that many non-core workers are women. There are *no* protective measures for various work patterns *per se*. Discretion remains in the hands of individual enterprises. But a number of areas concerned with pay have special relevance for some work patterns. These are set out below.

Enhanced earnings

There are two main ways in which basic earnings can be increased. The first is through working longer hours, or by producing more. Hence, overtime payments, commission, and different types of piecework earnings have a key role to play in many areas of work. The second is enhanced earnings based on the performance of the individual or the enterprise.

Earnings may be made up in the three ways shown in Table 7.2.

Table 7.2 Enhanced earnings

Activity	Method
Basic pay + Higher pay due to time worked/outputs	Overtime commission, piecework, bonuses
Higher pay due to better worker performance	Performance related pay, bonuses
Higher pay due to better enterprise performance	Profit sharing, PRP, share options

Most of the innovative schemes have focused on the 'core' workforce. Although the picture is changing, the public sector has also had less scope for manoeuvre in offering higher pay for better performance.

Pay related to hours worked/output

Access to overtime is a key area for many workers, especially part-timers, temporary and home-based staff. The availability of overtime has been particularly important in the public sector, being one of the few areas of enhanced payment for non-core staff. In occupations such as retailing, insurance and door-to-door sales work, part-time and casual workers have low basic pay, and commission has constituted the bulk of earnings. In some occupations there has been a major change. Studies of computing staff have shown that in this relatively new industry 'old' pay structures which favoured core workers are being replaced. Formerly pay was overwhelmingly based on increments but this is being replaced by schemes basing pay on performance. This enables new recruits or those on temporary contracts to progress quickly through the pay scales. The needs of a highly competitive industry with many articulate and ambitious workers have, in effect, required that pay systems of the core has been overtaken by new work patterns.

Other occupations show similar responses.

Example: May and Baker (Dagenham)
A major overhaul of pay systems included the introduction of wide market-related salary bands, maxima of salary being 50 per cent above minima. This could reflect performance assessment, which is carried out every six months.

Such approaches support and facilitate the use of new work patterns. That said, overtime availability remains a key area especially to part-time, job-sharers, and temporary workers. Employers have a number of options:

- Whether to allow access to overtime?
- At what stage and at what rate to pay overtime?

In the private sector, approximately two-thirds of employers give overtime opportunities to part-timers, over a quarter do not allow part-timers to do more than their basic hours. A number of enterprises allow part-timers to earn the higher overtime rates but only after they have worked the normal full-time number of hours.

The question of whether a part-timer has access to overtime payments turns on whether the part-time contract is seen as complete in itself (and thus any excess in the contract hours will qualify for overtime rates) or whether they are merely contractual 'parts' of a whole, i.e. a full-time contract. Clearly, any generosity to part-timers will have to be stressed in the light of overall make-up of the workforce. Lots of part-timers on overtime rates would distort labour costs, and the attitude of full-timers who might find the system unfair to them, will have to be assessed.

Overtime has become a thorny issue in job-share arrangements. It reflects the above dilemma and also questions the precise nature of a job-share contract. The differing responses can be seen from three job-share policy/contracts, all drawn from not dissimilar local government employers.

Examples
1 *Local Authority A*
'Payments at the appropriate enhanced overtime rates shall be made where additional hours are worked in excess of the individual job-sharer's normal contracted hours'.
2 *Local Authority B*
'Overtime – Enhanced payments for overtime working will be made only when the individual job-sharer exceeds the contracted hours for the equivalent full-time appointment'.

3 Local Authority C

'Overtime payments at the appropriate overtime rates will be made in the following circumstances:
- when a job-sharer works in excess of their contractual hours in any week where the total hours worked by the job-share partners exceed the contractual hours of the full-time job they share
- where a job-sharer works in excess of contractual hours at management's request in any week where their partner is absent or has not yet been appointed.

These examples illustrate the range of responses by management. Example A sees the individual job-share contract as complete in itself, but B sees sharers as interdependent parts of a full-time job. C aims to differentiate between 'emergency' overtime (payable after the individual sharers contractual hours have been worked), and 'normal' overtime (only available when the hours of the full-time job have been completed).

Many types of workers – job-sharers, part-timers, workers on flexi-hours – may prefer the option of time off in lieu. In the case of flexi-hours, this option is central to the whole concept. However the extent to which workers are free to exercise the time off option is a key issue, especially in smaller organisations, or departments where the absence of individuals could be disruptive. It may well be preferable to leave the discretion to management, while encouraging the employees to make a request.

Example

Job-sharers were employed to head an advisory unit with strong community links in a busy urban local authority. The work involved attending meetings both within and outside the authority, often in the evenings. This led to a build up of entitlements to time off in lieu which had reached a point where the sharers said, 'If we take all the time off we're entitled to the post won't be covered at all!'

Opportunities for enhanced wages for temporary and fixed-term employees appear, on current practice, to be very much more limited. Some employers do not pay the same basic rate to temporary as to permanent staff, and the vast majority tend to be on the lowest grades. A recent study of temporary workers provided examples of some typical practices in the area, especially regarding incremental rises.

Examples

Company A, a manufacturer of alcoholic drinks, which employs many temporary manual staff, allows for re-grading after one year's service and after a period of training. Obviously, virtually all temporary staff remain on the lowest grades.
Company B, an airline, employs many experienced in personnel service occupations. They are often ex-employees with considerable numbers of years of service. They always remain on the lowest incremental point, no matter how many times they are employed.

The study showed a tendency to give opportunities for overtime, for example, in leisure and retailing, but limited access to bonuses paid to permanent staff. Most managements are willing to give *pro rata* paid holiday entitlement. There is, therefore, a current unwillingness to provide enhanced payment, either in terms of putting 'regular' temporary staff on a higher incremental point, or access to regular bonuses paid to permanent staff, even in occupations where temporary work is widespread.

A research study

A study of temporary workers during the summer of 1983 well illustrated the situation of such workers. The work varied from seasonal sales staff to mini-cabbing and despatch riding, to work under a short fixed-term contract for an English language summer school. Many of the workers were 'regular' temps in their area of work. All were on basic weekly rates. All reported an unwelcome attitude concerning other workers and management. Some felt compensated by the possibility of a permanent job; and the availability of discount shopping facilities, travel expenses and the like, which the equivalent permanent staff enjoyed. Many expressed resentment at the inflexibility of the pay scale to build in any 'cash' recognition of previous experience, even though several were highly educated and articulate, compared to the permanent staff.

Overall, these questions of enhanced payments to the temporary and fixed-term staff reflect the dilemma of this type of work. Managers often see them as uncommitted, even feckless; the workers become demoralised and cynical about the work situation. Arguably, this does not produce efficiency. It may be possible to overcome these difficulties to retain a core of temporary staff who are highly motivated by some payment scheme which recognises experience and efficiency. Yet there are deep-seated traditions which may make this difficult.

Homebased workers are frequently in the same situation. As many traditional forms of homework are paid as piecework they can recognise efficiency and productivity. However, 'new' homeworkers, sometimes previous full-time employees on a salary, can present problems if overtime/bonus payments are available to in-house staff. Systems have to be established to define hours of work and thus the point at which overtime payment becomes available. All this relates back to the management and discipline of distance workers discussed in Chapter 6. It will also depend on the extent to which homebased work implies such flexibility in working hours so that they rule out the concept of overtime.

Example: Insurance staff

The life insurance market demands efficient sales and service to customers. Workers have to be motivated and effectively rewarded and, athough based at home, they have to receive appropriate training. Company A employed workers on a self-employed basis, describing them as 'associates' and providing them with 'warm' contracts but leaving the selling to individuals. All sales led to a percentage commission for the associate. Company B, also a multinational organisation, employed workers as agents, paid them a basic salary, provided them with 'warm' contracts but provided a bonus on a successful sale. Agents who achieved a good sale record received pens, scarves, and other prizes at official and lavish functions. The same perceived objectives led to diametrically different employment and pay policies.

Much depends on the homebased activity. Manufacturing and processing suggest pay based on piece rates. Though they need not exclude bonuses, selling suggests pay largely or exclusively based on commission or fee. Homebased work in the service sector therefore requires closer consideration of pay methods and administration.

Performance related pay

Increasingly, there is a tendency to relate the pay of core workers to performance. In theory, this must also aid groups of flexible workers such as job-sharers, homeworkers, and short-term workers. There is strong evidence of this change affecting the public sector, though often on a more selective basis. The development is also linked to acute problems of recruitment and retention, especially in the public sector and in specialist areas like computing. Even teaching (an occupation which has traditionally solely based pay rises on promotion or seniority) has begun to build in performance (efficiency) payments to reflect a growing incidence of staff appraisal and accountability.

Example: Performance pay at the Alliance and Leicester Building Society

An overhaul of pay at the UK's sixth largest building society established a system whereby a 'percentage level of performance' (PLOP) on a scale of 0 per cent – 200 per cent, with 100 per cent as the expected performance level for each job provides for those in excess of the 100 per cent to obtain a relatively higher share out of the 6 per cent of the total wage bill merit pool.

In theory performance-related pay systems can accommodate atypical staff. But part-time and temporary staff only rarely qualify. There are particular difficulties in appraising the performance of some groups, especially job-sharers, where their work is highly integrated. Yet part-timers are generally excluded and temporary staff rarely appraised, though some agency staff can earn higher salaries after a proven track record.

There is no reason why performance-related pay schemes cannot be adapted to accommodate some of these workers either on the basis of a minimum number of weekly hours or length of service. Both would provide adequate opportunities for performance appraisal and reflect the extent to which the workers have been properly assimilated.

Many employers report high absenteeism rates among part-time and temporary staff, and lower absence rates for men than women. As new work patterns have been attractive for and to women, especially in professional jobs, attendance bonuses and performance related pay is particularly appropriate. Unlike the provision of occupational benefits, which some employers, especially of temporary staff, see as an incentive to absenteeism, payment here could be used to *encourage* attendance and efficiency.

Pay related to performance of the enterprise

This is a rapidly expanding area, but one which presents special problems for the management of flexible staff. Some schemes are well documented. They provide for employees to share in the profit of an enterprise and are scrutinised and approved by the Inland Revenue.

Popular arrangements are:

- Profit sharing on a cash or shares basis
- Savings related share option scheme (SAYE)
- Approved designed share trusts (ADSI): profit sharing after holding shares in trust for a specified time
- Profit related pay

The approval of the Inland Revenue of all these schemes effectively limit them to fairly long-serving permanent workers (usually five years service and upwards). These can be particularly attractive to employees from a tax viewpoint and for managers 'as a reward for good employees they want to keep'.

Although there is evidence that these schemes are not growing quickly and that most are both complex to administer and hard to understand, they have a significant role to play in cementing employment relationships.

Yet it is difficult to quantify the extent to which these develop commitment, loyalty and hard work and reduce labour turnover. There is also reluctance to support schemes on the part of many trade unions, who would prefer to see increases in basic pay depend on the increased efficiency and profit of an enterprise. Even the Banking, Insurance and Finance Union (BIFU) has reported disquiet at some of the operational aspects of schemes particularly the wide discretion they generally provide for management.

How do these schemes relate to the new workforce? As yet, public sector employers have not operated these schemes on a wide scale and the problem of accommodating such workers has not arisen. In the private sector, the experience to date has been variable but some groups have been able to participate. A recent study showed that out of fifty-one organisations operating schemes, forty-three gave access to part-timers, though sometimes after a qualifying period.

PAY, BENEFITS AND CATEGORY B WORKERS

Most of what has been previously discussed has little or no application to workers not directly employed by the firm. Questions of tax, insurance and occupational benefits are the worker's own responsibility. Yet as these consultants, freelance and other self-employed staff are integrated in work units there may be merit in applying similar criteria regarding expectations and opportunities. This is clearly less pressing when a worker performs a discrete task for a limited period.

Some aspects of pay which can often be taken for granted with employees have to be spelt out for Category B staff.
These include:

- Clear agreement on the manner and time of payment. Uncertainties and delays can cause considerable annoyance and resentment
- There must be clarification of entitlement and date for payment of expenses and other outgoings
- If appropriate, there must be agreement for 'overtime' or enhanced payments. If pay is for a task, or is paid as expenses in a lump sum, there may be a need to anticipate possible extension of work and therefore pay. The mechanism at least, should be in place and not left to *ad hoc* arrangements
- There must be agreement on statutory and other deductions from pay: they must not be left to chance.

This chapter has suggested that practices relating to pay have tended to be based on tradition and have been inflexible. Although employers practices have varied enormously, many workers have suffered low pay and a limited package of employment benefits. Current practices continue to deter or exclude many atypical workers. Another factor is the inability to gain promotion and access to posts of seniority other than as full-timers.

Research continues to show that even job sharing stops at a certain level, despite evidence of managerial and policy orientated posts being undertaken on a part-time basis. A questioning of the assumptions which still tend to leave various groups of workers with relatively low pay and prospects may help and may make some work patterns more attractive.

SUMMARY POINTS

- The introduction of new work patterns should be accompanied by a conscious evaluation of pay and benefits. When such an exercise takes place, it should be linked to:
  - the nature and form of the contractual arrangement and its documentation
  - the management, appraisal and promotion/training facilities of the individual worker
  - discussions on any sabbaticals, career break or retainer policies applicable to non-work periods
- Employers' organisations should take into account special provisions for particular work patterns, including:
  - details of pay and deductions
  - pay in non-work periods
  - statutory guaranteed pay
  - pay during sickness or absence because of injury

o maternity pay
  o pensions
- Occupational pension provision is an important issue in the design of pay packages for atypical workers. Key points are:
  o the viability of the scheme, given the balance of core and non-core workers
  o the likely continuity of employment in each category of worker
  o the clarity of the criteria used to define and regulate membership of the scheme
- Organisations should ensure that the provision of pay and benefits, or lack of it, does not contravene anti-discrimination legislation. Any differential in payments should be based on objective and analytical considerations which do not perpetuate gender bias – this caution should apply to many existing job evaluation exercises which often stress characteristics more commonly exercised by men
- As with management and development systems, pay and benefits systems should aim to integrate atypical workers more closely into the organisation. Access to occupational pension schemes, bonus schemes and performance-related pay schemes should be actively considered in the case of Category A, and some Category B workers, following an objective consideration of how difficult or easy it is to adapt existing systems to accommodate their needs.

References

1 Leighton, P. and Winfield, M., *Does Job Sharing Work?*, Industrial Society and the Essex Institute of Higher Education, 1988.
2 Leighton, P., 'Observing employment contracts', *Industrial Law Journal*, 1984, p.94.
3 *McLeod v Hellyer Brothers Ltd* [1987] IRLR 232.
4 IDS Study 374, 'Private sector and part-timers', 1986.
5 IDS Study 351, 'Maternity and paternity leave', 1985.
6 *Worringham v. Lloyds Bank* [1981] IRLR 178.
7 *Bilka Kaufhaus GmbH v. Weber von Hartz* [1986] IRLR 317.
8 IDS Study 374, ibid.
9 *Jenkins v. Kingsgate Clothing Ltd* (No. 2) [1981] IRLR 388.
10 *Rainey v. Greater Glasgow Health Board* [1987] IRLR 26; *Bene Veniste v. University of Southampton* [1989] IRLR 122.
11 See the UK decision in *Bromley v. Quick* [1988] IRLR 249.

Source material

Atkins, S., Luckhaus, L. and Szyszczak, E., in McCrudden, C. (ed.) *Employment and European Equality Legislation*, Eclipse Publications, 1988.
Behind the Fringe: Unequal Access to Employee Benefits, Monks Publications, Saffron Walden, Essex, 1988.
Department of Employment, 1989, 'Employers' labour use strategies', *Research Paper* No. 63.

IDS, *Equal Value*, Study 359, Income Data Services, 1986.
IDS, *Private Sector Part-Timers*, Study 374, Income Data Services, 1986.
IDS, *Profit Sharing and Share Options*, Study 357, Income Data Services, 1986.
IDS, *PRP and Profit Sharing*, Income Data Services, 1988.
IDS, *Staff Benefits and Allowances*, Study 364, Income Data Services, 1986.
IDS, *Women's Pay and Employment*, Study 402, Income Data Services, 1988.
IRS, 1986, 1987, 1988, IR-RR *Annual Review*, Industrial Relations Services.
IRS, 'Integration and equality at Midland Bank', IR-RR 407, January 1988.
IRS, 'Occupational pensions face dual challenge', IR-RR 399, Industrial Relations Services, 1987, p. 11.
IRS, 'Part-timers – emerging from the shadows', IR-RR 424, Industrial Relations Services, 1987, p. 2.
IRS, 'Reaching for excellence: pay and performance at A and L', IR-RR 406, Industrial Relations Services, 1987, p. 2.
IRS, 'Taking the pulse of sickness absence', IR-RR 405, Industrial Relations Services, 1987, p. 13.
Policy Studies Institute, *Job Evaluation and Equal Pay*, Research Paper No. 58, Department of Employment, 1988.
Smith, I., *The Management of Remuneration*, Institute of Personnel Management and Gower, 1986.
Turner, D., 'Equal value as a bargaining lever', *Personnel Management*, June 1986, p. 38.
Women's Pay: Claiming Equal Value, Labour Research Department, 1986.

Chapter 8
The work environment

Health and safety at the workplace tended to be something of a neglected topic for both managers and lawyers outside traditionally dangerous occupations in manufacturing and processing. However, a number of major incidents involving massive loss of life have pushed occupational safety to centre stage. The sinking of the *Herald of Free Enterprise* and the King's Cross Underground fire in 1987, as well as the explosion on the Piper Alpha oil platform in the North Sea in 1988, were the most dramatic examples.

There has also been a growing consensus about the need to provide a healthy as well as safe working environment. The introduction of smoking and alcohol policies, health screening, awareness of the potentially harmful effects of noise, pollution and VDUs are common examples.

These policies and issues need effective discussion with, and co-operation from, the workforce. Policies to improve health and welfare need also to be fairly and rigorously enforced. The growing fragmentation of many workforces and the increasing use of non-employees at the workplace means that negotiations have to be undertaken with individuals and organisations with different employment concerns than those of the normal employer/employee relationship. The process of consultation, decision making and monitoring may become more difficult.

The whole topic has become wide ranging and complex, not least because the European Community has formulated several draft directives on safety and related issues which will apply broadly at the workplace and which will assume greater significance in 1992. New regulations and the interpretation of longer standing laws have a heavy influence in establishing or applying general standards. Less emphasis is now put on specific occupations or types of activity. For example, Section 2 of the 1974 Health and Safety at Work Act lays down general requirements on an employer to provide a safe workplace regarding premises, plant, supervision, equipment and the like. This is becoming much more prominent in case law than detailed occupation-specific provisions. You need to be aware of these trends and should therefore deal with the issues of safety and the new workforce in a 'broad brush' manner.

Although health and welfare issues have become more important in recent years, accident prevention remains the law's central concern. The accident statistics make gloomy reading. For example, the number of accidents in manufacturing and construction rose by 30 per cent and 45 per cent respectively during the period 1981–5. In analysing the likely causes of an apparent decline in safety standards in the UK an official of the Health and Safety Executive recently identified as a key factor:

'... the disappearance of major companies and the growth in many parts of the country of small new enterprises ... [which] are not only engaged in manufacture but also in sub-contracting, *serving the continuing trend towards the 'flexible firm' which depends increasingly on peripheral units and contractors to provide components and services which the 'core' no longer does.* Many companies under financial pressure have cut their maintenance activities to the bone and skimmed or dispensed with the services of safety specialists. ... And in hard times, it is training and supervision generally that are the first to go.'

Little direct research evidence has analysed the impact of changing work patterns on the incidence of accidents and health and welfare at specific organisations or more generally. It would be too simplistic to argue that employing more part-timers and temporary workers, and the growth in the use of Category C staff has inevitably led to declining standards. However, much anecdotal and systematic evidence suggests that such changes *are* sometimes contributory factors.

Changing work patterns tend to highlight different aspects of the work environment. In common with many other issues covered by this book, managers have to consider new topics and approach them in very different ways in comparison with the approach to health and safety for full-time employees. A wider range of responsibilities and possible liabilities arise. These include:

- Should medical screening relevant to permanent full-time staff apply to Category A and B staff?
- How can you ensure the effective enforcement of safety rules against Category A and B staff?
- What is the position when a consultant or agency worker suffers injury or loss on your premises?
- What is the position when, for example, a seconded worker negligently injures another person while working for you?
- Do Category B and C workers have a right to representation on your in-house safety committee?
- How does the use of Category B and C workers affect any legal requirements to take out effective insurance policies?
- What are the legal responsibilities for workers who work in their own homes?
- How do you make a smoking policy effective with considerable numbers of Category B and C staff at the workplace?

Clearly this is a complex area, made more so because trade unions, (which have traditionally been highly instrumental in promoting safety issues) are still less active in the 'new' workforce. Two types of primary issue arise:

(a) Those concerned with the health and safety responsibilities of an organisation *to* its workers and to others.
(b) Those concerned with responsibilities *for* workers when they injure or damage persons and property.

THE GENERAL LEGAL FRAMEWORK

Safety and welfare matters have a legal reality in the following ways:

Terms in contracts of employment

All employees have *an implied term in their contract of employment* that their employer will provide a safe workplace. This relates to safe premises, equipment, adequate supervision and appropriate training. These duties, owed only to employees, are reinforced by an implied contractual term of mutual trust and confidence. If an employer fails to respond to repeatedly expressed concerns of a safety or health nature by an employee, that employer may be in breach. Examples are failures by employer to provide safety equipment, or guard against the risk of violence or theft to an employee. These duties exist regardless of occupation, sector of employment and place of work, but they are clearly modified by work specific factors, especially level of risk.

In extreme cases, breach of these duties can lead to a complaint of constructive dismissal and entitle an employee to make a claim for unfair or wrongful dismissal. (See Chapter 10).

The law of negligence and breach of statutory duty

The law of negligence entitles claims to be taken against anyone who has failed to take 'reasonable care' in undertaking a particular activity. Breaches of the law of negligence arise if anyone ought to have foreseen that negligent conduct might injure another. The law is not confined to the employer/employee situation. Indeed, all the employers and workers covered by this book are affected by this area of law. The standard expected is simply that of the reasonably competent manufacturer, builder, caterer, architect and the like. Relatively fewer resources available to an employer might lower the standard reasonably expected and more can be required of a large employer. This has only a slight impact on standards.

If an employee injures a third party in the course of their employment, the employer is in normal circumstances vicariously liable to pay compensation to victims. Vicarious liability only arises for employees: all other workers are personally liable for their negligence. The conduct of Category B workers, for example a consultant, will only rarely involve responsibility on the part of their employer.

Damages can also be claimed if an employer inflicted harm through a breach of a specified piece of safety legislation. The Factories Act, 1961, and the Office, Shops and Railway Premises Act, 1963, are the obvious examples of legislation which can give rise to claims for damages.

The health and safety statutory framework

This includes the Health and Safety at Work Act, 1974 (HSWA) and statutes and regulations applying to specific areas of work. Enforcement of the HSWA (and other statutes) is via criminal sanctions (fines imposed by Magistrates' and Crown courts). Improvement and Prohibition Notices imposed by the Safety inspectorates and, apart from HSWA itself, through claims for breach of statutory duty.

This legislation is *not* confined to protecting employees. Duties are applicable to protect, for example, consultants, casual, agency staff, sub-contractors. But there are still significant differences as between the impact of law on the self-employed compared to employers and to employees. Employees are entitled to expect greater protections. Duties are also imposed on employees and others though they tend to be less comprehensive than duties on employers. The distinction between Category A and B workers is a real one for health and safety purposes. But unlike the approach of law to other issues and protections considered in this book, Category B workers do have significant legal rights (and duties).

Duties under the Act

The duties on *employers* are to:

- Maintain safe plant and systems
- Provide safe storage of substances and articles
- Provide adequate instruction, information, supervision and safety training
- Maintain safe premises
- Provide a safe working environment
- Provide a safety policy
- Facilitate and consult with safety reps
- To establish a safety committee if requested
- To protect self-employed persons from risk.

The duties of *employees* are to:

- Take reasonable care for him/herself and for others who may be affected
- To co-operate with others in the discharge of their statutory duties (S.7)

The duty of the *self-employed* is to:

- Ensure, so far as is reasonably practicable, that others are not exposed to risk (S.3).

Section 4 of the 1974 Act also establishes a duty on those concerned with premises used for work by persons other than their employees. This clearly applies where Category B and C workers use an organisation's premises. It requires that:

- The premises and means of access are reasonably safe
- Plant or substances are safe and without risks to health.

This duty is clearly confined to premises and property and does not extend to liability for activities, lack of supervision of employees, etc. This duty in part duplicates duties under the Occupier's Liability Act, 1957, to ensure safe premises for visitors. All Category B and C workers are 'visitors'.

A summary of the legal position

Category A employees are protected through:

(a) Employment contracts
(b) Law of tort
(c) S.2 HSWA 1974 (by employer)
(d) S.3 HSWA 1974 (by self-employed person).

Category B workers are protected through:

(a) Specific contract terms, if any
(b) Law of tort
(c) S.3 HSWA

Category C workers are protected through:

(a) Their contract of employment, if an employee,
(b) Specific contract terms, if self employed
(c) Law of tort
(d) By S.4 HSWA regarding certain risks on another's premises
(e) By specific Training Agency regulations if a YTS trainee.

Other provisions

So far we have described the legal minimum. Many other protections and procedures can be established by contract or otherwise at individual workplaces. Where there are risks and problems not specifically identified by law, these need to be provided for by contract or otherwise. The existence of risks and apportionment of responsibilities has obvious insurance implications, and needs careful attention.

RESPONSIBILITIES TO THE WORKFORCE: SOME SPECIFIC TOPICS

Establishing safe systems

An organisation needs to create a positive attitude towards safety matters. This need is increased where the workforce contains workers who only work part-time or on a temporary basis. Safety issues for those who work at home ought not to be neglected.

Effective communication is vital, as is the need to induct new workers into the safety system. The law's basic requirements regarding employees is to provide such information as is 'reasonably practicable' to ensure health and safety.

Information can be communicated by notice boards or by providing written information on an individual basis. The information ought to identify persons with safety responsibilities; safety procedures including fire and other hazard procedures; and deal with use of safety equipment. Notice boards will normally be accessible to Category A workers, but it should be borne in mind that temporary and part-time staff will have less opportunity to read and absorb material. Any safety bulletin or in-house journal which refers to safety matters must be distributed to those employees. When they join an organisation, they need to be specifically notified of these facilities.

Example

A worker was taken on as a summer play organiser for handicapped children. His work included driving children around in a specially designed minibus. On one occasion a child was injured on a picnic/excursion. The worker had no idea of the procedures to be followed and was reprimanded for his failure to notify certain persons after the incident. The child was satisfactorily dealt with regarding emergency help, although it was unfortunate that the temporary worker was unaware of such procedures in an obviously problematic area of work.

A safety policy

All employers must prepare and bring to the notice of employees a written policy relating to health and safety. Many employers have responded by providing a document which, broadly, reiterates statutory duties. A policy is, of course, tangible evidence of the employer's commitment to safety, much like equal opportunities policies. Such documents can be specific, and provide basic information relevant to the individual workplace. They need not be bland. They can identify risks, medical facilities, define individual work responsibilities, e.g. to report hazards, or incidents, or problems. They can confirm that the same responsibilities and entitlements apply to Category A workers. An employer with a significant number of temporary job-share and part-time staff, might include a section as follows:

'All employees, including those on temporary and part-time contracts, are reminded of their individual responsibilities for safety under S.7 of the

Health and Safety at Work Act. Those who spend less time at the workplace are particularly required to familiarise themselves with safety procedures, to seek advice when unclear and to recognise that a more limited involvement with ... does not imply any lowering of safety standards'.

There is a need to ensure effective distribution, updating and coverage of issues in the policy. Strictly, these policies need not be available to Category B and C staff. However, the use of self-employed or consultant workers, especially where they are integrated in the workforce might suggest that the same or similar material should be provided for them.

Section 3 of the HSWA established the general duty of an employer 'so far as is reasonably practicable to ensure safety 'for persons not in his employment'. Distribution of information and the safety policy to Category B, and even Category C, workers would help discharge by this duty. Policies dealing with, for example, smoking, alcohol, sexual harassment, must be available to *all* workers.

Use of contract documentation

Curiously, Section 1 of the EPCA, 1978 does not require communication of safety rules. However, insofar as part-time and temporary staff qualify for S.1 statements, the document could refer to safety issues. Research suggests that employers in retailing, catering, farming and leisure, and others who have traditionally made extensive use of temporary and seasonal staff produce useful material for such workers. However, other employees, even in more hazardous areas of work such as transport, construction and manufacturing, appear to provide relatively little written material for workers and are less likely to feature safety issues. If material is available and clearly written it should be uncomplicated to provide it for Category B and C staff.

Where contract terms are provided in a handbook and include safety procedures and safety disciplinary rules, the handbook must also be given, or be accessible to, Category A workers, and preferably to Category B staff also.

Safety monitoring

Under the Safety Regulations and Safety Committee Regulations, 1977, certain workplaces can establish particular procedures to monitor safety. A recognised trade union may appoint a safety representative from among employees. Normally that person should have been employed for at least two years at the workplace or in a similar occupation. Technically, only recognised unions can nominate the representatives. Non-unionised workplaces are not under this statutory duty.

Realistically, temporary and even part-time staff are unlikely to be nominated by unions. However, with the increasing awareness of the needs of the new workforce by trade unions this situation is changing. Indeed, unions might well be encouraged to appoint at least one representative drawn from this group of workers who could identify their specific safety requirements. Category B workers have no entitlement, though an employer could invite a self-employed or freelance worker to represent them at meetings or to discuss matters with the organisation's safety officer.

Safety representatives have various statutory functions, such as investigating potential hazards and complaints, consulting with management, and sitting on the safety committee. To undertake these duties, the representative is entitled to reasonable time off work with pay.

'Hazards' include problems associated with management supervision and information, as well as the more obvious hazards connected with plant and machinery. Lack of information and inadequate supervision of temporary, seasonal and part-time staff would provide legitimate grounds for complaint, especially as hazardous work is by no means confined to occupations with a dominance of full-time, permanent employees. Even if a representative is not specifically appointed to deal with temporary and part-time staff he or she is still entitled to represent them on 'general matters'.

Safety committees have to be established if requested by safety representatives. In practice, many exist in non-unionised employments and where there are no safety representations. No statutory requirements exist regarding such things as minimum numbers or the committee's composition, regularity of meetings, or agendas. Practice reveals variety in these matters, with some committees in manufacturing industry meeting on a weekly basis and others only meeting when there is a specific item for discussion. If a meeting revealed concern over the safety of temporary and similar staff, an employer would be unwise to ignore it. In some areas of employment, especially health care and local government, problems have been referred to committees by in-house workers regarding the application of safety procedures to Category C workers, especially those provided by a sub-contractor.

Example

The employer was a city health authority. Laundry work had been sub-contracted to X Ltd but was still performed at the employers' premises using the employers' laundry facilities. A 'no smoking' rule applied to in-house staff, as did fire procedures including a requirement to participate in fire drills. These rules were ignored by the sub-contract workers, much to the concern (and annoyance) of in-house employees. The matter was raised at the safety committee. Although, legally, the contract workers were not covered by, or entitled to, membership of the committee, the contractor was invited to send a member who could be co-opted to the committee so as to discuss the problem of 'harmonising' practices.[1]

The safety officer

Health and safety is often the front-line managerial responsibility of the personnel department. Safety training is dealt with more generally under training. Individual organisations will have developed their own procedures and ensured that officers have the facilities to deal with safety in a comprehensive way. Where Category B and especially where Category C workers are being used, it is vital that the safety officer is consulted prior to contracts being drawn up so that safety matters can be addressed in the negotiations and agreement. Questions of cost, job specification, performance indicators and dispute resolution have been discussed in Chapters 3 and 4. Safety procedures and safety discipline are often neglected. Safety standards should be agreed, as should disciplinary procedures and monitoring applicable to these workers. Specifically, the role of the organisation's safety office *vis-à-vis* consultants, self-employed persons, and the agency, sub-contractor and seconding organisation should have been clarified.

The induction of these workers regarding safety is equally important. Failure to deal with them can cause major problems (and legal action).

Example

This extract is drawn from the published account of a cleaner who worked for a short time for a well-known NHS contract cleaning firm. It describes her recruitment and the cursory investigation of her own health record. The firm has very high labour turnover. She was sent to hospital and directed to a ward, 'There was no explanation of the colour coding system which should operate in every hospital as a precaution against infection'. She moved to another ward the following day, still having received no training or health check. She then worked on a ward with infections and, because of the outbreak, was told not to use toilet buckets in the patient area. The rest of the account catalogues confusions, infection risks and the continuing lack of training. It clearly showed a lack of co-ordination between the health authority and contractor, inadequate communication of health risks to both patients and workers and limited training.[2]

The safety officer of the host enterprise has a key role regarding not only the liaison with the Category C employer, but also for induction and communication where the other employer (agency, contractors, secondary organisations) may not be effective. The right to inspection (or not) of the work or premises used by non-employees is a matter which must be resolved, especially where activities such as maintenance, catering, installation and health care are involved.

Health screening

This is an important issue. Most employers require some form of medical examination for full-time permanent staff. This may be because of the occupation and/or to do with occupational sickness and pension schemes. It is often a condition of employment. Should such procedure be applied to Category A staff? Clearly, if the work requires fitness or lack of disability, the fact that it is being performed on a part-time or limited basis will have no relevance. Effective health screening can be costly, and so if it is to be used for *all* employees the screening itself has to be appropriate and economic.

It is just as vital that health checks are effective regarding Category B and C staff, though here requirements will form part of the commercial contract between organisation and, for example, agency, and subcontractor. This is not so much because the health of these workers is your responsibility but because there may be a 'knock-on' effect on your own employees for whom there *is* responsibility.

Establishing safe systems: a checklist

- What is the safety and health record of the workplace? Has there been an increase, or wider range of accidents and other problems since new work patterns were introduced?
- If there has been an increase, has the organisation carried out or begun an investigation?
- Does the safety policy reflect, if appropriate, the impact of new work patterns?
- Is it available to all workers?
- Are safety communications and notice-boards accessible to all staff?
- Are there needs and issues relevant to these workers not being effectively channelled to management through committees or reps?
- Do safety rules and their enforcement apply equally to all staff?
- Are safety matters adequately reflected in induction programmes?
- Have safety matters been drawn to the attention of Category B workers, and C workers, and their employer?

Maintaining safe systems

The contract of employment and the statutory framework require that safety is an on-going issue. The safety system must be monitored and enforced in a rigorous way. It must respond to problems and react to change, not least in the nature and composition of the workforce.

The legal requirement to maintain the system requires such steps to be taken as are 'reasonably practicable'. All Category A and B workers are entitled to safe machinery, material and supervision and effective maintenance and monitoring. As regards Category A staff, the failure to respond to complaints about danger, including danger of a non-accidental nature, such as violence from the public or fellow workers, might not only constitute a breach of safety legislation but also a possible breach of contract. It can lead to a constructive dismissal, and the fact that the worker is not full-time or permanent will not be relevant.

The relative inexperience of employees or the part-time nature of the contract are factors which may have to be responded to by *extra* training and supervision. If an employer actually knows that temporary staff are accident prone because of lack of familiarity with equipment, confusion about safety rules or first-aid equipment, then the situation must be remedied.

A particular issue is that of enforcing safe systems when the employee is off-site, using their own equipment, or working at home. These workers are entitled to the same safety standards, subject only to the rubric 'reasonably practicable'. It may be less 'practicable' to provide the same level of monitoring as for on-site staff. There has been particular concern for homeworkers engaged in manufacturing processes. They are dependent on their employer for materials and the provision and maintenance of equipment. Although the risks may appear less dramatic, safety of home computer staff is dependent on similar factors. Regular visits can be made, and the list of tasks for these visits ought to formally include a checking of equipment and enquiries as to health and welfare of homeworkers.

Where off-site work involves transport, a regular inspection and maintenance programme will probably be in use, not least for vehicle insurance reasons. Although research indicates that the inspectorates established under safety legislation to visit premises concentrate their energies on larger employers, especially those in 'high risk' occupations, protection of off-site or homeworkers should not be neglected.

Non-employees at the workplace

Where Category B and C workers come to your premises and use equipment and facilities, the situation is complex. Technically, they are entitled to some statutory protections regarding safe systems, especially the premises themselves. In addition, Category C staff can claim protections from their own employer. Experience shows that when injuries occur, such workers are often faced with problems in enforcing legislation.

Example

A few years ago, a relief farm-worker was sent to a farm by an agency who fixed the fee and terms under which she was to carry out her duties. She was treated as self-employed for National Insurance purposes. The job was explained by the farm manager over a two day period and then she was left alone. She suffered an accident, apparently due to failure of the farm manager to maintain a tractor in a safe condition. The relevant safety regulations only applied if the relief was their farm's employee. She was not, and thus the farm manager escaped prosecution. He could have been prosecuted under HSWA, had the Act been operative at the time. Any duty under the law of negligence was probably subject to a lower standard of care than that owed to an employee because you can expect skilled agency workers to be aware of risks. The agency was clearly not responsible for the dangerous tractor, so the entitlement of the relief worker to any form of compensation was negligible.

The general question which arises for Category C workers is the degree of protection which you owe them. If they are provided by an agency or seconded from another employer can you expect that they will be safety conscious and adequately prepared? Is it necessary to supervise activities in detail and ensure that their standards are compatible with those of your own employees?

Although it is difficult to provide clear guidance where workers come as individuals it would be prudent to monitor safety issues as closely as for employees. When a group of workers are provided by a sub-contractor their main protection must come from their own employer. Safety equipment and monitoring should have been considered in the pre-contract negotiations and the contract.

The legal position when non-employees work and suffer injury on your premises is complex.

Example
Cleaning had recently been sub-contracted for in a large urban hospital district. The contract specification defined the tasks to be carried out, but did not directly deal with responsibility for safe systems. One morning a cleaner slipped and was badly injured when she fell on a floor. It appeared that the cause was patient vomit which had not been cleaned up. The hospital claimed that the duty to ensure safe floors was that of the contractor. The contractor claimed that dangers specifically caused by patients remained the safety responsibility of the hospital. It emerged that similar though minor accidents had occurred during the previous weeks and had led to a series of irate conversations between the hospital manager and the sub-contractor. However, the focus of discussion was whether the cleaning contract had been broken, rather than safety. It is likely that under statute and common law the hospital continued to have responsibility for the safety of premises, though might well have a claim against the contractor for breach of contract.[3]

A final matter, not unrelated to the above example, is responsibility for recording and notifying accidents. There is a duty to notify the safety inspectorate of any death or major injury to an employee. All other injuries have to be recorded. Employers also have to notify the death or major injury of *any person*. Effective monitoring by the employer is necessary for this duty to be discharged not only for their own employee but for Categories B and C workers in the case of death and major injuries.

Maintaining safe systems: a checklist

- Is safety monitoring adequate for casual, part-time and flexitime staff?
- Are problems and complaints being properly responded to?
- Are there adequate safety checks for homebased workers?
- Has the contract providing Category C workers adequately clarified responsibility for maintaining safe systems regarding equipment, substances, discipline, and monitoring?
- Is there an effective mechanism for dealing with complaints and issues from Category B and C staff?

Accidents and injuries to the workforce: some specific issues

Although duties are more extensive and detailed regarding Category A workers, employers have duties to protect other workers, especially in relation to safe premises. For many areas of law, the key factor is whether the injured worker was your employee or not. The legal tests of employment status remain difficult and unsatisfactory (see Chapter 4). However, in cases where injuries have occurred, there has been a tendency to apply the legal tests so as to decide that the injured worker was an employee, despite contrary indications.

Examples

1 *A building worker was taken on by a building contractor after the briefest of conversations. It amounted to the phrase 'no cards'. He started work immediately and was supervised by the contractor's foreman. He suffered major personal injuries when he fell from hazardous equipment. The contractor argued that as both they and the worker intended the employment relationship to be one of self employment, he could not now claim compensation which was only due if he was an employee. The Court of Appeal disagreed. It decided that despite the clear intentions of the parties, the legal reality was one of a contract of employment. He had been subject to the control of the contractor while he was working.*[4]

A similar approach might well apply to freelance, consultant and similar workers if they suffer injury at the workplace, especially where they are integrated in the host workforce. Courts tend to adopt a more flexible approach to the issue of employment status when dealing with injury cases than industrial tribunals.

2 *A seaman was employed as a deckhand. Soon after he started work, he was transferred to work on a tug owned by a Dutch company. The tug's captain was an employee of that company and the deckhand was injured when the tug was being untied from alongside a dredger. He was dragged into the water and crushed. He claimed compensation from his own employer. It appeared that the cause of the accident was the system of communication between deckhand and captain when the tug was being untied. The deckhand was to knock on the lower wheelhouse when untying had been completed. The House of Lords felt this was unreliable and did not ensure a safe system. The judges noted the overall responsibility to provide this and although the performance of this may be delegated, the employer remains liable for its non-performance.*[5]

The case illustrates the fact that the law regards safety responsibilities as wide-ranging and not limited to the employer's own workplace or excluding the influence of third parties.

Accident insurance

The Employer's Liability (Compulsory Insurance) Act, 1969, obliges most employers to insure against liability for personal injury to employees in the course of their employment. The exempted employers are mainly in the public sector. Failure to insure is a criminal offence. Although the legal requirement is confined to all employees, and therefore covers all Category A staff, it might be sensible to have wider coverage in view of the decision taken in the building trade case above.

RESPONSIBILITY FOR THE CONDUCT OF WORKERS

Where workers inflict damage or injury on others, the law provides relatively clear guidance on responsibilities. If the worker in question was an employee and the incident took place in the course of employment, the employer is vicariously liable to compensate victims. The nature of the contract of employment is not material and liability can be imposed for part-time, homeworking, or temporary employees as much as for full-time, permanent staff. Liability insurance policies must adequately cover the whole workforce.

While employees are subject to the direction of another (for example, they are seconded to an organisation, or are agency staff) the basic legal position is that their own employer remains vicariously liable providing they were employees (and many are not) and the incident was in the course of their employment. These principles apply to accidents but may not do so when the employee in question commits an intentional act.

Example
B, an employee of a contract cleaning firm, worked at an office premises for six months. While working there, he made unauthorised overseas telephone calls to the value of £1400. The client claimed the money from the contract cleaning firm, alleging that they were responsible for the deliberate, though foreseeable, conduct of their employee. It was argued that the cleaning contract contained an implied undertaking to compensate clients for any losses they suffered. The Court of Appeal disagreed. They decided that simply because the cleaner had the opportunity to make calls (he dusted and disinfected phones) using the phone took him totally outside the course of his employment.[6]

If a material cause of an accident or injury was the failure of the employer to provide proper information or instructions to the worker, the employer may also be liable. For example, if a consultant, architect or a freelance computer programmer was not warned about oddities and hazards in the electrical system, the employer might well have to pay compensation if a third party was injured by the worker.

SUMMARY POINTS

- Responsibility for a safe and healthy working environment extends to everyone connected with the workplace. Classifying workers is less important than identifying the hazards associated with their activities and minimising the risks involved.
- Employing a more varied workforce requires a wider discussion of the health and safety issues, careful anticipation of potential accidents and complaints and a consistent application of standards. Although some workers may have to take more responsibility for their own safety, everyone at work has basic legal entitlements to a safe workplace.

- Considering and developing systematic health policies should be a central part of any introduction of new work patterns. Expert advice should be drawn on and matters never left to chance.
- In this process, temporary and Category B and C workers will expect equivalent treatment. They will be less likely in the future to shrug off injuries and the discomfort of being regarded as 'risks of the business'.
- Successful health and welfare policies should reflect an active consideration of the characteristics of new work patterns. In some situations, policies will have to be explained to agencies, subcontractors and self-employed workers and become incorporated into contracts. In others, there will be a need for more effective communication and display of information and monitoring.

References

1 Leighton, P., 'The subcontracting of services', a report to the International Labour Office, Essex Institute of Higher Education, 1985.
2 *I was a mole in Mediclean*, London Health Emergency, 1984.
3 Leighton, P., ibid.
4 *Ferguson v. John Dawson Ltd* [1976] 1 WLR 346, IRLR 346.
5 *McDermit v. Nash Dredging Reclamations Ltd* [1987] IRLR 334.
6 *Heasmans v. Clarity Cleaners* [1987] IDS Brief 346, p. 15.

Source material

Davies, P. and Friedland, M., *Labour Law – Text and Materials* 2nd edn., Weidenfeld and Nicolson, 1984.
Health and Safety Executive, Annual Reports, 1983–87, HMSO.
James, P. and Lewis, D., 'Health and safety at work', in Lewis, R. (ed.) *Labour Law in Britain*, Blackwell, 1986.
Munkman, J., *Employers' Liability*, 10th edn., Butterworth, 1985.
Wedderburn, Lord, *The Worker and the Law*, 3rd edn., Penguin Books, 1986.

Chapter 9
Industrial relations

Trade union responses to the introduction of new work patterns have been neither consistent nor unified – a reflection of the more general difficulties the movement has had in adjusting to changes brought about by shifting labour market trends.

Traditionally, trade unions have been deeply suspicious about any moves to increase atypical employment in the workplace. The cause is practical rather than ideological. Recruiting and organising part-time, off-site, temporary and contract workers has always been more difficult for individual unions to achieve. Atypical workers are perceived to be more isolated from the workplace, less able to play an active part in union activities. They also have needs and interests which often conflict with those of full-time members – something which, combined with many full-time workers' suspicions of atypical working, is seen to endanger collective solidarity.

Legal protection for atypical workers is very modest in the UK compared with the rest of Europe – if anything, their security under the law has been eroded during the 1980s (see Chapter 1). This leaves unions more reliant on collective bargaining to push for better conditions at a time when their bargaining strength is weakened by the relative over-supply of these kinds of worker on the external market.

The introduction of flexible working has always been associated with low pay and an erosion of working conditions in many union officials' eyes. A 1986 survey into bargaining practices commented: 'Essentially, the "flexible labour market" means lower labour costs. This is a central aim of the present government which it has pursued through policies such as reduction in the scope of the wages councils, privatisation, with low-paying employers responsible for services, removal of the fair wages resolution which could lay down minimum terms and conditions.'

The concept of 'core-peripheral' working only served to confirm this view. A TUC response to the NEDO report *Changing Working Patterns* in 1986 commented: 'The notion that a secure and flexible "core" of workers is being created on a wide scale is undermined by the general degree of insecurity and worsening conditions experienced by all groups of workers.

... The concept of "numerical flexibility" is very much "old wine in new bottles". Certainly, there has been a growth in insecure forms of employment in recent years, but this is not new. Moreover, those industries most associated with this kind of work, such as docks and construction, are hardly models to follow.'

Yet in its response to the NEDO report, the TUC did acknowledge the growth in use of temporaries, part-timers, self-employment and sub-contracting. The document also expressed the growing feeling of its more prominent members that union bargaining strategies should ensure that such workers are employed under the same conditions as permanent full-time staff and should, wherever possible, receive union representation.

This acknowledgement reflects a recent pragmatism about introduction of new work patterns which extends beyond the defensive postures adopted by unions during the late 1970s and early 1980s.

A growing number of individual trade unions are seizing the initiative in this field by bargaining for working arrangements which meet the social and professional needs of their members (rather than the economic needs of the employing organisation); and by seeking to recruit and represent the interests of non-unionised atypical workers. These include many blue-collar unions which were implacably opposed to the introduction of new work patterns in earlier years, such as the TGWU and the GMB.

This shift reflects a response to the realities imposed by a changing labour market. Trade union membership suffered badly from the recession and the deregulation of employment practices which followed. Trade union membership in the UK reached a peak of 13 289 000 in 1979. From 1981 and 1983, there was a sharp fall followed by a continued decline up to 1986. Total union membership at the end of 1986 was 10 539 000 – 20.7 per cent lower than its 1979 peak.

The sharp decline during the two years of recession was a product of short-term labour cut-backs. The steady decline since is part of a much longer-term trend. Put at its simplest, the kind of worker traditionally attracted to trade union membership – male, blue-collar, full-time and conveniently on-site – has been in decline for over thirty years. The kind of worker which has steadily increased in numbers of the same period – female, white-collar and often off-site – is not joining in sufficient numbers to make up the deficit.

Faced by a decline in their bargaining strength, individual unions are not seeking to recruit atypical workers who had so far remained outside their orbit, both to make up their numbers and to allay the threat of undercutting and substitution. Further pressure has been added by the steady integration and mergers of unions throughout the 1980s which has eroded job demarcations and fuelled competition to recruit members from workers in the same workforce by different unions.

The willingness of trade unions to bargain actively for the introduction of new work patterns has been further encouraged by the realisation that many arrangements benefit their existing full-time members. White-collar unions with a high proportion of female members have been particularly keen to push for job sharing, career break schemes, homeworking and professional part-time working, often as part of broader equal opportunities programmes, despite the fact that many of these arrangements are not wholly supported by the TUC. The instances of unions taking a lead in the introduction of 'social push' schemes are likely to increase as more women achieve senior bargaining positions in their unions and the decline in both male and young entrants to the labour market bites deeper.

SPECIFIC RESPONSES TO NEW WORK PATTERNS

Given these circumstances, how are trade unions likely to respond to specific initiatives introducing new work patterns to the workplace? As we have already seen, trade unions do not speak with one voice and the likely response will depend on a number of specific factors. The most important are:

- the specific work pattern being introduced
- the individual union(s) affected
- the balance of local, regional and national interests represented in the bargaining team.

Responses to different work patterns

Individual union responses to flexible working have varied enormously according to the specific pattern being introduced. Key factors in their response have been the extent to which:

- the arrangement benefits their existing full-time members
- it compromises the job security of their existing members and potentially undermines current terms of employment
- the new workers fall entirely outside the bargaining unit of the union – and therefore reduces their bargaining influence
- the arrangement compromises existing health and safety and other workplace procedures
- the union has been consulted in its introduction.

Responses to different unions

Attitudes towards the introduction of new work patterns still vary markedly from one union to another. John Atkinson from the Institute of Manpower Studies and Denis Gregory from the Trade Union Research Unit attempted a summary of the gut reactions of differing individual unions.[1] This included:

- *the ostrich approach*: which holds that the widespread introduction of new work patterns is not happening and that no change to traditional union approaches to organisation and recruitment of members is required

- *the dinosaur approach*: which accepts that significant changes are under way but considers them a by-product of recession and deregulation – as such they are a temporary phenomenon and all the unions need to do is hang on until a Labour government and/or economic stability restore the status quo
- *the bourbon approach*: which holds that flexibility deals are simply a 1980s version of productivity deals – not only did unions survive productivity dealing but some workers prospered under them and thus, it is argued, the introduction of new work patterns poses no substantive problem
- *the opportunist approach*: which recognises that there are substantial advantages to be secured for individual workers, and for the union which can represent them – this approach often trades the acceptance of new work patterns for an employment security pledge and possibly a single union agreement.

As we have already seen, some unions have progressed beyond these purely defensive postures to actively bargain for new work patterns which benefit their existing members; or actively seek to represent atypical workers to increase their bargaining influence, make up their numbers or allay the threat of undercutting and substitution.

Local versus central bargaining interests

Despite the frequent rejection of flexibility initiatives by many union initiatives nationally, local negotiations have often accepted management-led changes. This gap between 'the rhetoric of resistance and the reality of the workplace'[2] has taken a number of forms:

- reluctant acquiescence in the face of a weakened bargaining position
- cynical acquiescence as part of a calculated negotiation stance (as in the case of local branch officials 'turning a blind eye' to the use of contract or agency staff in return for management concessions elsewhere)
- wholehearted co-operation, often when the interests of local branch officials are closer to those of local management than those of their national union.

As we have already seen, local branches (with or without the co-operation of their national union) may also push for the introduction of new working practices themselves when in the interests of their members.

Union responses to specific work patterns

It is worth taking a closer look at union responses to specific work patterns in recent years.

Flexibility: weekly or annual hours

Trade unions generally have no firm policies on these arrangements, but their attitudes may be influenced by the fact that they often exceed the eight-hour day, creating problems of undue fatigue for their members, and possibly doing away with the principle that hours in excess of eight per day should be paid at enhanced overtime rates. Evans and Bell of the Institute of Personnel Management[3] cite the example of British Rail's proposals for flexible rostering, involving a day of between seven and nine hours, which were strongly opposed by ASLEF who saw it as an attack on the guaranteed eight-hour day achieved in 1919.

Temporary working: short-term contracts and sub-contracting

Since the determination of the pay and conditions of the workers employed in these patterns often falls entirely outside the bargaining unit of many unions, many have often felt threatened by their wider use. Their introduction has often been seen as a means of weakening trade union organisation at the workplace, as a threat to permanent employment or as a means of cutting overtime earnings. Recent attempts by individual unions to recruit temporary and contract workers (see below) have resulted in agreements which link their pay to those of full-time workers. In some organisations, the employment of temporary staff has been the subject to joint agreement where a maximum possible number, in terms of a percentage of the local workforce, has been set out. Sometimes this kind of agreement has been negotiated to provide greater job security for the permanent workforce, with temporaries having less job security and being more likely to be laid off if the business suffers a downturn.

Sub-contracting

IPM Research in 1986[3] indicates that both temporary work and sub-contracting have often been introduced without consultation and with little influence on the outcome. Where its use is subject to union agreement, such as in the construction industry, they often lay down that sub-contract staff must become members of the specific union and receive pay linked to full-time rates. This kind of agreement has also been agreed directly with employment agencies contracting out staff to clients – most notably with Manpower Limited.

Part-time work

Many unions' ambivalence towards part-time work reflects a conflict of priorities. Like temporary and contract staff, part-time workers are difficult to recruit and organise. They are heavily concentrated in poorly unionised occupations with high levels of turnover. Many are employed in small firms where trade unions have only a weak foothold. In addition, the shortening of the full-time working week remains a priority and the expansion of part-time work (particularly if instituted by management) has been seen as endangering a general reduction in hours. Increasingly, there has also been the fear that part-time jobs will be substituted for full-time ones. However, more progressive unions recognise that this process of substitution will only be intensified while part-timers remain a poorly paid unorganised sector of the labour force. This has been a prime motivation behind the recent initiatives by the TGWU and GMB to represent the interests of part-timers outside their present bargaining orbit – described in greater detail below.

Job sharing

A key factor of job sharing has been its potential to improve the conditions of part-time work. Yet trade unions still have mixed feelings about the concept, with many being openly hostile. A study of job sharing in 1986[4] found evidence of worries about 'dilution' of the workforce and the decline of full-time posts which many trade unionists thought their proper concern. There were additional anxieties about increased complexities in collective bargaining as well as fear that job sharers as part-timers would be less likely to be active trade unionists. At the same time, several trade unions, especially in the public sector, have actively supported and pushed for job sharing as a major plank in an equal opportunities programme (see below). A further study two years later[5] found that many of these attitudes, while still cautious to job sharing, were softening, but that some of the central anxieties about the move away from full-time regular employment remained. At a collective bargaining level, the study found that job sharing was not hard to accommodate. Both personnel managers and trade union officials surveyed expressed themselves satisfied that the practical issues of job sharing regarding pay and other terms of employment were resolvable, though sometimes after lengthy negotiations. The growing 'fund' of job share policies is clearly aiding this process.

Union initiatives to recruit atypical workers

As we have already seen, the proportion of atypical workers who choose to join trade unions is well below that of their full-time counterparts – a significant problem at a time when union membership has dropped generally.

We have also examined the reason why. Atypical workers are more difficult to recruit and their interests more difficult to promote – particularly because they may conflict with those of existing full-time members. Atypical workers tend to be concentrated in industries with low levels of unionisation and high levels of turnover. Often away from the workplace, their ability to play an active role in the union is thereby rendered more problematic.

Yet a few pioneering examples, most notable the efforts made by the shop-workers union USDAW, have suggested that, with deliberate and sensitive orchestration of priorities and methods, atypical workers can be brought into membership and effectively represented.

In the late 1980s, a number of new initiatives have emerged. The most noteworthy are:

NALGO (The National and Local Government Officers' Association: which has pushed for the rights of their part-time members to be given priority and called for an emphasis on negotiating improvements at a local level. In a recent report, it also argued that much more effort should be devoted to involve part-time workers at a branch level, commenting that branches should: 'hold meetings at times and places convenient to part-time staff (and) consider assistance with travel expenses, providing lifts and assistance with child-minding costs for part-time staff attending meetings'.

GMB (The General Municipal, Boilermakers and Allied Trade Union): which announced in May 1987 that it intends to put women's issues far higher on the bargaining agenda, actively pushing for the right to family leave, inclusion of part-timers in sick-pay arrangements and payment of unsocial and additional hours premia to part-time workers. GMB's FLARE campaign (Fair Laws and Rights in Employment) calls for:

- Workers to be protected from the first minute of the first day of employment under employment protection legislation – minimum qualifying hours per week and minimum periods of service being removed
- Protection of all workers, regardless of the size of the firm
- All workers to be protected by a guaranteed minimum wage expressd as an hourly rate to ensure that part-time workers are properly protected.

The union has also launched a nationwide programme of women's Workplace Discussion Groups which are modelled on the Swedish study circles. Their purpose is to build confidence among women and encourage greater participation in the trade union.

TGWU (Transport and General Workers' Union): which launched in February 1987 its 'Link-up' campaign to recruit part-time and temporary workers, producing a model agreement which stipulated that these categories of workers should enjoy the same terms and conditions as full-time workers, on a pro-rata basis where appropriate.

The 'Link-up' Campaign

The TGWU 'Link-up' Campaign provides a good illustration of the bargaining position likely to be taken by future unions actively seeking to recruit and represent atypical workers.

In its model agreement for part-timers, it calls for the following negotiating priorities:

- pro rata pay and conditions with full-timers
- payment for unsocial hours
- premium payments for hours worked in excess of contracted hours
- payment for call-out and travelling when asked to work at short notice or extra shifts
- improvements in training opportunities
- equal access to all fringe benefits.

The emphasis on call-up payments and on overtime and unsocial hours payments reflects the union's growing concern with the use of part-timers as a flexible and cheap labour force to be drawn on as and when needed. Their response is to argue that part-timers should be adequately compensated for the disruption to their lives and for working unsocial hours.

Equally interesting is the TGWU's response to the bargaining priorities with temporary agency workers. The TGWU currently (1987) has about 11 500 members who obtain their work through employment agencies. Many work in firms with a high level of unionisation. An existing agreement with the work contractor, Manpower Ltd, may well prove the model for future agreements with other employment agencies or contractors. The agreement provides that:

- all staff employed by the agency should be union members
- no workers should be used to undermine or break industrial disputes
- all workers should receive pro rata rates of pay, holiday pay and other benefits.

The agreement is felt by the union to have greatly benefited the TGWU and that it is superior in many respects to a number of agreements covering permanent workers.

The union's decision to better represent atypical workers is both an acknowledgement of the changes taking place in the labour force and an attempt to forestall the threat this poses to their existing members. At the time of the campaign's launch, TGWU Assistant General Secretary, Larry Smith, commented:[6]

'... Times change, and with them the composition of those areas of the workforce where we have a natural constituency. Today, we have higher levels of female employment, higher levels of part-time and temporary employment, higher proportions of ethnic workers, and so on. We need to move with these times ... In addition, the existence of an organised and unprotected sector of the workforce is itself a threat to the maintenance of terms and conditions among the better organised sectors. The threat of undercutting and substitution is a very real one for many of our members, as the incursion of the self-employed, sub-contracting drivers into the road haulage so obviously demonstrates ...'

Just how successful the TGWU and other unions prove in seeking to recruit and represent atypical workers remains to be seen. It is too early to gauge how effectively the Link-up and FLARE campaigns are proving. As one commentator put it:[7] 'The critical issue facing the TGWU and GMB, both traditional blue-collar unions, is how easy they will find it to change their methods. With an overwhelming male officialdom, a macho attachment to the rough and tumble of the big concentrations of manufacturing industry and a tradition of site-based activism, it is hard to believe they will find it easy ...'

CONCLUSION

In the past ten years, traditional union hostility or suspicion of atypical working has not prevented the introduction of new work patterns in the workplace by many firms. In a 1987 ACAS survey, only 33 per cent of managers reported they were constrained in their organisation of work and that a trade union presence had not generally inhibited the introduction of new working practices. Indeed, as Table 9.1 shows, the survey found a recent tendency to more flexibility in unionised organisations than in their non-unionised counterparts.

Yet it is important to draw the right conclusions from this trend. Most flexibility agreements which damaged or undermined the job security or terms of employment of individual trade unions' members were introduced at a time when traditional bargaining strength had been weakened by falling workplace respresentation.

The introduction of new working practices did, in fact, attract a high proportion of disputes. A survey of 140 firms by the Labour Research Department in 1986, which covered flexibility of task as well as working time, found that 40 (29 per cent) reported industrial action in response to flexibility deals during the previous five years. Six of these reported two disputes and one (a Scottish local authority) reported three.

The respondent from Metal Box, Crawley, was clearly speaking for many when he said: 'Flexibility should only be agreed upon if it is to the benefit of the worker (i.e. job security, better conditions of employment and pay, and not put another worker out of a job). It should be to the mutual benefit of all, not just to the management and shareholders.'

This remains the basis on which most unions approach flexibility agreements, although they themselves are proving far more flexible in the way in which they interpret 'mutual benefit for all'.

Two final examples illustrate more recent trade union bargaining responses.

Table 9.1 Flexibility and unionisation

Type of flexibility adopted	Percentage of employers recognising trade unions	Percentage of employers not recognising trade unions
FLEXIBILITY IN NUMBERS		
Part-time working	71	69
Temporary working	67	44
Fixed term contract working	20	9
Homeworking	5	8
Outside contracting	84	63
FLEXIBILITY IN CRAFT AND SKILLS		
Production workers do routine maintenance work	29	16
Craftsmen do work usually performed by other craftsmen	41	20
Relaxation of divisions between manual technical and clerical skills	29	17
Other types of flexibility in crafts and skills	13	9
FLEXIBILITY IN HOURS OF WORK		
Shiftworking	30	23
Annual hours working	4	2
Job sharing	11	8
Flexible working hours	14	13
FLEXIBILITY IN PAY AND REWARDS		
Payment systems rewarding the acquisition of new skills	25	13
Merit pay	23	25
Profit sharing/share options	31	16
Integrated job evaluation	5	6

Source: ACAS, The 1987 ACAS Study

British Caledonian – 'The Way Ahead' programme

In 1986, British Caledonian negotiated agreements under its programme 'The Way Ahead' designed to eliminate overtime and overtime pay by substantially increasing basic wage rates and providing time off in lieu for any additional hours worked.

The agreements removed an unpredictable and variable labour cost for the company and gave employees higher security of earnings. They covered a very wide range of workers represented by, among others, the AEU, EEPTU, TGWU, TASS, GMB, ASTMS and APEX.

A key factor in the agreement was the acceptance of directly employed temporary workers to cope with seasonal demand. Every effort is made to contain work within the existing workforce but temporaries, in preference to agency staff, are now used especially to cover the peak winter workload associated with aircraft maintenance.

The number of these temporaries is jointly agreed from time to time but the previous practice of offering unlimited overtime to permanent workers before contractors may be used was ended.

Temporaries' terms are no more or less favourable than those of B Cal workers. It was agreed that there would be no reduction in staffing levels as a result of employing temporaries, although they clearly introduced a new variable element into labour costs.

The agreements also incorporated initiatives from the unions. A 'time wastage' form was introduced at their suggestion to identify 'down time' and there were numerous examples of employee-inspired moves to make better use of the working day.

As a result of the agreements, the demands placed on the manager and supervisor have now changed from one of close monitoring and direct supervision to one of efficient planning and organisation. There is a greater degree of involvement before decisions are made.

B Cal's experience in negotiating the agreements shows that unions are prepared to accept new working practices designed to reduce or better manage labour costs provided there is a tangible pay-back for their members. In particular, their acceptance of temporary workers to cope with seasonal demand was due to a number of factors:

- Workers gained, as well as management, from the sacrifice of overtime the change entailed – they received a higher fixed salary and therefore greater security of earnings
- The numbers of temporaries were subject to joint agreement
- Their terms of employment were linked to those of full-time workers
- The use of temporaries involved no reduction in permanent staffing levels.

NALGO's strategy on job sharing

The use of job sharing, and the negotiation of job sharing policies has been more widespread in local government than in any other sector, public or private. A survey by the organisation 'New Ways to Work' in 1987 found that fifteen London boroughs and thirty-eight local authorities outside the capital have job sharing policies.

NALGO has played a key role in negotiating job sharing arrangements for its members. It has a high proportion of female members and a growing number of women in senior bargaining posts. The national union was therefore an early advocate of greater rights for part-time workers. They were quick to see the potential benefits in job sharing as a means of improving the quality of part-time work at a time when most other unions were deeply suspicious of the concept.

Their negotiating guidelines comment: 'Even if the branch doesn't endorse a policy in support of job sharing, branch negotiators should still offer individuals who want to organise a job share help and representation. Some branches have won equal opportunities agreements which cover job sharing, and this can be an excellent way to safeguard sharers' rights to training, promotion and career development. However the job sharing agreement is structured, branches can use the advantages and safeguards secured for job sharers to the benefit of other part-timers who often miss out in negotiations on better terms and conditions.'

NALGO's branches have generally bargained for job sharing on the basis of eight key negotiating points:

- *full union involvement and consultation* when job sharing agreements are negotiated or one-off arrangements established
- *no exploitation* by employers trying to use job sharing as a compulsory alternative to redundancy or as a way to down-grade the pay and conditions normally associated with a full-time post
- *guarantees* that posts or parts of posts are not lost through job sharing
- job sharing arrangements initiated at the *incentive of the employees involved*
- *a written contract and job description for each sharer*
- *a sixteen-hour working week* for sharers to safeguard their rights under employment protection legislation
- *pro rata entitlement* to the same pay and conditions as colleagues in equivalent full-time posts and equal opportunities for training
- *the right to return to full-time work* after a period of job sharing.

If possible, NALGO branches are instructed to insist on a further four points which, the union feels, will make the introduction of job sharing more successful. These are:

- *all posts at all levels* should be open to job sharing
- *detailed information and training for personnel officers* should be provided on the practicalities of job sharing
- establishment of a *job share register*
- *job advertisements* stating that applications from sharers are welcome.

These bargaining points feature in many of the agreements the union has negotiated with local authority employers.

SUMMARY POINTS

- While traditional suspicion or hostility to the introduction of new work patterns remains in many trade unions, these attitudes are being re-evaluated
- As a result, trade union responses to management initiatives will be varied and subject to a number of local factors. The most important are:
  - the specific work pattern being introduced

- the national policy of the union(s) affected
  - the balance of local and national interests represented in the bargaining team
- Trade union responses to proposals for specific work patterns will also depend on the extent to which:
  - the arrangement benefits their existing full-time members
  - it compromises the job security of their existing members and potentially undermines current terms of employment
  - the new workers fall entirely outside the bargaining unit of the union – and therefore reduces their bargaining influence
  - the arrangement compromises existing health and safety and other workplace procedures
  - the union has been consulted in the matter of its introduction
- A growing number of trade unions are now seeking to recruit and represent greater numbers of atypical workers. Their bargaining stance has been based on the negotiation of pro-rata pay and conditions with full-timers coupled with calls for equal rights to employment protection and job security
- Whilst they have had mixed success in their endeavours, these developments suggest that trade unions will increasingly take the initiative in negotiations over new work patterns and push for terms and arrangements which balance the worker's interests more effectively with those of the organisation.

References

[1] 'Unions and the flexible workforce: ostriches or opportunists?' *Manpower Policy and Practice*, Vol 1. No. 4. Summer 1986.

[2] (See ref. 1).

[3] Curzon, C. (ed.) *Flexible Patterns of Work*, Institute of Personnel Management, 1986.

[4] Leighton, P. and Rayner, C., *Job Sharing in South-East Essex*, Employment Relations Research Centre, Essex Institute of Higher Education, 1986.

[5] Leighton, P. and Winfield, M., *Does Job Sharing Work?*, Industrial Society, 1986.

[6] Smith, L., 'Linking up with the new worker', *Manpower Policy and Practice*, Vol. 2. No. 4, Summer 1987.

[7] Atkinson, J., 'Heads down ... hope for the best', *Manpower Policy and Practice*, Vol. 2, No. 4, Summer 1987.

Chapter 10

Disputes and termination of contracts

This chapter deals with legal and managerial issues arising from disputes and the ending of an employment relationship. In many cases, the end is painless. The contract is ended through its expiry or the completion of its purposes. In other circumstances the end comes through complaints and/or dismissal. The law is complex in this area, particularly in its application to new or atypical work patterns. Employees in some work patterns, especially short-term engagements, face considerable legal problems if they challenge the employer. There are few legal constraints on an employer wishing to end the relationship providing the necessary notice is given, correct procedures are followed and, if relevant, the employer had good grounds for deciding to end the contract.

ENDING CONTRACTS WITH CATEGORY A AND B WORKERS

The legal framework

This is drawn from two major sources:

- Long established common law rules enforced through the ordinary civil courts
- Statutory protections relating to unfair dismissal and redundancy payments

The statutory protections are only available to employees who work at least sixteen (eight) hours per week and who have been continuously employed for two years or more by the same employer. The following workers are therefore excluded:

- Self-employed workers
- Many part-timers (though most job-sharers *are* covered)
- Most fixed-term and temporary workers.

The issues associated with distinguishing between employees and self-employed have already been discussed in Chapters 4 and 5. Other legal issues are discussed here.

'Continuously employed': searching for a definition

This is a notoriously difficult area of law. Here are some indicative situations recently considered by tribunals and courts:

(a) A peripatetic photography teacher employed by an LEA had a series of contracts, none of which amounted to sixteen hours per week, but added together they did. *No continuity*.
(b) A worker in a photo-processing laboratory with a long-term but highly fluctuating work pattern characterised by irregular gaps in employment. *Continuity*.
(c) School dinner staff who worked hours which sometimes dipped below the required eight, but which generally exceeded eight. *Continuity*.
(d) Fuel delivery drivers with a long-standing working relationship with their employers. However, the nature of their work meant that they normallly worked only through the winter months (for an average of thirty weeks) and then had twenty-two weeks off. *No continuity*.
(e) Scientists employed by central government had been employed over a number of years in investigating and eradicating diseases affecting bees. They had worked on an irregular basis. When the need for their work ended they were dismissed. *No continuity*.

As has been touched on in Chapter 5, continuity can be preserved by a continuing contractual relationship through non-work periods, e.g. through payment of a retainer, a career break scheme or a 'global' contract. More commonly, it is achieved through the operation of Paragraph 9, Schedule 13, EPCA. The Schedule provides for continuous employment during illness, maternity leave and similar. It also provides that 'temporary cessations' of work or 'customary' breaks do not interrupt continuous employment.

Continuity and temporary fluctuating work

What is 'temporary'? It is when there are periods without work but an expectation that when work becomes available again the employee will be re-employed. In a context of flexible work, continuity is only preserved when there is no work available. For example, work sharing schemes do *not* provide for continuity of employment during the lay-off period, as the work is still available for others to perform.

The expectation of continuing employment over a period of time, especially in an occupation prone to fluctuation, is clearly important. This explains the decision in *Flack* v. *Kodak Ltd.*[1] However, if the periods of non-work are lengthy, as in *Sillars* v. *Charrington Fuels*,[2] or are characterised by an uncertainty that work will be renewed,³ it is likely that employees will not be able to establish continuity of employment.

Continuity and part-time or fluctuating hours

Normally continuity is broken when weekly hours fall below the statutory minimum of sixteen or eight. The law does not allow for crude averaging of hours over a given period. However, there have been cases when occasional shortfalls in the prescribed hours have occurred, especially where hours were anyway somewhat variable, and where courts have not been too literal in their approach. Thus, the case of the dinner ladies, established continuity of employment.⁴

The law is currently less flexible when an employee has separate contracts with one employer, none having the required minimum hours in themselves. The House of Lords has decided that contracts cannot be aggregated, so that the peripatetic photography lecturer⁵ lost her case.

Continuity and job sharing contracts

For several years there have been doubts (though no directly relevant case law) as to whether job-share arrangements of a 'week-on week-off' or 'fortnight on-off' nature ensure continuity of employment through the non-work period. Although it is not possible to be definitive, continuity is probably preserved either because the employee remains governed by the contract during non-work periods; or because the gap is clearly 'temporary' in that the sharer will take over the work at the prescribed time. 'Workless' days, or even a workless week, will not necessarily break continuity.

Continuity and homeworking

Job location should have no impact on continuous employment. In so far as work is intermittent, the same principles regarding temporary work will apply. Much homework, including teleworking, is intermittent, and the issue of continuity will only arise providing the workers are considered employees under the 'mutuality of obligation test' (see Chapters 4 and 5).

Whether certain groups of workers are able to make a statutory claim for redundancy or unfair dismissal will hinge on the history of the employment relationship, the traditions of an occupation and the expectations and assumptions of the parties. The very nature of temporary, seasonal or casual work does not necessarily mean that a decision to end or not re-engage employees will leave employees with no legal rights.

Common law and statute law

Industrial tribunals have occasionally tried to adopt a sympathetic attitude to claims by Category A workers who are not obviously on the 'fringe' of legal protections. But only a minority will be able to do so.

222 NEW WORK PATTERNS

If an employer decides to end contracts does this mean employees can make no legal challenge? Clearly the answer is 'no', for the 'ordinary' law courts have recently become more active, a phenomenon described in Chapter 1. A range of procedures are available in certain circumstances:

- A claim for breach of contract
- An injunction to prevent the dismissal
- A declaration of rights
- An order from public law to quash a decision to dismiss
- An action for wrongful (as opposed to unfair) dismissal.

Some of these legal actions have been discussed in Chapter 4 in the context of re-organisation and deployment of the workforce. They are sometimes available as an addition, as well as alternative or only option for employees. These alternative legal mechanisms, though capable of responding to similar situations adopt very different approaches to issues from industrial tribunals.

Contrasting approaches

The key questions are shown in Figure 10.1.

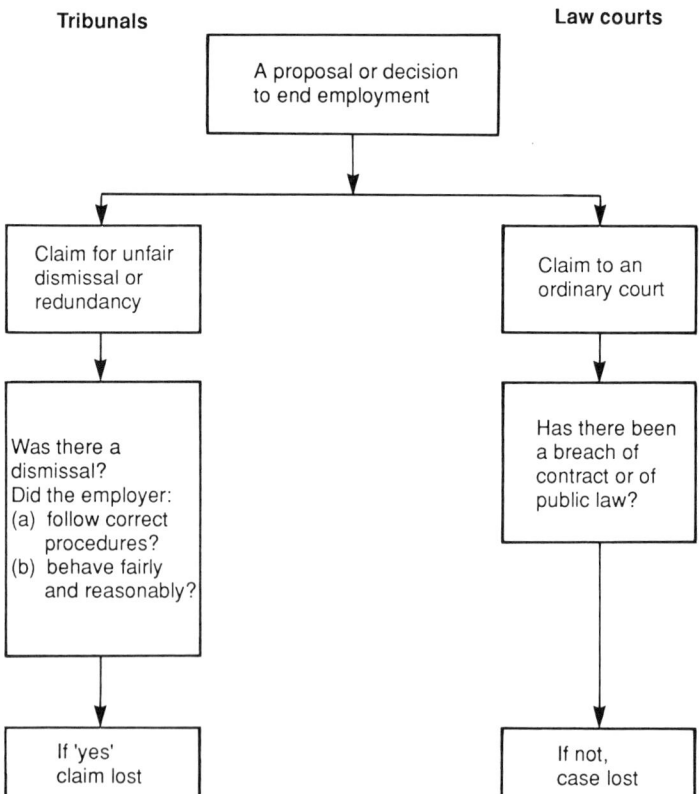

Figure 10.1 *Approaches of tribunals and law courts*

The essential difference between the two areas of law is that tribunals will explore the motives, and the reasonableness of the employer's conduct in a context of expected managerial standards. By contrast, courts are overwhelmingly concerned with the legal technicalities and correctness of the proposal or decision to end contracts. Most importantly, courts are potentially available to *all* employees, regardless of length of employment and hours of work. In addition, County Court and High Court claims can be supported by legal aid, unlike claims to industrial tribunals.

BREACHES AND TERMINATION OF CONTRACTS: THE COURTS

All employees, whether full or part-time, temporary or permanent are entitled to the correct period of notice to end the contract. Minimum periods (one week for each completed year of service) are prescribed by the EPCA though they can be extended by the individual contract. Failure to provide the correct notice amounts to a breach and can also be viewed as a wrongful dismissal. Additionally attempts to unilaterally change working conditions, as well as directly ending contracts can, of course, amount to a dismissal of the employee. This is through the process of constructive dismissal, where law regards the conduct of the employer as repudiating the contract and entitling the employee to 'accept' the repudiation and end the contract.

Wrongful dismissal

Lack of, or incorrect, notice entitles the employee to claim for wrongful dismissal in the County Court or High Court and to obtain damages referring to the foreseeable loss they have suffered. Damages can reflect the difficulties associated with finding another job. Courts might take the view that damages will be lower for many Category A workers because, for example, part-time and temporary jobs might be thought easier to get in many cases.

Wrongful dismissal has relevance to disciplinary procedures. If the contractual document makes available certain facilities, for example, a right to an appeal against a penalty, the failure to apply them may amount to repudiation of contract and therefore constitute dismissal. Care must always be taken in these procedures if they apply to Category A workers. They have the same rights to be treated correctly.

The employer can argue that the employee previously broke the contract, e.g. by gross misconduct, and the employer was merely reacting appropriately. However, it is difficult to see the argument being sustained when the substance of the employee's complaint is that contractual disciplinary procedures were not followed. The fact that there are no formal procedures applying to certain groups of workers does not preclude courts implying fair and reasonable processes through the rules of natural justice.

Examples
*1 A part-time gardener who had a previous good record was instantly dismissed for swearing at the employer's wife. It appeared that he had been provoked. He won a claim for wrongful dismissal as, given the circumstances and his previous work record, the incident did not amount to a repudiation of the contract by the employee.[6]
2 A registrar in a further education college was dismissed without his employers following correctly the code of discipline. He obtained damages.[7]*

Relatively few employees, especially those who anyway had somewhat tenuous links with the organisation, will seek this type of remedy. However, some types of new workers (especially those excluded from statutory procedures) may well see advantages in claims for wrongful dismissal. For example,

- Highly paid and specialist workers, who may be faced by relatively few job opportunities
- Employees on fixed-term contracts, wrongly ended during their duration, where the damages are easy to assess
- Employees who provide equipment or use their own premises where they need compensation for losses suffered through the wrongful termination, especially where this happens soon after they have made purchases or carried out modifications to their home.

Other remedies

In principle, the experience which has built up relating to full-time staff is equally applicable to new workers. For example, if an employer breaks the contract of the employee by failing to provide a safe workplace, pay the agreed wages, or makes demands on the employee which go well beyond the scope of the contract the employee has a choice:

(a) to claim they have been *constructively dismissed* and leave the job
(b) to remain in the job but claim for *breach of contract.*

Assuming the latter, attitudes and responses will vary, especially where there are disputes involving temporary workers who may not want the expense and inconvenience of a legal action. Claims may be made for highly paid workers or by those dependent on maintaining reputation and status. Damages may become more common, but nonetheless it is likely that those whose employment relationship is limited by length of contract or limited involvement in the organisation will be less likely to go to law.

Injunctions

The traditional view has been that when things go wrong in employment contracts the best outcome is to end the relationship. Courts have been reluctant until very recently to keep the contract 'alive' when disputes have arisen. However, greater variety in the labour market has been reflected in growing options for legal action (see Chapter 1). Injunctions may be available to restrain a breach but only if a court considers sufficient goodwill remains between the parties. They have been granted in the following circumstances:

- To halt the unagreed move of social workers from one job location in London to another[8]
- To halt the dismissal of a health worker until the correct disciplinary procedures had been followed[9]
- To prevent a newspaper production manager working for a rival until he had given the contractually required period of notice[10]
- To require a local authority to carry into effect a promotion offered and agreed to over the telephone.[11]

Will injunctions be equally applicable to new work patterns? In principle, they are available to all workers. However, injunctions are discretionary and it may be (although there is no directly applicable case law as yet) that, in the cases involving limited engagements or part-time work, courts will be inclined to require the continuation of the contract. On the other hand, the lower level of integration and interdependence of some work patterns, such as homeworking and short-term engagement may suggest breaches by one side or the other can be more easily dealt with by injunctions. It remains open, but managements would be unwise to ignore this possibility.

Declarations of rights

Until recently the role of courts in this respect has also been fairly low key. The procedure is used to put a brake on proposed actions, including suspension and dismissal of employees or others. The court is here called upon to determine the contractual entitlements of the parties, for example, to state the agreed date of termination, to clarify entitlements under rules of discipline or to decide upon the exact nature of the engagement, e.g. whether the contract is a 'task' contract. It does not, of itself, provide for compensation or other redress, but can be a useful preliminary step. With the increasing flexibility, variety and complexity of new work patterns, employers and employees may increasingly seek guidance from courts. As yet, this is a fairly rare legal action but one with which trade unions, especially those in the public sector, are becoming more familiar.

Public law remedies

This is a complex and much debated topic. Courts will carry out a judicial review of decisions to dismiss workers, vary their terms of work or introduce new working conditions, providing the employer is exercising statutory duties and powers. Employees in the NHS, local authorities, central government and education are potentially covered. However, for courts to intervene in an employment question it must involve something more than simply the contract of employment. There has also to be an 'public law element', such as the correct application of statutory consultative processes or recruitment carried out according to statutory rules, such as those established by the Education Act, 1986, and the Education Reform Act, 1988.

Employees may apply to the High Court for an order to quash a decision, or require employers to carry out correct processes. It does not provide for compensation for individuals but can be effective to challenge dismissals, suspensions and other proposals. The public sector employs vast numbers of part-time, casual and similar workers. Some have already successfully challenged the processes by which their work was changed or they lost jobs. The 'dinner ladies cases' have been discussed in Chapter 4 and illustrated the essential 'holding operation' of most cases.

BREACHES AND TERMINATION OF CONTRACT: THE TRIBUNALS

Protection is provided for by possible claims for unfair dismissal and redundancy payments under EPCA. Apart from establishing that they are qualified to bring a claim, the claimant must:

- Prove, if necessary, that they have been dismissed
- Bring a claim within the time limit set by law.

Has there been a dismissal?

In most cases this is not problematic. The employer unambiguously ends the contract by word or in writing, with or without notice. Alternatively, the conduct of the employer constitutes a repudiation of the contract which the employee accepts by resigning. However, three circumstances which bring a contract to an end do so other than by dismissal. This prevents a claim for unfair dismissal or redundancy.

Frustration of the contract?

This occurs when there is a supervening external event which makes it impossible for the contract to continue. This might occur through chronic illness or periods of imprisonment. To decide whether the contract has been frustrated, a tribunal will examine the impact of the 'event' on the contract's performance. Case law suggests that it is more likely that a short or fixed-term engagement will be frustrated. For example, serious illness requiring six months hospitalisation may well frustrate a twelve or eighteen month engagement.

Examples

1 *An apprentice was sentenced to Borstal training for twelve months. He had a four year apprenticeship. In view of the length and purpose of the contract it was held to be frustrated.*[12]

2 *An employee was seen as a key worker. He had been ill for four months, and his work had been covered by a temporary arrangement. At this point the employer found a permanent replacement, and the EAT held that it was not necessary for them to find another temporary worker. The contract was frustrated.*[13]

Both of these examples show that if employees are taken on for particular purposes or perhaps operate in specialised ways, external events can more easily frustrate the contract. It is possible that the destruction of the home of a homeworker would frustrate the contract if they had to move into hotel accommodation while it was being rebuilt: or that the lengthy illness of a part-time job-share or casual worker would have a quicker impact on the contract than on that of a full-timer.

An agreed termination?

Basic legal rules allow for the parties to agree that a contract ends. However, appraisal agreements must not be used so as to deny potential claims for unfair dismissal and redundancy. It has been recently confirmed that the concept of 'self quit' (e.g. 'If I don't return from leave or meet performance standards I have agreed that the contract ends!') is inappropriate.[14] However, if the employee resigns following negotiations for enhanced severance pay or to take up another more attractive post (e.g. moving from on-site to a home-based job) the situation may be different. Fixed-term contracts are to be subject to special rules over and above those set out in the EPCA. These establish that an engagement of two years or more can be subject to a waiver clause entered into before its expiry indicating that the employee agrees to exclusion from statutory job protection procedures.

Examples

1 *Two employees of Liverpool University requested early retirement (in a context of likely compulsory redundancies) if insufficient volunteers came forward. They accepted the retirement but then made claims for redundancy payments. It was decided by the Court of Appeal that this was an agreed termination rather than dismissal. The relatively attractive terms of the retirement scheme and the adequate period they were given for consideration were significant factors.*[15]

2 *Two research fellows had been employed by the University of Strathclyde on a series of fixed-term contracts stretching back to 1970 and 1974 respectively. The last contract was due to expire on 31 December 1985. During 1985, negotiations had taken place to establish a company to exploit research findings. They began to work with the new company in January 1986 but found the contract unsatisfactory. They claimed they had been dismissed for redundancy by the University. The EAT held that the contracts had ended through agreement. The tribunal thought that the*

researchers had had sufficient details and time to consider the new posts and were under no pressure to leave the university (other researchers had stayed).[16]
3 A fixed-term contract producer/researcher for Thames Television agreed on the expiry of her contract to accept a sum of money for non-renewal of the contract. It was decided she had not voluntarily agreed to end the contract. She had had no choice but to leave, and had been dismissed.[17]

The implications of these cases is that tribunals will examine carefully the following matters before deciding that the apparent agreement to leave is real:

- The existence or otherwise of options to stay or go
- The attractiveness or otherwise of those options
- The existence of adequate information and time before making a decision
- The genuineness of the motives of the parties.

It is likely that employees in new work patterns will be viewed similarly to other workers for these purposes.

A 'task' contract?

If an employment relationship requires the performance of a particular task, the contract ends when that has been achieved. Even if the employer sends notice to end it, the law will not consider this a dismissal. 'Task' contracts are a fairly new phenomenon but one relevant to some new work patterns. Where a contract is to perform a specific function (e.g. carry out a research project or install equipment) the law states that that function characterises the contract. The task rather than a set period of time will dictate the end of the relationship. Case law is limited as yet, but may develop.

Example
Lecturers in a further education college were redeployed to work on courses funded by what was then the MSC. Many had lengthy periods of employment at the college. Funding was withdrawn and when they were dismissed they claimed redundancy payments. The EAT decided that they had not been dismissed: the specific task of teaching courses subject to external funding had come to an end.[18]

Effective dates of contract termination

The EPCA defines the effective date of termination (EDT) for unfair dismissal and redundancy purposes. It defines the starting point of the period within which claims must be brought. The position is as follows:

(a) Where a contract is determined by notice, whether by employer or employee, the EDT is the date on which the notice expires (SS. 55(4)(a) and 90(1)(a).
(b) Where there is no notice, the EDT is the date on which the dismissal took effect (SS. 55(4)(b) and 90(1)(b) – usually when the employee actually left.

(c) Where the contract is for a fixed-term, the EDT is when the contract expires (SS. 55(4)(c) and 90(1)(c)).

Where pay is given in lieu of notice and the employee told not to come to work, the EDT is probably when that notice runs out. If an employer dismisses imediately but with money to cover the notice period this could be seen as compensation. The EDT is then the day the employee actually leaves. The attitude of the parties is crucial to determine the correct interpretation of evidence.

Date of termination and new work patterns

Most employees will be subject to the ordinary legal rules, or to the special rules affecting fixed-term engagements. Where the fixed term is dependent on an event rather than a specific date (e.g. the last evening class, or the satisfactory installation of equipment), the EDT will be on the happening of that event provided this is not considered a 'task' contract.

Job-share contracts

The matter has not been tested but there may be difficulties in fixing the EDT where the job-share is on a week on/fortnight on/off basis. Where dismissal is instant, or subject to notice expiring on a specific date, the situation is clear. Where pay is given in lieu, the situation is uncertain. The options are:

(a) If the contract is seen as providing continuity through non-work periods, the EDT will be the end of the relevant pay period, regardless of whether the job-sharer was scheduled to work or not.
(b) If the contract is inoperative during non-work days the EDT will be the last day the job-sharer was scheduled to work.

Similar problems may arise over the EDT for negotiated annual hours contracts, work patterns which vary considerably (say, on a nine day fortnight) or complex shift working leaving significant number of non-working days over, perhaps, a calendar month.

Temporary and casual contracts

These have proved problematic. Where there is an expectation that work will be resumed but notice is given, the EDT will usually be when the notice expires. If no notice is given, the EDT is the last day the employee worked. Even if it was possible to argue that the contract itself continued through gaps due to the operation of a 'global' contract, it would be hard to argue that the EDT occurred the first date that work could be reasonably expected to be available but actually was not wanted. No court or tribunal has accepted that argument, even though there could be circumstances where an employee was making themselves available for work by turning down other offers.

Claims for redundancy payment

As discussed earlier, new work patterns are introduced for a variety of reasons, not least to cope with fluctuations and uncertainties. Some employers will have increased their dependence on temporary, casual and part-time staff as a direct response to these factors. If the organisation's fortunes decline or it feels in need of further restructuring or cutbacks, what is the legal position of the affected workers?

The EPCA contains a definition of redundancy. It identifies the employee entitled to a redundancy payment. Compensation is based on a formulae which computes length of service with weekly earnings. Since 1986, all but the smallest employers no longer qualify for a rebate from the Redundancy Fund. Redundancy occurs in any of the following circumstances:

- A business moves its work location
- The cessation or diminution of a business
- The requirements of a business for employees to carry out work of a particular kind have ceased or diminished.

The law relating to redundancy payments adopts an approach linked to the needs of the organisation, rather than looking at the impact of change on the individual. It attempts to take an objective view of the organisation and look at factual and tangible matters, rather than exploring the reasons for the changes and whether they were strictly necessary. Manpower demands are paramount. Simply introducing (or abandoning) particular work patterns will not usually create a redundancy situation.

A change in the hours when work is to be carried out will not fall within the definition. Hence, changes to flexi-hours or their abandonment will not be regarded as a redundancy situation.

Redundancy and part-time work

If the decision of the employer is to replace part-timers by full-timers it may create a redundancy. This will be the case if the overall strategy of the employer is to reduce the number of employees.

Example
Mrs Brown, a part-timer, was told she could only keep her job if she worked full-time. She refused and was dismissed. This was held to be redundancy because the aim of the reorganisation was to reduce the number of employees.[19]

If the objective is simply to replace part-timers with an equivalent number of full-timers, there is no redundancy situation. However, if the process involves the replacement doing work of a different kind to that done at present by part-timers, there may be a redundancy situation.

Example
An employer replaced a part-time secretary with a full-time personal assistant. Unlike the part-timer, the personal assistant was required to have a driving licence and carry out additional duties. This was a redundancy situation because of the change in job content.

If there is a redundancy situation, the law can examine the employer's response to it. It may do this if an employer, faced with economic problems, dismisses all part-time or temporary staff first.

It may amount to an unfair dismissal if the selection of these workers was contrary to a contractual or customary agreement. If a policy at the workplace declares that part-timers, job-sharers and temporary staff should be considered alongside full-timers, and that length of service is the overwhelming criterion, selection of these workers before ordinary full-timers would be an unfair dismissal. The selection of one or both job-sharers for redundancy in preference to full-timers would possibly be not only illegal but also unfortunate, given the objective of job sharing being to secure an equal but different employment relationship to full-timers.

Anti-discrimination legislation and selection for redundancy

Given the high representation of women in the new workforce, it is possible that selection of, for example, part-time workers first for redundancy may be regarded as unfair selection and unfair dismissal, as discussed in Chapter 4. Even though much might hinge on conditions in the individual organisation and occupation, employers would be ill-advised to rely on previous practices. An agreed procedure can be challenged as discriminatory. The composition of the workforce, especially in new or flexible work patterns, needs to be carefully borne in mind before dismissals for redundancy are issued.

Redundancy and temporary work

Only temporary workers with two or more years continuous employment can claim. If they were recruited in 1986, for example, for two and a half years, and put on a temporary contract because there were continuing uncertainties, a lower demand for staff could well lead to their being dismissed before or at the end of the agreed period. It appears a declining demand for manpower will lead to the conclusion that selecting temporary staff first may be fair (unless, as mentioned previously, there is a policy to the contrary or it would be discriminatory).

Is the dismissal for redundancy unfair if there was inadequate consultation or consideration of the employee's position? The attitude of tribunals appears to be that this is unlikely providing the employee was aware that the engagement was temporary.

Should the employer consider the employee for other vacancies? This area is one which gives rise to frequent disputes. If a temporary worker has been in post for several years – perhaps on a series of fixed-term engagements – *prima facie* they have a proven track-record and ought to merit some serious consideration, perhaps even priority for any remaining posts. On the other hand, managements will probably be aware that full-time permanent staff often resent temporary staff being given consideration. It can amount to 'leap-frogging', repress open competition for posts and, where the job is at a senior level, deny promotion opportunities. The law will only rarely say that the employer is obliged to go further than 'consider' the temporary worker for a vacancy.

Examples

1 A lecturer had been on a temporary contract which was not renewed. It was held that this was because of redundancy and an industrial tribunal decided that the dismissal was unfair because the employers had failed to find an alternative job. The EAT thought that was 'going too far'. The need to find other work might apply to a redundant permanent worker but not to an employee who was fully aware that the job was insecure.[20]

2 Mrs Beard was a temporary needlework teacher. Work was reorganised and when she was declared redundant she was not considered as a candidate for a new permanent post. She was well qualified and experienced. A less qualified candidate was appointed. This was held to be unfair dismissal.[21]

The overall position appears to be that a temporary or fixed-term worker faced with a redundancy situation will be able to claim a redundancy payment if they meet the law's requirements. The employer has to make a selection fairly, handle it correctly and, if appropriate, consider the employee for other posts. It may well be that valued temporary workers will be retained in any event. Responsible managers may well feel that there is an obligation to reward them, *pro rata*, when redundancy, relocation or redeployment affects the workforce.

Redundancy and homeworkers

A decision may be made to move homebased workers on-site or to require them to work at another location. If home is their agreed and only workplace this will amount to a redundancy situation. Even if the situation is not so clear cut and the decision to move workers on-site is not a breach of contract, might it be a change in requirement for 'work of a particular kind'? If the work's job content changes it will probably be a redundancy situation. If not, it will be an open question whether the fact that work is performed at home, using the employee's facilities and subject to increased employee discretion makes it 'work of a particular kind'.

Offers of alternative employment

The legislation provides that an employer faced with redundancy can make an offer of 'suitable alternative employment'. If the relevant employee 'unreasonably refuses', their entitlement to a redundancy payment is lost (S.82(5)). The employer has to establish these facts.

Case law, generally affecting full-time staff, has laid down guidelines as to what constitutes 'suitable' and what might be legitimate grounds for 'refusal'. Factors other than pay, benefits and job description can be relevant. A job may be unsuitable because it has lower status or 'perks', has risks, or a lack of career opportunities, compared to the original. Tribunals have also taken into account the domestic circumstances of the employee to determine whether they rejected the offer 'unreasonably'.

How might this apply to Category A workers? To what extent would an offer to a job-sharer to work full-time (or move to 'ordinary' part-time work), or to a homeworker to move on-site, or an employee currently working on flexi-hours to change to a job on standard hours, affect the interpretation of 'suitable'? The question probably turns on the extent to which tribunals take on board the essential characteristics of each work pattern. This is especially likely where (as in the case of job sharing, annual hours contracts or some types of homeworking) they have been carefully negotiated to accommodate employees' as well as employers' needs. Tribunals have tended to expect a degree of flexibility and co-operation from employees who are offered alternative work. How far this might go in affecting new work patterns will have to be seen. It is essential that if the work pattern involves a high level of participation and decision making, the offer of alternative work must be subject to comprehensive discussions. The process ought also to reflect the culture of the workplace and equal opportunities policies.

The impact of the Wages Act, 1986, in removing the redundancy rebate may cause employers to defend cases of dismissal on grounds other than redundancy. Attention must be turned to these.

Claims for unfair dismissal

This area of law is more extensive and more likely to protect Category A workers than redundancy. Some types of dismissal, for example, discriminatory dismissals, do not demand the two year qualifying period. Additionally, the law requires that an employer shall not only have to establish grounds to dismiss an employee, but that they handled it fairly. In effect, the law focuses as much on procedures as on the conduct or circumstances of the employee.

Claims can be brought if an employee is dismissed:

- With correct notice
- Without notice (including constructive dismissal)
- Through the non-renewal of a fixed-term contract.

Claims must be brought within three months of the EDT (see p. 228). The employee has a right to a written statement of reasons for dismissal (S.53 EPCA).

Fair reasons to dismiss – the major grounds are:

Capability or qualifications

This entitles the employer to dismiss an employee if he/she is incapable of performing the job through incompetence or due to physical or mental factors.

There is no need to expand on this area. Many standard employment law texts set out the relevant criteria to decide whether the employer had sufficient grounds. However, in the context of Category A staff, a few matters may be relevant:

- The extent to which the higher level of autonomy and self-management often required of new workers will be reflected in this area of law. For example, would it be legitimate to dismiss a homeworker who failed to adequately organise work, report problems and faults in equipment? What would be the impact of greater difficulties in monitoring and appraisal? Has there been a lack of effective communication and liaison between job-share partners? Does one impliedly expect lower standards of performance from temporary staff?
- If incapability arises through physical or mental illness, tribunals may well accept that the nature of some work patterns would entitle an employer to take action more promptly than if the employee was an ordinary full timer. It may be more difficult to provide temporary cover. If the engagement was short or highly specialised, the employer may need to react quickly.

On the first point, it would clearly be important for the employer to establish that the expected performance standards had been made clear; that they related not only to the specific job content and necessary skills, but also to the mode of performance. Many work patterns have additional responsibilities. If the employer takes the view that these are not being carried out properly, they must be sure of their ground and demonstrate that appropriate training and support was provided, if relevant. A tribunal will not be impressed with a situation where the employee is being blamed and dismissed for what, at the end of the day, were faults in the management system rather than the individual.

On the second point, job-share arrangements often have built into them temporary cover by the remaining partner, therefore an over-hasty response by the employer might be thought unfair in some circumstances. It will depend on the impact of illness, be it long-term or intermittent, on the efficiency of the employer's operations. Short-term engagements are most likely to suffer and require a response from management if the employee becomes very ill during an early stage of the contract. The effect of illness on part-timer and other work patterns is hard to predict. Much would depend on the actual job, the extent of illness, and various organisational factors.

Misconduct

Category A workers are no different from normal employees regarding many kinds of misconduct. Lateness, violence, drunkenness, theft, etc., will clearly entitled the employer to react. But in the light of the increased self-managing nature of some work patterns, failure to comply with broader work requirements could be also viewed as misconduct. A homeworker who delegates work to another, who fails to properly record work, who is not available for routine visits or who refuses skill updating or training might be committing an act of misconduct. A job-sharer who provided misleading information for their partner, failed to co-operate on the 'joint' aspects of work or who consistently and incorrectly blamed their partner when they went wrong might be similarly viewed. The regular reluctance of an employee on a negotiated or core hours contract to respond to the employer's request for the additional hours or overtime might well be acting unlawfully. Much would depend on the extent to which these factors were expressly or implicitly recognised in the contract. It is the responsibility of management to be sure on this. Careful consideration of the demands of the work and a well-drawn contract document will clarify the issues.

'Some other substantial reason' for dismissal (SOSR)

This has proved the most relevant and the most controversial aspect of unfair dismissal law *vis à vis* the new workforce. Some of the case law has been previously discussed in Chapter 4. It shows, broadly, that an employer can dismiss an employee if there are convincing organisational reasons for so doing. Additionally, highly disruptive employees, or those whose behaviour adversely affects the reputation of the enterprise can also be fairly dismissed in some circumstances. It may well be that some new work patterns impose additional requirements on employees to be co-operative, supportive and flexible. If so, SOSR could be used to justify ending their contract if such qualities are missing.

Much case law has evolved over matters other than the working arrangements of Category A employees. Tribunals continue to accept the expressed need for regular full-timers or permanent workers and may concede the entitlement of an employer to revert to more traditional work patterns if they consider it appropriate.

Examples

1 Ms Grant worked three days a week as secretary to an architect's practice. She was asked to work full-time but was dismissed when she said she was unable to do so. The tribunal decided the practice could not be run satisfactorily without extra help. The assumption was it had to be by a full-timer.[22]

2 Mrs Lock was a part-time secretary, but was replaced by a younger full-timer when she was off sick. The tribunal held that although she could be dismissed for SOSR it had been unfairly handled.[23]

3 C was recruited as a temporary kitchen porter, originally for six to eight weeks. In

fact, he stayed for more than six months. He was then replaced by a permanent worker. He claimed unfair dismissal (then the qualifying period was twenty-six weeks) and the tribunal rejected SOSR. They could not see why he could not be retained, as the work was clearly still available and the employer did not have different recruitment and personnel practices for temporary and permanent staff.[24]

4 Mr Terry was employed on a fixed-term contract as a lecturer. It was not renewed. The EAT decided that the employer could potentially establish SOSR where there was a genuine need for a specific short-term engagement.[25]

5 G was a consultant radiologist engaged as a locum for a specified period. The contract was not renewed. It appeared that the Regional Medical Officer disliked 'permanent locum appointments'. No interest had been shown in G's future and the tribunal thought the employer's attitude 'heartless and inexcusable'. SOSR was not established and her dismissal was unfair.[26]

It is difficult to draw general guidelines from these cases, but key factors which have been held influential by tribunals appear to be:

- Proven and genuine reasons for making changes to working practices
- Consideration of, and discussion with, the employee regarding their position
- A justifiable reaction to an employee who had been made fully aware of the wider, as well as job specific, demands of the post.

Economic and organisational factors are treated seriously by tribunals. It remains to be seen how they react to problems encountered by employers regarding specific work patterns. This is particularly true where working arrangements have been evolved through a policy document, perhaps in conjunction with equal opportunities initiatives: and involve high levels of employee consultation and participation. It would be ironic if tribunals adopted a 'hard line' approach to ending a particular work pattern and failed to recognise the forces, such as need for skill retention, which had motivated its introduction.

Dismissal and job sharing

If the job-share contract has specified the procedures which follow the departure of one job-sharer, there can be no question of unfair dismissal so long as they are adhered to. If the contract is silent and the employer decides to redeploy or even dismiss the remaining sharer (for example, because of the difficulties of finding a replacement or because of staff reduction or redeployment) what is the position?

There may be a redundancy situation if the employer wants fewer staff. However, it is possible that the problems of finding a replacement and of accommodating the needs of the remaining sharer may constitute SOSR, especially if there have been attempts to solve the problems. As yet, there is no case law. But it is likely that even if tribunals are sympathetic to management's dilemmas they will still require them to properly consult and discuss with the job-sharer.

Handling dismissals

Even though an employer has adequate grounds for ending the contract, it is still necessary for the dismissal to be handled fairly. The handbook from ACAS, *Discipline at Work*, is particularly helpful in suggesting appropriate procedures. It does not deal with some of the specific problems which new and atypical work patterns give rise to, though its general approach is useful. In most circumstances, the following steps ought to be taken:

- A proper investigation of the facts which are asserted to provide grounds to dismiss. In the case of homeworker or job-share arrangements, it may be necessary to carry out a series of interviews and visit work premises as well as examining disciplinary and performance records
- Discussion and consultation with the employee in question. With new work patterns (especially if they have been recently introduced) it is necessary to examine the managerial and support structure to be able to clearly identify the likely cause of problems
- A consideration of improvement of the support structures, help for the employee, and, if necessary, redeployment of the employee
- A consideration of length of service and prior work record of the employee
- A strict adherence to any contractual disciplinary or consultative contractual procedures. Failure to do so will tend to a finding of unfair dismissal.[27] An argument by employers that there would have been no point in using the procedures will be normally irrelevant.

Remedies for unfair dismissal or redundancy

A few special points arise from new work patterns. For redundancy payment there is a statutory formula of compensation, based on computing length of service with weekly pay to a maximum of £164. For unfair dismissal, there is the possibility of re-instatement or re-engagement by the employer after a successful claim. Very few employees are awarded or able to exercise this entitlement. The possibility of return to the workplace for, say, part-time and temporary workers, is even less likely. If personal relations had broken down between job-sharers and/or their colleagues, a similar conclusion may be drawn.

Compensation is the most likely outcome. The basic award is the same as for redundancy payments, though it is difficult to assess the effect of new patterns on the additional compensation award for unfair dismissal. These awards, when applied to full-time permanent staff, reflect loss of occupational benefits, job security and future employment prospects, as well as loss of future earnings. It is possible that the more flexible and transient nature of many work patterns will attract lower awards.

ENDING CONTRACTS WITH CATEGORY B AND C WORKERS

Only employees are protected by common law rules or EPCA against breach of contract and job loss. Category C workers, even where the impetus for the dismissal came from the host/client enterprise, will only have a claim against their own employer. This is beyond the scope of this book. The law is involved if the services of a consultant, freelance or similar worker, or the performance of a sub-contractor, proves unsatisfactory. This depends on the extent to which the legal rules for termination of contract are complied with (as discussed in Chapters 3 and 4, the original contract should have established procedures for dealing with complaints, disputes, settlement and compensation).

- Any procedures established by contract must be followed, including those for notice and arbitration
- Any breach of contract by one party which is sufficiently serious to amount to fundamental breach will entitle the other to accept the contract as ended
- Any breach which is not serious will entitle the other party to damages. There will be costs and losses foreseeably flowing from the breach.

Whether a contract has been broken will be a question of fact and interpretation. Especially difficult are alleged breaches involving poor performance, abuse of position, disputed facilities and opportunities, and unspecific targets. It is invariably better to attempt to resolve them by negotiation or arbitration than resort to law.

References
1. *Flack v. Kodak Ltd* [1986] IRLR 255.
2. *Sillars v. Charrington Fuels* [1988] IRLR 180.
3. *McHugh v. Thoresen Car Ferries Ltd*, EAT 239/80.
4. *Deary v. Secretary of State for Employment* [1984] ICR 413.
5. *Lewis v. Surrey County Council* [1987] IRLR 509.
6. *Wilson v. Racher* [1974] ICR 428.
7. *Gunton v. Richmond LBC* [1982] IRLR 321.
8. *Hughes v. Southwark LBC* [1980] IRLR 321.
9. *Irani v. Southampton and South-East Hampshire H.A.* [1985] IRLR 203.
10. *Henderson v. Evening Standard* [1987] IRLR 64.
11. *Powell v. Brent LBC* [1987] IRLR 466.
12. *Shepherd and Co Ltd v. Jerrom* [1986] IRLR 358.
13. *Hart v. Marshall* [1977] ICR 539.
14. *Igbo v. Johnson Matthew Chemicals Ltd* [1986] ICR 505.
15. *Birch and Humber v. University of Liverpool* [1985] ICL 470.
16. *Manson and Johnson v. University of Strathclyde*, EAT 23, 22 [1987] (356/87).
17. *Thames Television v. Wallis* [1987] IRLR 136.
18. *Brown v. Knowsley Borough Council* [1986] IRLR 102.
19. *Brown v. Dunlop Textiles Ltd* [1967] ITR 53.

20 *Gwent CC v. Lane* [1977] IRLR 337.
21 *Beard v. Governors of St Joseph's School* [1978] ICR 1234.
22 *Grant v. Thompson*, COIT 1150/246.
23 *Lock v. THF Hotels Ltd*, 1174/114.
24 *Chandler v. J. Sainsbury Ltd*, COIT 952/77.
25 *Terry v. East Sussex CC* [1976] IRLR 332.
26 *West Midlands Regional Health Authority v. Guirguis*, EAT 567/7.
27 *Polkey v. A.E. Dayton Services Ltd* [1987] IRLR 503.

Source material

IDS, *Employment Law Handbook 31, Part-timers, Temps and Job Sharers*, Income Data Services, 1985.

IDS, *Employment Law Handbook 35, Continuity of Employment*, Income Data Services, 1986.

IDS, *Employment Law Handbook 39, Contracts of Employment*, Income Data Services, 1987.

IRS, *Temporary, Casual and Agency Workers*, IRLIB 325, p.2, Industrial Relations Services, 1987.

Wedderburn, Lord, *The Worker and the Law* 3rd edn., Weidenfeld and Nicolson, 1986.

Index

Absenteeism, 170, 186
 labour costs, 24, 25
Accidents at work, 192, 202–3
Accommodation, 58
 allocation of, 146–7
Additional Voluntary Contributions (AVCs), 174
Administrative costs, 25
 career break schemes, 43
 job-sharing, 47, 58
 sub-contracting, 37, 38
Advertising
 job-sharing, 104, 106, 108, 110, 124
 recruitment, 103
Agencies, employment, 137
Agency workers, 149–50
 contracts, 138–9
 pay, 177
 preparing for, 69–74
 and promotion, 157
 and trade unions, 213
Alternative employment, offers of and redundancy, 232–4
Annual hours contracts, 90, 127, 209–10
Anti-discrimination legislation, 6–7, 43, 87–90
 and occupational benefits, 175–6
 and selection for redundancy, 231
Appraisal procedures, 57, 58, 151, 152–4
 and agency workers, 73
 career appraisal programmes, 63
 homeworking, 134
 job-sharing, 124
 secondment, 67
Apprenticeship contracts, 129
ARC (Action Resource Centre), 49
Assessment procedures, 57
Association of Teachers of Management, 112
Atkinson, John, 208
ATO (Approved Training Organisation), 41, 80, 111
Attitudes to employment
 atypical workers, 10–11
 young people, 7

Atypical workers
 attitudes to employment, 10–11
 and employment legislation, 12
 trade union attitudes to, 206–18

Banks
 recruitment problems, 8
 and secondment, 49
Benefits, *see* Occupational benefits
Briefing
 agency workers, 72–3
British Caledonian
 'Way Ahead' programme, 215–16
British Computing Society, 112
British Institute of Management study (1988), 7

CAC (Central Arbitration Committee), 94, 95
Cadbury, Sir Adrian, 7
Career appraisal, 153–4
Career break schemes, 42–5, 142
 and occupational pensions, 172
 preparation for, 62–3
 training on return from, 156
Career continuity
 maintaining, 27–9
Careers officers
 and recruitment of YTS trainees, 111
Case studies
 advertising for job-sharing, 110
 on employee status, 117–18
 on introducing change, 83–6
 job-sharing, 62, 126–7
 Project Fullemploy, 68–9, 149, 150
 on secondment, 51–3
 self-employed workers, 33
 on status of workers, 92–3
Casual workers, 91, 129
 contracts for, 136–7
 pay, 132, 167, 170, 171
 equal pay legislation, 179
Category A (directly-employed workers), 15, 16, 22

appraisal, promotion and training, 151
contracts for, 118, 119, 121–34
  ending, 219–37
health and safety issues, 192, 194, 195, 196, 197, 199, 200, 202–3
integration information, 143–4
labour costs, 26, 27
pay and benefits, 166–87
practical difficulties, 148
promotion, 157
recruitment, 100, 104, 114–15
supervision of 161–3
training, 155
and wrongful dismissal, 223–4 workers
Category B (Self-employed workers), 16, 22, 26, 27
appraisal, promotion and training, 151
contracts for, 119, 134–7, 139
  ending, 219–23
health and safety issues, 192, 194, 195, 197, 198, 199, 200, 201–2, 205
integration information, 143–4
and organisation culture, 149
pay and benefits, 166, 187–9
practical difficulties, 148
recruitment, 100, 104, 114–15
reporting systems, 146
supervision of, 162–3
training, 155
Category C (external workers), 16, 22, 26
appraisal, promotion and training, 151
contracts for, 137–9
  ending, 238
health and safety issues, 192, 195, 197, 198, 199, 200, 201–2, 205
integration information, 143–4
and organisation culture, 149
supervision of, 162–3
CEI (Centre for Employment Initiatives), 49, 149
Change
consultation, negotiation and notification of, 94–100
introducing, 83–7
to management systems and procedures, 55–9
restraints on, 87–94
Chapman, Rhiannon, 3, 14
Charitable organisations
and consultancy fees, 113
Civil Service
new work practices, 7, 9–10
Clients, relationships with, 150, 151
Codes of practice, 151
and sub-contracting, 137
Collective bargaining, 60, 94, 96
Commercial contracts, 137–8
Committees, safety, 198
Communication systems, 55–6
health and safety issues, 196
Company cars, 56, 146

COMPASS (Community Project Assignments), 49–50
Compensation payments
for injuries, 193, 204
for redundancy and unfair dismissal, 237
Complaints procedures
and sub-contracting, 80
Computing Services Association, 112, 137
Conduct of workers
misconduct as grounds for dismissal, 235
responsibility for, 204
Construction industries
analysis of labour costs, 24
contracts, 137
Consultants, 33–6
contracts, 112–13, 134–6, 163
and equal pay legislation, 179
preparing to use, 66–7
recruiting, 111–13
reporting systems, 146
see also Category B
Continuity of employment
legal position on, 220–1
Contract staff
homeworking, 48
see also Sub-contracting
Contracts
agency, 138–9
annual hours, 90, 127, 210
for Category A workers, 118, 119, 121–34
for Category B workers, 119, 134–7, 139
for Category C workers, 137–9
changing status of workers, 91–4
commercial, 137–8
consultants, 112–13, 134–6, 163
core and variable hours, 127–8
disputes and termination of, 219–38
documents, 118–21
health and safety issues, 193, 197
homeworking, 133–4
length of, 128–33
for secondments, 138–9
variation or termination of individual, 97–9
for YTS trainees, 139
see also Fixed-term contracts
Control systems, 55–6
Core/peripheral working, concept of, 10
and trade unions, 206–7
Costs
of self-employed workers, 31, 32
of sub-contracting, 76
see also Administrative costs; Labour costs; Personnel costs
Counselling, 158–9
Courts, decisions of
on breaches and terminations of contracts, 222, 223–6
on changes to working practices, 96–100
on employee status, 117–18
on status of workers, 91–4

on temporary contracts, 131
CSR (Corporate social responsibility)
  and secondment, 48
Culture, organisational, 149–50

Damages, claims for, 194
Demand
  of individual workers, 5–8, 27–9, 153
  and labour costs, 18, 23–7
Demographic trends, 8–11
Development policies, 57–8
Directly-employed workers, see Category A
Disabled people
  recruitment of, 101
Discipline, 160–3
Discretionary return to work
  career break schemes, 44–5, 142
Dismissal
  grounds for, 234–6
  see also Unfair dismissal; Wrongful dismissal
Distance workers, 14, 15, 158, 159
  recruitment, 100, 104
DLOs (Direct Labour Organisations), 74, 79, 115
Dress regulations, 149

Earnings, enhancement of, 181–7
Economic goals
  of organisations, 22
Economic push, 4
EDT (effective dates of contract termination), 228–30, 233
Education
  formal programmes, 61–2
  see also Teachers; Training
Education Act (1986), 226
Education Reform Act (1988), 226
Employer Responses to the Decline in School Leavers in the 1990s (Meager and Metcalfe), 8–9
Employment Act (1982), 94
Employment agencies, 110–11, 137
Employment Appeal Tribunal (EAT), 88
Employment Protection (Consolidation) Act, 1978 (EPCA), 119, 120, 127, 129, 131, 133
  and contract termination, 220, 226, 233, 238
  health and safety, 197
  and pay, 167, 168
  and redundancy, 230
Employment Protection Act (1975), 94
Epstein, Joyce, 142
Equal opportunities
  and contract compliance, 139
  and new work patterns, 19
  policies, 83
  programmes, 142–3
  and YTS trainees, 80–1
Equal pay legislation, 179–81

European Community
  Draft Directive, 96
  employment legislation, 12, 22, 90, 175
  and part-time contracts, 124
  on safety, 191
External policy constraints
  and new work patterns, 19, 22
External workers, see Category C

Facilities, allocation of, 146–7
Factories Act (1961), 194
Fair Wages Resolution of the House of Commons, 87
Fees, consultancy, 112–13
Finance Act (1987), 173–4
Financial control, 59
Fixed-term contracts, 122, 130–1
  and contract termination, 227
  sick pay, 168, 170–1
Flexitime arrangements, 7, 184
  contracts, 123
Formal policies
  job-sharing, 64–5
Formal programmes, 61–2
Formal reporting systems, 56, 145, 159–60
'Full-time only' policies, 88–9
Full-time staff
  gaining support of, 60–1
Functional flexibility, 2, 29

GMB (General Municipal, Boilermakers and Allied Trade Union), 207, 211, 212
Goals, organisational
  and new work patterns, 18–29
Government policy
  and new work patterns, 11–13, 19
Gregory, Denis, 208
Guaranteed re-entry
  career break schemes, 42–3, 142

Hackney Job Share Project, 64
Health and Safety, 90, 191–205
  and agency workers, 70
  and YTS trainees, 80
Health and Safety at Work Act (1974), 191, 194–5, 196–7
Health screening, 199–200
Henley Management College
  analysis of labour costs, 24, 25
Holidays
  labour costs, 24, 25
Homeworking, 47–8
  and career break schemes, 45
  change of status to, 94
  and continuity of employment, 221
  contracts, 119, 133–4
  and equal pay legislation, 179, 180, 181
  health and safety, 90, 201
  high-technology, 14
  and liability, 204
  maternity pay, 171

and organisational goals, 23
pay, 171, 176, 177, 185
pension rights, 174
as peripheral work, 10
and redundancy, 232
Host organisations
  and secondment, 67–8, 138
Hours of work
  advertising, 104
  change in, 90
  and continuity of employment, 221
  contracts, 90, 98, 122–8, 127, 209–10
  flexitime, 7, 123, 184
  homeworking, 133
  job-sharing, 65
  law regarding, 119
  time off in lieu, 184
  see also Overtime

Illegal contracts, 119
Illness
  and contract termination, 226
  as grounds for dismissal, 234
In-house units
  and sub-contracting, 37–9, 74, 76, 78, 79, 80
Individual workers, demands from, 7–9, 153
  and career continuity, 27–9
Induction packages, 143–4
  for agency workers, 72–3
Industrial injuries claims, 93
Industrial Relations Act (1971), 12
Industrial tribunals, see Tribunals
Injunctions
  and contract termination, 224–5
Injuries at work, 193, 202–3, 204
  self-employed workers, 136
Insurance policies
  accidents, 203
  liabilities, 204
Integration
  of atypical workers, 3, 143–4

Job centres
  advertising in, 110
Job evaluation schemes, 56, 181
  job-sharing, 126
Job specifications, 59
  job-sharing, 65
  sub-contracting, 77–8
Job-sharing, 45–7
  accommodation and equipment, 58
  advertising, 104, 106, 108, 109, 124
  and anti-discrimination legislation, 12
  appraisal systems, 57
  and career break schemes, 45
  case studies, 62
  and continuity of employment, 221
  contracts, 119, 122, 124–7
    ending 219, 229
  costs, 58

and dismissal, 234, 236
and external relationships, 150–1
in Holland, 61
law on, 98
in local authorities, 11
management objections to, 89–90
maternity pay, 171
'overlap' time, 56, 65
and overtime, 183–4
pension rights, 126, 174
as peripheral work, 3, 4, 12
and policy statements, 74
practical difficulties, 148
preparation for, 64–6
and promotion, 58, 124, 157
Stock Exchange scheme, 49, 101–2, 157
teachers, 87
and trade unions, 211, 214
  NALGO's strategy on, 216–22

Labour costs
  and job-sharing, 47
  and new work patterns, 18, 23–7, 59
  sick pay, 170
  sub-contracting, 37
Labour market requirements
  and new work patterns, 19
Labour sources, 100–2
Legislation, employment, 3, 11–13
  on consultation, negotiation and notification of change, 94–100
  contracts on changing status of workers, 91–4
  on ending of contracts, 224–8
  health and safety at work, 90, 191, 194–5, 196–7
  and pay, 166–81
  restraints on change, 87–94
  and worker contracts, 117–40
Liaison
  agency workers, 72
Line managers
  and agency workers, 72, 74
  attitudes of, 61, 141, 143
  and homeworkers, 48
  and job-sharing, 126
  and new work patterns, 59
  and sub-contracting, 75, 80
Local authorities
  advertising, 105
  job sharing, 126–7
  new work practices, 7, 10
Local Government Act (1988), 13, 87, 139
Local labour markets, 9
Loyalty, organisational, 31, 32

Management
  levels of supervision, 159–63
  systems
    and agency workers, 71
    changes to, 55–9

Managers
  local, 141–3
  role of, 158–9
  and secondment, 49
  women, 6
Maternity leave, 8, 47, 165
Maternity pay, 171–2
Medical examinations, 199–200
Meetings, 145, 149
  career break schemes, 63
Minimum wages, 119
Monitoring, systems, 143, 145–6, 163
  safety, 197–8

NALGO (National and Local Government Officers' Association), 174, 212, 216–17
National insurance
  self-employed workers, 118, 136
Negligence, law of, 193–4
Networkers
  recruitment of, 100, 101
NHS (National Health Service)
  new work practices, 7
  sub-contracting, 37, 39, 75
Noticeboards, 145–6, 196, 200
Numerical flexibility, 29, 207

Occupational benefits, 165–90
  homeworkers, 134, 174
  job-sharing, 126, 174
Occupier's Liability Act (1957), 195
Office costs
  and homeworking, 48
Offices, Shops and Railway Premises Act (1963), 194
Organisation
  gaining support of, 59–62
  goals of, 18–29
OSP (Occupational Sick Pay), 168, 169–71
Overtime
  and Category B workers, 188
  job-sharing, 126
  and part-time workers, 121, 124, 183
  payments, 181–4, 185

Part-time working, 45–6
  accommodation for, 58
  advertising, 104
  attitudes of full-time staff, 144
  and career break schemes, 45
  and continuity of employment, 221
  contracts, 119, 121, 123–4
    ending, 219
  and dismissal, 87–8
  and equal pay legislation, 180, 181
  and liability, 204
  in local authorities, 10
  maternity pay, 171
  and overtime, 121, 124, 183
  and occupational pensions, 173, 175
  pay and benefits, 167, 168, 169, 169–70, 177–8

pension rights, 174
and redundancies, 230–1
teachers, 87
and trade unions, 210–11
and women, 5–6, 12, 13
Pay, 56–7, 167–72
  agency contracts, 138
  consultants, 136, 137
  deductions or withholding of, 161
  enhanced earnings, 182–7
  equal pay legislation, 179–81
  of homeworkers, 133, 171, 176, 177, 185
  for non-work periods, 176–9
  performance related, 177–9, 187
  redundancy, 237
  and temporary contracts, 132
  see also Overtime
Pensions, occupational, 126, 165, 172–5
Performance appraisal, see Appraisal systems
Performance related payments, 176–9, 186–7
Performance targets
  job-sharing, 126
Peripheral workers
  core/periphery working, 4–5
Perks, traditional, 56–7, 146
Personnel costs, 25
  job-sharing, 47, 58
  sub-contracting, 38
Personnel data
  career break schemes, 63
Personnel departments/managers
  and agency workers, 72, 74
Practical difficulties, 148–9
Press advertising, 104
Pricing
  of sub-contracts, 76–7
Private sector organisations
  job-sharing, 64
  and overtime, 183
  sub-contracting, 74–5
Professional associations
  and consultant recruitment, 112
  and sub-contracting, 39, 137, 139
Professional jobs
  advertising, 104, 105
  bargaining strength in, 60
  job-sharing, 46
  requirements of individuals, 28
  temporary, 29, 30, 31
  women in, 5–6, 100–1
Profit sharing schemes, 186–7
Project Fullemploy, 68–9, 149, 150
Project management, 158
Promotion, 58, 156–7
  job sharing, 58, 124, 157
Psychological attitudes, 147–8
Public relations
  and secondment, 48–9
Public sector organisations, 4
  and consultancy fees, 113
  and contract changes, 99
  contract compliance in, 139

and contract termination, 225–6
and employment legislation, 11
equal opportunities programmes, 142
job-sharing, 46, 64, 124
new work practices, 7, 10
and overtime, 182
self-employed workers, 34
sub-contracting, 36, 37, 39, 74, 75, 76
temporary work, 31
Public subsidy trainees, see YTS

Radio advertising, 104
Re-entry
  and secondment, 50, 51
Recruitment, 100–14, 150
  advertising, 103, 104–10
  of consultants, 111–13
  costs, 27
  external, 103
  internal, 102–3
  and job-sharing, 47
  policies, 59
  and self-employed workers, 32
  and trade unions, 211–14
  and YTS workers, 39
Redundancies
  claims for payment, 226, 228, 230–3
  and contract changes, 100
  negotiation of, 96
  obligatory consultation on, 95
  and part-time work, 230–1
Redundancy Payments Act (1965), 12
Reed Employment survey (1988), 7
Regional labour markets, 9
Relationships, working
  external, 150–1
  internal, 147–50
Reporting systems, 145–6, 149
Retirement
  recruitment of retired people, 101
  secondment as perparation for, 49, 50
'Return ticket' schemes
  of secondment, 50–1, 156
Rothwell, Sheila, 25–6

Sabbatical schemes, 44
Safety officers, 198–9; see also Health and safety
School leavers
  reduction in numbers of, 9–11
Secondment, 48–53
  contracts, 137, 138–9
  and organisation culture, 149
  preparing for, 67–9
  recruitment for, 101
  training on return from, 156
Self-employed workers, 31–3
  categorisation of, 117–18, 140
  change of contract status to, 91–4
  ending contracts, 219
  health and safety issues, 194–5

homeworking, 48
increase in, 7
recruitment of, 101
see also Category B
Service sector
  part-time working, 46
  replacing school leavers, 8–9
  status of workers in, 91
  women employed in, 5
Sex Discrimination Act (1986), 43, 90
Shiftworking
  and organisational goals, 22, 23
Sick pay, 168–71
  consultants, 135
  homeworkers, 133
  and job-sharing, 126
  and part-time working, 124
'Single ticket' schemes
  of secondment, 50
Smith, Larry, 213
Smoking regulations, 149, 192
Social goals
  of organisations, 22
'Social pull' factors, 5, 42–53
Social security
  and flexible workers, 57
Social Security Act (1986), 170, 173–4
SOSR 'Some other substantial reason'
  for dismissal, 240–1
Stock Exchange
  job-sharing scheme, 49, 101–2, 157
Students
  recruitment of, 101
Sub-contracting, 14–15, 34, 36–9
  and agency workers, 70
  choosing a sub-contractor, 113–14, 115
  commercial contracts, 137–8
  preparations for, 74–80
  in the public sector, 13
  and trade unions, 210
Subsidised services
  labour costs, 24, 25
Supervision, levels of, 159–64
Supply teaching, 105

TA (Training Agency), 39, 40
Task contracts, 129, 225, 228
Taxation
  of flexible workers, 57
  self-employed workers, 118, 136
Teachers
  contracts, 128, 130
  supply, 105
  terms of contract for, 87
Teachers Pay and Conditions Act (1987), 87, 128
Teaching
  supply teaching, 105
Teamworking, 56, 158
Technical specifications
  and sub-contracting, 76, 78

Telephone answering machines, 58
Temporary work, 29–31
  accommodation for, 58
  and agency workers, 72
  as choice
    by office workers, 7
  and continuity of employment, 220–1
  contracts, 122, 129–33
    ending, 229–30
  and liability, 204
  and occupational pensions, 172
  pay and benefits, 167, 184–5
  and redundancy, 231–2
  sick pay, 169, 170–1
  status of workers, 92
  and trade unions, 210
Tendering process
  and consultancy fees, 113
  and sub-contracting, 74, 75
TGWU (Transport and General Workers' Union), 207, 211, 212–14
Time, *see* Hours of work
Trade associations
  and sub-contracting, 39, 137
Trade unions, 19
  attitudes to new work patterns, 10, 11, 206–23
  and consultancy fees, 113
  consultation with, 60–1, 94, 95
  and contract changes, 98, 99
  health and safety issues, 193, 197–8
  and industrial action, 96
  and occupational pensions, 174
  and performance related pay, 187
  and 'social pull' factors, 42
  and sub-contracting, 38, 79, 210
  and YTS workers, 40, 41
Training, 154–6
  costs, 27
  formal programmes, 61–2
  for homeworkers, 48

  and job-sharing, 126
  policies, 57–8
  YTS trainees, 81
Tribunals, 95, 120
  on breaches and termination of contracts, 221, 226–37
  on employee status, 117–18

Unfair Contract Terms Act (1977), 131
Unfair dismissal, 193, 226, 227, 228–30, 231, 233–6, 237
  and anti-discrimination laws, 88

Wages Act (1986), 161, 172, 176, 233
Wages councils, 37, 119
Women
  and anti-discrimination legislation, 12–13
  career appraisal, 153, 154
  career break schemes, 43, 44
  demands from, 5–6
  maternity pay, 171–2
  part-time workers
    to replace school leavers, 10–11
  in professional jobs, 5–7, 100–1
    advertising for, 104
  as sources of labour, 100–1
  as temporary workers, 29
  and trade unions, 207–8, 212, 213–14, 216
Working conditions, 56–7
  agency contracts, 138
Wrongful dismissal, 193, 223–4

Young people
  attitudes to employment, 7
  school leavers, 7–9
YTS (Youth Training Scheme), 39–42
  contracts, 139
  preparation for trainees, 80–1
  recruitment, 111
YTS Certification Board (YCB), 41